WHO DO YOU THINK YOU ARE?

365 meditations + the books they came from

chad prevost

Copyright © 2020 The Big Self School

The Big Self School is a learning community whose central mission is to help change-makers and visionaries deepen their self-awareness and relationships so they can sustainably impact the world. We create digital courses, online community, books, and media designed to activate self-awareness, deeper connections, bold action, and healthy habits so you can play big without burning out.

www.bigselfschool.com

Printed in the United States of America

Text layout and design: Averil Eagle Brannen

Library-of-Congress Control Number is available upon request.

ISBN: 978-1-945064-26-5

eISBN: 978-1-945064-27-2

WHO DO YOU THINK YOU ARE?

365 meditations + the books they came from

chad prevost

How this book came to be
and how it should be used

This book materialized out of the ashes of various personal and professional failures, and a reassessing of who I am, what I value, and what I choose to live for each day. My wife and I have shared a lot together in this journey, and after several leaps of faith, launched the Big Self School, a part of which is the manifestation of this book. This book also bears the impression of the social and psychological scars we experienced while putting it together: a global pandemic, economic chaos, and civil and social unrest unlike anything seen in our lifetimes.

The idea is simple. If someone really wants to change, to grow as a person, what is the best medicine? What are the most direct routes? How do you discover who you are? How do you find the courage to share it with the world once you know?

Reading is one. We read to understand. We read to learn, to find something we didn't even know we were looking for. We read to find community — both with past and present authors, and with the others who read with us. We read to be enriched.

Meditating is another. Here you have, at your disposal, 365 different quotes and the books they came from, along with a question (or two or three) for meditation. The world does not need another grabbag of quotes. We wanted a book more like the kind it was influenced by. We wanted it to contain the transformative potential it celebrated, discussed, and meditated upon.

This book is designed to bring you clarity, not clutter. We live in the information age. Marcus Aurelius says, "What doesn't transmit light creates its own darkness." On the other hand, Erasmus points out, "Give light, and the darkness will disappear of itself." We're infiltrated by information fighting for our attention, fighting to persuade us, to manipulate us, to shape who we are, how we think, believe, and behave. This book is intended — with a focus on self-exploration and personal identity — to help you construct who you are, and how you want to feel, think, believe, and behave for yourself.

The process of compiling this material has been a transformative experience in its own right. I was challenged to read new texts being presented to me all the time, as well as revisit many greats from the past, all through the lens of transformation and the power of the text to shine a light down a path that would otherwise be dark. The experience gave me purpose and kept my own meditations and processes in line with the powerful material I was constantly considering.

The readings come from psychology, philosophy, poetry, essays, biographies and autobiographies, memoirs, dictionaries, treatises, and literature. The quotes are meant to inspire, comfort, and challenge. They represent a wide diversity of experiences and ideas. They are intended for you to actively think, reflect, feel, and meditate upon. The day's quote is no attempt to summarize the book from where it's sourced. The quote is the quote. Leave the book out if it gets in the way of simply considering the quote and the meditation questions.

While my intention is to get you excited about each given book's possibility to work within your life, I have kept the summaries slim. Reviewing each book would extend far beyond the intended purpose. Think of the book summary as a possible source for further consideration. Every now and then a book will speak to you. When that happens it will feel more like an exciting opportunity, and less of yet another of a thousand microdecisions you already have to make each day, or pressure to do more.

Depending on how you want to engage with the questions, you might consider reading and reflecting through simple meditation. You might also consider reading and reflecting through short, timed writing. You can journal alongside some of the thoughts. You might combine the readings and meditations with other rituals or habit experiments. You might pray, or just stop and think for a few minutes here and there. That is really between you and yourself.

Meditation is a practice anyone can do and can transform our lives by bringing us greater resiliency, creativity, peace, clarity, and balance. It is generally understood that a meditation practice leads to three key skills: concentration, mindfulness, and lovingkindness.

Start wherever you feel led. See how often you can meet yourself with each day's reading. Make this your year. This is your commitment to pause for a moment each and every day.

This book meets you where you're at. Only you can decide where that is. The power of reading with a purpose, combined with meditating's transformative potential, will bear fruit in your life. What that fruit is, how long it will take you to arrive, how dedicated you are to the process, all that is up to you. It all depends on the seeker, the curious one, why you're seeking, and what you're going to do about what you discover. This book is a guide, a traveling companion. This book is about you.

How committed are you to yourself?

Who do you think you are?

january

"Those who don't know must learn from those who do."

WHY I LOVE THIS QUOTE:
A strong quote to begin the new year, a powerful, aphoristic thought. Want to learn to think for yourself? Learn from the masters. Find a few great thinkers and go deep. This quote also suggests that if you remain ignorant, you will end up learning from those who know more than you do anyway. You can learn one way or the other.

WHY THIS IS A TRANSFORMATIVE BOOK:
The Republic is an inquiry into the notion of a perfect community and the ideal individual within it. Huge questions are raised and examined: What is goodness? What is reality? What is knowledge?

It also addresses the purpose of education and the role of both women and men as guardians of the people. With lucidity and clever use of allegory, Plato arrives at a depiction of a state bound by harmony and ruled by philosopher kings.

QUESTIONS FOR MEDITATION:

What is outside of your control that you are frustrated by, blocked, or feel like you're at an impasse?

Is it possible that your response to the situation is keeping you blocked?

What can you learn from the situation?

"The doors to the world of the wild Self are few but precious. If you have a deep scar, that is a door, if you have an old, old story, that is a door. If you love the sky and the water so much you almost cannot bear it, that is a door. If you yearn for a deeper life, a full life, a sane life, that is a door."

WHY I LOVE THIS QUOTE:

It's a beautiful expression of following your desire out the door and into a bigger framework of considering your life. You find the larger, saner life by pursuing your desire, listening to your longing. You can also find the bigger life out there waiting for you through where you've been wounded. It's not overly romanticized, either. She is telling us that there are limits. There aren't endless doors of opportunity. They are few, and they are important because they are few. There is something at stake. There are choices for you to walk through.

WHY THIS IS A TRANSFORMATIVE BOOK:

Clarissa Pinkola Estes', *Women Who Run With the Wolves*, is Jungian psycho-analytic theory applied to folktales and fairy tales from around the world. It is for everyone who feels confined, constrained, and soul-sick. This book helps you to reconnect with your intuition, reevaluate what it means to live authentically and reimagine what your life can look like when you live it wild and free. It's a guidebook to the picture language and the narrative logic of our right brain. The subject is fascinating. This book also has a highly prag-matic, powerful core that can change the quality of your life.

QUESTIONS FOR MEDITATION:

What are the doors through which you would walk if you could?

"Real courage is when you know you're licked before you begin, but you begin anyway and see it through no matter what."

WHY I LOVE THIS QUOTE:

Courage is always hard. So many fight against injustice and oppression and remain nameless. They are beaten, jailed, denied jobs and educational opportunities, and even though their fight for justice may not manifest for them, even though they know they won't win, still they rise. This quote encourages us to be among those willing to take a stand for what we know is right, even if we're in the minority.

WHY THIS IS A TRANSFORMATIVE BOOK:

Harper Lee's *To Kill a Mockingbird* is one of the most important novels ever written in the United States. In 1930s rural Maycomb, Alabama people were pretty much set in their way of life. Town folk had received an education and worked as lawyers, doctors, bankers, and businessmen. Country folk may or may not have received an education because they had to work the fields and many were illiterate. Even the majority of those educated white folk still saw themselves as superior to blacks, and few, if any, had the audacity to take a black's word over a white's even if it were the correct moral thing to do. Yet, the crux of Lee's novel is a court case threatening to disrupt this way of life, having the town divide along both racial and moral lines, and having each character step into others' shoes and view the world from another's perspective.

It reads like a coming-of-age novel but is also just excellent storytelling. Packed with powerful and resonant themes, it does not moralize. It leaves us with a portrayal of how racism works in the collective culture — in this case under Jim Crow-era laws during the Great Depression. It is as relevant and important today as ever.

QUESTIONS FOR MEDITATION:

How could you be more courageous in your own life?

"The chief element of happiness is this: to want to be what you are."

WHY I LOVE THIS QUOTE:
This is such an excellent distillation of what so many try to say on the subject of happiness. And to think Erasmus wrote this in 1510 (at the age of 43). Notice, all wrapped up into this English vernacular at once: (1) that happiness has a primary element; (2) that it is rooted in striving to be something (a pursuit); and (3) that you are a somebody, that you possess an identity, a real or truer self. That's a lot to pack into the punch of 14 words.

WHY THIS IS A TRANSFORMATIVE BOOK:
Erasmus is so overlooked and undervalued. He was practically a century before Shakespeare (98 and a half years if you're starting from birthdates). He preceded Voltaire by 130. *In Praise of Folly* stands out as a mature and inspired satire taking on all manner of misled philosophical topics of the time. I read it at a time in seminary when the undermining of perfection came as a breath of fresh air theologically. I immediately loved Erasmus's supremely styled satirical punches.

I have wondered why Erasmus has been so overlooked in so many ways, and a clue probably lies in his illegitimate birth from a father who was under holy orders. He had already been stuffed into a monastery during his teens. He learned Latin as well as any "home" tongue. Critics say the future even then was already with the use of vernacular tongues. Also, no country could claim him as a true native son, and while he lived in Belgium, England, Germany, Italy, Switzerland, and Holland, it was rarely in any one place for very long.

QUESTIONS FOR MEDITATION:

Do you have a good idea of who you are?

"The crisis facing men is not the crisis of masculinity, it is the crisis of patriarchal masculinity. Until we make this distinction clear, men will continue to fear that any critique of patriarchy represents a threat."

WHY I LOVE THIS QUOTE:
Patriarchal masculinity is a term that describes ideas about, and practices of, masculinity that emphasize the superiority of masculinity over femininity and the authority of men over women. These ideas perpetuate and maintain gender inequalities. By assuming that femininity is weak or lesser than, men deny (or are embarrassed by) such qualities within themselves, even though we all find wholeness in embracing both aspects into ourselves.

WHY THIS IS A TRANSFORMATIVE BOOK:
To know love, men must be able to look at the ways that patriarchal culture keeps them from knowing themselves, from being in touch with their feelings, from loving. In *The Will to Change: Men, Masculinity, and Love*, bell hooks shows men how to express the emotions that are a fundamental part of who they are — whatever their age, marital status, ethnicity, or sexual orientation.

Hooks addresses the most common concerns of men, such as fear of intimacy and loss of their superior status in society, in new and challenging ways. She believes men can find the way to spiritual unity by getting back in touch with the emotionally open part of themselves — and lay claim to the rich and rewarding inner lives that have historically been the exclusive province of women. *The Will to Change* is designed to help men reclaim the best part of themselves.

QUESTIONS FOR MEDITATION:

How can we honor and encourage masculinity while undermining the flawed assumptions of patriarchal masculinity?

"I pray to the God within me that He will give me the strength to ask Him the right questions."

WHY I LOVE THIS QUOTE:

The character who says this conveys two key concepts. First, is the idea that God is everywhere, even within every individual, and the idea that faith is based on questions, not answers. Eliezer, the narrator, struggles with his faith. He continually asks where God has gone and questions how such evil could exist in the world. The quote tells us that these moments demonstrate ongoing spiritual commitment even in the face of unspeakable evil.

WHY THIS IS A TRANSFORMATIVE BOOK:

Born in the town of Sighet, Transylvania, Elie Wiesel was a teenager when he and his family were taken from their home in 1944 to Auschwitz concentration camp, and then to Buchenwald. *Night* is the terrifying record of Elie Wiesel's memories of the death of his family, the death of his own innocence, and his despair as a deeply observant Jew confronting the absolute evil of man. *Night* can also be read as an attack against silence. So many times in the work, evil is perpetuated by a silent lack of resistance or by ignoring reports of evil. The novel bears witness to tragedy in order to warn others, to prevent anything like the Holocaust from ever happening again.

QUESTIONS FOR MEDITATION:

What are the right questions to ask about your current circumstance?

"If you are like most people, then like most people, you don't know you're like most people."

WHY I LOVE THIS QUOTE:
In some ways we realize we're all very much alike. That's why we can get behind big, bold statements like: "All men are created equal." But research shows that regardless of IQ or education level, we are all susceptible to similar errors in our reasoning. As a result, most people believe they are the exceptions to the rule. Most overestimate their abilities and underestimate their weaknesses. Some researchers call this "illusory bias." It reminds me of William Saroyan's statement: "Everyone has got to die, but I always thought an exception would be made in my case."

WHY THIS IS A TRANSFORMATIVE BOOK:
Daniel Gilbert's, *Stumbling on Happiness*, brings to life the latest scientific research in psychology, cognitive neuroscience, philosophy, and behavioral economics. Gilbert reveals what scientists have discovered about the uniquely human ability to imagine the future, and about our capacity to predict how much we will like it when we get there. (Hint: we're not very good.) He explains in detail the cognitive errors we make in trying to predict our future happiness. He also outlines one technique that has been effective in predicting future happiness, but then goes on to discuss the reason why the vast majority of humans won't use it.

QUESTIONS FOR MEDITATION:

Do you have an easier time giving feedback than receiving it? Most people do. Why do you think that is?

"Problems that remain persistently insoluble should always be suspected as questions asked in the wrong way."

WHY I LOVE THIS QUOTE:

We can think about this quote in grand, philosophic ways about the nature of the universe and human behavior. We can also think about it in terms of our own identity and actions and experiences.

WHY THIS IS A TRANSFORMATIVE BOOK:

In *The Book on the Taboo Against Knowing Who You Are*, Alan Watts argues with equal parts conviction and compassion that "the prevalent sensation of oneself as a separate ego enclosed in a bag of skin is a hallucination which accords neither with Western science nor with the experimental philosophy-religions of the East." He explores the cause and cure of that illusion in a way that flows from profound unease as we confront our cultural conditioning into a deep sense of lightness as we surrender to the comforting mystery and interconnectedness of the universe.

The book explores many of the core inquiries which religions have historically tried to address — the problems of life and love, death and sorrow, the universe and our place in it, what it means to have an "I" at the center of our experience, and what the meaning of existence might be. Watts offers a new understanding of personal identity. It reveals the mystery of existence, presenting an alternative to the feelings of alienation that is prevalent in Western society, and a vision of how we can come to understand the cosmic self within every living thing.

QUESTIONS FOR MEDITATION:

How do we learn to ask better questions?

What questions am I afraid to ask?

"Life will give you whatever experience is most helpful for the evolution of your consciousness. How do you know this is the experience you need? Because this is the experience you are having at the moment."

WHY I LOVE THIS QUOTE:

There's something direct and practical about the idea Eckhart Tolle expresses here. If you consider yourself as a lifelong learner, what more can you learn from than your own experiences? If experiences aren't your teacher, what is? Books and meditation? Good answer! But those are your experiences as well. Whether or not your experience is necessary or meaningful or whether this is "best of all possible worlds" (which Voltaire ruthlessly satirizes in *Candide*), isn't the point. It's about the evolution — or persistent gradual growth — of your consciousness.

The idea also connects with Nietzsche's quote about loving everything: "My formula for greatness in a human being is amor fati: that one wants nothing to be different, not forward, not backward, not in all eternity. Not merely to bear what is necessary, still less conceal it...but love it."

WHY THIS IS A TRANSFORMATIVE BOOK:

Eckhart Tolle's message in *The Power of Now* is simple. Living in the now is the truest path to happiness and enlightenment. Tolle is a world-class teacher. More importantly, within a chapter of reading this book, you are already holding the world in a different container, more conscious of how thoughts and emotions get in the way of your ability to live in genuine peace and happiness.

QUESTIONS FOR MEDITATION:

What experience are you having right now?

How are you prepared for it?

"In a very real sense we have two minds, one that thinks and one that feels."

WHY I LOVE THIS QUOTE:
Research over the past 25 years especially has shown us that our brains feel as much as they think, and that we don't actually "think" as much as we think we do. The new work in emotional literacy draws a more holistic view of our social interactions, decision-making, and behavior overall.

WHY THIS IS A TRANSFORMATIVE BOOK:
In *Emotional Intelligence: Why It Can Matter More Than IQ*, Daniel Goleman reports from the frontiers of psychology and neuroscience. The book offers startling new insights into our "two minds" — the rational and the emotional — and how they together shape who we really are. Everyone knows that high IQ is no guarantee of success, happiness, or virtue, but until Emotional Intelligence, we could only guess why.

Goleman delineates the five crucial skills of emotional intelligence, and shows how they determine our success in relationships, work, and even our physical well-being. What emerges is a new way to talk about being smart. The best news is that "emotional literacy" is not fixed early in life. Every parent, every teacher, every business leader, and everyone interested in a more civil society, has a stake in this compelling vision of human possibility.

QUESTIONS FOR MEDITATION:

Some say, "I think, therefore I am." Others say, "I feel, therefore I can be free." How can you "be" in your feelings? Are you comfortable there? Does it come at the expense of thinking rationally?

"Every action you take is a vote for the type of person you wish to become. No single instance will transform your beliefs, but as the votes build up, so does the evidence of your new identity."

WHY I LOVE THIS QUOTE:
This about sums it up, doesn't it? You become your beliefs one small vote at a time. It's a good reminder that if you really want to establish a habit, you should inhabit the identity of what you are becoming.

WHY THIS IS A TRANSFORMATIVE BOOK:
In *Atomic Habits: An Easy & Proven Way to Build Good Habits & Break Bad Ones*, James Clear emphasizes that, "You do not rise to the level of your goals. You fall to the level of your systems." He certainly makes a powerful argument as to why. There are a lot of books on habits, and a lot of great ones, but recency bias notwithstanding, Clear is convincing. He tracks his own progress in such a systematic and orderly way. He covers the bases. He gives credit where credit is due, and he constantly re-evaluates ideas and interprets them into his own originally constructed ideas.

QUESTIONS FOR MEDITATION:

As you continue to explore "who do you think you are," what habits do you already consistently enact? What habits have you broken? How did your identity play a role in establishing the habit or breaking it?

"I have never missed a meditation in thirty-three years. I meditate once in the morning and again in the afternoon, for about twenty minutes each time. Then I go about the business of my day."

WHY I LOVE THIS QUOTE:

When I first read this statement, I was overwhelmed by the very concept of such highly-trained discipline and especially the unknown potential power of meditating. I didn't know what to do with it, so I underlined it in my book, but didn't do anything with it. Now that I have started a meditating routine of my own, I realize Lynch is right about how we do waste our time on so many other things throughout the day, that if you establish the routine, it can fit in naturally.

WHY THIS IS A TRANSFORMATIVE BOOK:

In *Catching the Big Fish*, filmmaker David Lynch provides a window into his methods as an artist, his personal working style, and the immense creative benefits he has experienced from the practice of meditation. Lynch describes the experience of "diving within" and "catching" ideas like fish — and then preparing them for television or movie screens, and other mediums in which he works, such as painting, music, and design. Lynch writes for the first time about his more than three-decade commitment to Transcendental Meditation and the difference it has made in his creative process.

He writes: "If you have a golf-ball-sized consciousness, when you read a book you'll have a golf-ball-sized understanding; when you look out of the window, a golf-ball-sized awareness, when you wake up in the morning, a golf-ball-sized wakefulness; and as you go about your day, a golf-ball-sized happiness. But if you can expand your consciousness, make it grow, then when you read that book, you'll have more understanding, when you look out, more awareness, when you wake up, more wakefulness; and as you go about the day, more inner happiness."

QUESTIONS FOR MEDITATION:

What efforts do you make to expand your self-awareness?

"The necessary thing is after all but this; solitude, great inner solitude. Going into oneself for hours meeting no one — this one must be able to attain."

WHY I LOVE THIS QUOTE:

It's not just for a young poet to go deep into one self and "disconnect," as we say today. It's good for all of us. We're social creatures, but that is not the problem. We are always social. We live on social media. We live constantly in and around the interruptions and urgencies of others and life's demands. It is healthy and necessary for self-integration to go deep inside oneself, at least for intervals, at least from time to time. Rilke also writes: "Nobody can advise you and help you, nobody. There is only one way. Go into yourself."

WHY THIS IS A TRANSFORMATIVE BOOK:

Rainer Maria Rilke is a fascinating personality and transcendent poet. I first came across *Letters to a Young Poet* as an undergraduate. I was overcome by the sincerity and deep thoughtfulness of these letters. They moved me then and I came back to them time and again, often when I was struggling with a desire to write mixed with how to make a living doing something fulfilling (and not sure what that meant either).

In 1903, a student at a military academy sent some of his verses to a well-known Austrian poet, requesting an assessment of their value. The older artist, Rainer Maria Rilke, replied to the novice in this series of letters — an amazing archive of remarkable insights into the psychology and depth of Rilke, not published as a whole until four years after his death in 1929. The ten letters were written during an important stage in Rilke's artistic development, and they contain many of the themes that later appeared in his best works, like *The Duino Elegies*.

QUESTIONS FOR MEDITATION:

Do you resist or long for time alone? If you resist it and find yourself seeking distraction when you have it, take this opportunity to ask yourself why? What is making you uncomfortable? Behind that insight is a door for growth.

"I'm consumed with regret for the things I didn't do, the choices I didn't make, the things I didn't say. We spend so much time being afraid of failure, afraid of rejection. But regret is the thing we should fear most. Failure is an answer. Rejection is an answer. Regret is an eternal question you will never have the answer to. 'What if...' 'If only...' 'I wonder what would have...' You will never, never know, and it will haunt you for the rest of your days."

WHY I LOVE THIS QUOTE:

He has a major point about what we project so much paralyzing fear and attention on, rejection. It's a good reminder that failure and rejection give us feedback. They can't say yes if you don't ask. They can't say yes if you're afraid of a few no's. Maybe a lot of no's. Each time you get a no, you can reassess your approach, your delivery, your content, and/or try again, start over. He's saying what you really should fear is the regret you're going to have when you chose not to try things, not to "put yourself out there," as they say.

WHY THIS IS A TRANSFORMATIVE BOOK:

Born a Crime: Stories From a South African Childhood is fresh and authentic. Noah is of mixed race, born right before the end of apartheid, which made his birth illegal due to racist laws against blacks and whites having sex (punishable by up to five years in prison). He struggles to find himself in a world where he was never supposed to exist. His fervently religious mother provided him with an unconventional upbringing, one that obviously shaped him into the man he would become as an adult. She in particular is a standout. Her parenting made him strong, and helped him escape the cycle of poverty, violence, and abuse that would ultimately threaten her own life.

QUESTIONS FOR MEDITATION:

What do you most wish you had done that you didn't?

"We insist on being Someone, with a capital S. We get security from defining ourselves as worthless or worthy, superior or inferior. We waste precious time exaggerating or romanticizing or belittling ourselves with a complacent surety that yes, that's who we are. We mistake the openness of our being — the inherent wonder and surprise of each moment — for a solid, irrefutable self. Because of this misunderstanding, we suffer."

WHY I LOVE THIS QUOTE:

We are all guilty of this: exaggerating and belittling ourselves and telling ourselves that in fact that is who we are. It is the work of the ego and it is rooted in constant self-comparison. While the "self" requires a healthy ego, we need reminding just to be open to the being and mystery of life itself. Strip it all away and that is the Someone we are.

WHY THIS IS A TRANSFORMATIVE BOOK:

If you haven't heard of Pema Chödrön by now, it's time. A profound thinker, charismatic speaker, and prolific author, she is a wonder. In this book, *The Places That Scare You: A Guide to Fearlessness in Difficult Times*, she encourages us to see problems as spiritual opportunities. Instead of trying to run from discomfort, she advocates staying put and learning about ourselves. Instead of habitually reaching for whatever palliative gives relief — always temporary — she suggests feeling and observing our discomforts, becoming more fully present in our lives, learning how to be truly here now. Only through this process, she says, can we experience the deep joy of being alive. This is a great companion volume to her book *When Things Fall Apart*. Above all, she encourages the consistent practice of meditation.

QUESTIONS FOR MEDITATION:

How can meditation or small acts of mindfulness help you escape the tyranny of constant self-comparison?

"The courage to be happy also includes the courage to be disliked. When you have gained that courage, your interpersonal relationships will all at once change into things of lightness."

WHY I LOVE THIS QUOTE:
There are certain threads that you can pull and all at once numerous things fall away and a new reality can be experienced. While many aspects of growth are long processes, sometimes you can hit upon something that immediately lifts you onto a higher plateau with a greater vision. In my personal journey over the past several months, shifting career paths and fields of study, as well as speaking out more about injustice and the rights of others, I have discovered how very real it is to want to be liked, and to fear rejection. If we are authentically finding our courage, we will feel lighter.

WHY THIS IS A TRANSFORMATIVE BOOK:
The Courage to Be Disliked: How to Free Yourself, Change Your Life and Achieve Real Happiness by Ichiro Kishimi and Fumitake Koga sends a reverberating message for our times. If you really have a feeling of contribution, you will no longer have any need for recognition from others. Because you will already have the real awareness that "I am of use to someone," without needing to go out of your way to be acknowledged by others. A person obsessed with the desire for recognition does not have a community feeling yet, and has not managed to engage in self-acceptance, confidence in others, or contribution to others.

QUESTIONS FOR MEDITATION:

If you are completely honest with yourself, what choices do you make on a regular basis that are about pleasing others?

"Abiding faith does not depend on borrowed concepts. Rather, it is the magnetic force of a bone-deep, lived understanding, one that draws us to realize our ideals, walk our talk, and act in accord with what we know to be true."

WHY I LOVE THIS QUOTE:

This idea impresses on us the importance of our connectedness to everything and everyone around us. We won't see this unless we are willing to get up close, close to ourselves and our experiences. She also says, "It's not the existence of beliefs that is the problem, but what happens to us when we hold them rigidly, without examining them, when we presume the absolutely centrality of our views and become disdainful of others."

WHY THIS IS A TRANSFORMATIVE BOOK:

Sharon Salzberg's, *Faith: Trusting Your Own Deepest Experience*, is an extremely personal account of her experiences with faith. As a Buddhist, her faith is not based on an object or an external subject. She argues that true, unwavering faith can only be found in trust and courage within oneself. The faith that Salzberg refers to is trusting your own deepest intuition, having self-confidence, and knowing that doubting is not a sign of being faithless. Instead, it should be seen as a key to spiritual strength.

QUESTIONS FOR MEDITATION:

When you think of the genuine people you know, are they people of faith?

What makes them stand out from the people you think of fake or inauthentic?

"The function of education is to teach one to think intensively and to think critically. Intelligence plus character – that is the goal of true education."

WHY I LOVE THIS QUOTE:

We should always be learning. We learn about others. We learn about ourselves. I have known highly educated people with little character. When I worked with selfish or egotistical ministers or narcissistic and small-minded professors with their Ph.D.'s and specialties, I was always surprised, sometimes disillusioned. There is more to learning than facts and the accumulation of knowledge that goes into building true knowledge. Perhaps that is why you're here, visiting this book regularly.

WHY THIS IS A TRANSFORMATIVE BOOK:

Today's quote comes from Martin Luther King Jr. himself, but the book selection is the biography from Stephen B. Oates, *Let the Trumpet Sound: A Life of Martin Luther King Jr.* I first read this biography when I was fifteen, back in 1987. I especially enjoyed the book's exploration of MLK Jr.'s philosophical underpinnings. King's approach to civil rights came as a result of his schooling and voracious appetite for theological, political, and philosophical reading. Oates' coverage of the Montgomery Bus Boycott and the Selma Marches in particular are superb. He is most known for the delivery of his "I Have a Dream" address, which followed the peaceful march on Washington, D.C. of 250,000 people, and as the youngest winner of the Nobel Peace Prize (at age 35). He also served for eleven years as elected president of the Southern Christian Leadership Conference, an organization formed to provide new leadership to the then burgeoning civil rights movement. He travelled over six million miles and spoke over 2500 times, appearing wherever there was injustice, protest, and action. His message rings out with great moral clarity to this day.

QUESTIONS FOR MEDITATION:

What does it mean to live a virtuous life?

"I've never done anything but dream. This, and this alone, has been the meaning of my life. My only real concern has been my inner life."

WHY I LOVE THIS QUOTE:

If we are considering identity and the transformation and exploration of the self through the inner life, one of the most profound thinkers and writers of the 20th century — and all time for that matter — would be none other than Fernando Pessoa. While there is a tendency toward entropy in Pessoa's work and self-conscious self-examination, the inner work that he does is often revelatory. Here is someone constantly peering through the veil of perceived reality and calling it out.

WHY THIS IS A TRANSFORMATIVE BOOK:

Fernando Pessoa attributed his prolific writings to a wide range of alternate selves, each of which had a distinct biography, ideology, and horoscope. When he died in 1935, Pessoa left behind a trunk filled with unfinished and unpublished writings, among which were the remarkable pages that make up his posthumous masterpiece, *The Book of Disquiet*, an astonishing work that, in George Steiner's words, "gives to Lisbon the haunting spell of Joyce's Dublin or Kafka's Prague."

Published for the first time some fifty years after his death, this unique collection of short, aphoristic paragraphs comprises the "autobiography" of Bernardo Soares, one of Pessoa's alternate selves. Part intimate diary, part prose poetry, part descriptive narrative, stands out as one of the most distinctive works of the twentieth century. These heteronyms — as Pessoa called them — were masks of Pessoa himself, although it would probably be more accurate to say that they were no one's masks, as Pessoa often described himself as "no one."

QUESTIONS FOR MEDITATION:

What is the meaning of your life? Would others agree or disagree? Does it matter what others think?

"In order to change conditions outside ourselves, whether they concern the environment or relations with others, we must first change within ourselves."

WHY I LOVE THIS QUOTE:

This is a concept we learn from a wide variety of sources. From Socrates' "Know thyself" statement when asked to summarize the aggregate of all the work philosopher's do, and on down the line into every strain of eastern and western thought. When it comes to awakening, transformation, the metamorphic process of changing and growing into awareness, it all begins with gentle but courageous work on the self.

WHY THIS IS A TRANSFORMATIVE BOOK:

Thoughts Without A Thinker: Psychotherapy From A Buddhist Perspective by Mark Epstein is a wonderful book because, among other things, it brings us studies and valuable information about meditation itself, and certainly doesn't promise simple or easy cures. Meditation, in fact, is shown to help people become less defensive in all situations, but alone it doesn't necessarily help with emotional issues. In that case, the guide of directed learning through reading and reflection, as well as mentors, community, and psychotherapists are all parts of the equation. This is a powerful distillation that he brings us to: Humans fear three essential things: other humans, our own minds, and death. The book is also a powerful corrective about the concept that growth entails "disavowing" the ego and transcending it into egolessness. You need your ego. You need it in its place, healthy and integrated into your whole self.

QUESTIONS FOR MEDITATION:

In what ways do you seek satisfactions in things outside yourself, like food, comfort, sex, or success?

"Failure, when it comes to future risk-taking, is a gift. Successful risk-takers are often motivated by failure — it's what tells them that they aren't done preparing yet. It's inspiration to work harder, to train better, and to learn more."

WHY I LOVE THIS QUOTE:

I love the optimism and clarity this idea has. When something isn't going right, when I am effectively failing at something, I want to deny it, get angry at it, possibly quit it, feel embarrassed, etc. What was I thinking? How silly? I might tell myself. Who do I think I am? But when I know I'm on the right track, when I know it's something important, or meaningful, then ideas embodied in this quote remind me to listen well and respond well. Take it as a gift means I'm receiving feedback that is valuable. Feedback is an opportunity to learn, and learning is a gift.

WHY THIS IS A TRANSFORMATIVE BOOK:

The Art of Risk: The New Science of Courage, Caution, and Chance by Kayt Sukel takes some of the ideas we've been touching on in this book to a whole new level. It's not about throwing caution to the wind, but really about pushing beyond our comfort zone. The majority of the book focuses on the science behind risk, with the objective of showing us how our brain reacts to risk taking, and transforming that into how we can use that information to nurture our risk-taking capabilities. She also dives into common misconceptions around people who take risks as a routine part of life.

QUESTIONS FOR MEDITATION:

What are you struggling with, frustrated by, or failing at? How can you see it as a gift, an opportunity for feedback? How can you take the information and reframe and make it better?

"Ask anyone what she means when she says 'God' and chances are that you will learn a lot more about that person than you will learn about God."

WHY I LOVE THIS QUOTE:
As meditation practices go, they tend to open the door to open-heartedness and a lack of defensiveness. Such practices are a kind of maturity, even if guides and mentors and deep thinkers are still necessary for direction. This thinking demonstrates a maturity of both. It is a thought representative of deep meditation and guided reflection. This idea connects me to Sharon Salzberg's idea of deep, personal faith as really being about what goes on deep in the privacy of your innermost self, not from holding tightly to rigid and unexamined beliefs.

WHY THIS IS A TRANSFORMATIVE BOOK:
Holy Envy: Finding God in the Faith of Others by Barbara Brown Taylor is more about finding common ground with those of other faiths and allowing it to deepen your own. Many of us are ignorant of other faiths besides our own (if we adhere to one at all). By learning about what others believe, we can be more accepting of them, and more clear about why we ascribe to what we do.

"Spending extended amounts of time inside other religious worldviews has loosened the screws on my own, which is beginning to seem like a good thing," she writes. "Disowning God has been a great help to me. Owning my distinct view of God has helped me understand it much better. Although I can see the places where religious truth claims collide, this does not bother me as much as it could. I am far more interested in how people live than what they believe...When my religion tries to come between me and my neighbor, I will choose my neighbor. That self-canceling feature of my religion is one of the things I like best about it. Jesus never commanded me to love my religion."

QUESTIONS FOR MEDITATION:

Who is God to you? What does your definition of God say about you?

"The place to improve the world is first in one's own heart and head and hands, and then work outward from there."

WHY I LOVE THIS QUOTE:

Change begins within your own self. It's a message we hear in a variety of contexts and from a diverse array of thinkers time and again. Here, it's expressed interestingly about beginning with your heart (feeling), your head (thinking), and also your hands (actions). The Big Self School is about doing the inner work, which will eventually lead to an outward manifestation and impact in the world. This is well expressed here.

WHY THIS IS A TRANSFORMATIVE BOOK:

Zen and the Art of Motorcycle Maintenance: An Inquiry into Values by Robert Pirsig is a classic. I read it in high school and college, and particularly love the first 100 pages or so when Phaedrus engages in the difference between the romantic and the classic minds. The situation: Phaedrus and his son take a motorcycle tour around Bozeman with two friends. The friends, John and Sylvia are depicted as representing the superficial values with an inability (and unwillingness) to fix their own bikes. They tune out when he explains how to fix John's $1800 BMW bike. Phaedrus stands there, holding a tin piece he pulled off a beer can to fix the problem expertly. John sees things for what they are defined as. It can only be a beer can. It is impossible to fix a machine with that. BMW bikes need precision parts. Phaedrus sees things in terms of adaptable atomic particles. It's a wild ride as Phaedrus inquires into values and what's important in the micro and macro scheme of things.

QUESTIONS FOR MEDITATION:

Why do you think the best way to improve the world begins with your own heart, head, and hands?

"I have one outstanding trait in my character, which must strike anyone who knows me for any length of time, and that is my knowledge of myself. I can watch myself and my actions, just like an outsider. The Anne of every day I can face entirely without prejudice, without making excuses for her, and watch what's good and what's bad about her. This 'self-conscious-ness' haunts me, and every time I open my mouth I know as soon as I've spoken whether 'that ought to have been differ-ent' or 'that was right as it was.' There are so many things about myself that I condemn; I couldn't begin to name them all. I understand more and more how true Daddy's words were when he said: 'All children must look after their own upbringing.' Parents can only give good advice or put them on the right paths, but the final forming of a person's charac-ter lies in their own hands."

WHY I LOVE THIS QUOTE:
Part of the power of Anne Frank's diary is her honest self-assessment. She seems beyond her years writing as a 13 and 14-year-old girl in these pages.

WHY THIS IS A TRANSFORMATIVE BOOK:
The Diary of a Young Girl by Anne Frank is as haunting as her insights were precocious. As Jews in Nazi occupied Holland, Anne and her parents and sister Margot, fled their home in Amsterdam to escape capture. From 1942-1944 they occupied rooms in an old office building, which they called 'The Secret Annexe'. Anne's diary details daily life within the confines of their safe house. The diary was left behind and found by the office cleaner. After being interned in two concentration camps, Anne and her sister Margot were finally sent to Bergen-Belsen where they both died. Anne was just 15 years old. Only Otto Frank, the girls' father, survived, and the diary was returned to him.

QUESTIONS FOR MEDITATION:
How do you take care of your personal character now?

"One of the best ways to make yourself happy is to make other people happy. One of the best ways to make other people happy is to be happy yourself."

WHY I LOVE THIS QUOTE:

It's easy to think of happiness as merely trite, shallow, or at best impermeable. Or even that happiness is fake, but what we really need is joy or wisdom or satisfaction. From Mother Theresa to Gandhi to the numberless and name-less who care for others, there is a tremendous amount of research and biographical detail about the power of compassion and service to others as being a key source of happiness and life satisfaction. The beginning of wisdom is to know yourself, and have compassion and understanding for yourself. The next step in that journey is to focus outwardly on others.

WHY THIS IS A TRANSFORMATIVE BOOK:

The Happiness Project: Or Why I Spent a Year Trying to Sing in the Morning, Clean My Closets, Fight Right, Read Aristotle, and Generally Have More Fun by Gretchen Rubin is a well-written year of resolutions and actions with the intent to become happier. It may seem trite and self-involved at first glance, but much of what Rubin sets forth is the generous and other-directed path to make those around her happy. As she notes, if you make others happy, you become happier in the process. The fact that Rubin starts the year not feeling particularly unhappy makes her research and self-study all the more valid. To be reasonably happy but to make efforts to become happier is a solid premise that Rubin builds on through empirical, as well as anecdotal research.

QUESTIONS FOR MEDITATION:

Does it come easily for you to serve others, or is the very idea uncomfort-able?

"Thus Western man enacted an extraordinary dialectic in the course of the modern era — moving from a near boundless confidence in his own powers, his spiritual potential, his capacity for certain knowledge, his mastery over nature, and his progressive destiny, to what often appeared to be a sharply opposite condition: a debilitating sense of metaphysical insignificance and personal futility, spiritual loss of faith, uncertainty in knowledge, a mutually destructive relationship with nature, and an intense insecurity concerning the human future. In the four centuries of modern man's existence, Bacon and Descartes had become Kafka and Beckett."

WHY I LOVE THIS QUOTE:
A powerful, complex thought, and one that may also be examined in *The Denial of Death* along these same lines. This quote gives us a wide angle lens to consider the shift in our worldview regarding our purpose and identity in this world. We need the optimism in our potential. We need reminders of the world within us and how that informs us as we move about in the world.

WHY THIS IS A TRANSFORMATIVE BOOK:
The Passion of the Western Mind: Understanding the Ideas that Have Shaped Our World View by Richard Tarnas helps readers understand how the modern mind developed from the Greeks to the present era. It is erudite and stylistically graceful. He makes clever associations between thinkers from diverse periods and contexts. The most profound material, and most of the book, Tarnas traces our thinking from Plato to postmodernism. The missing key in the philosophical quest, he argues, can be found in depth psychology and the unconscious.

QUESTIONS FOR MEDITATION:

If you had to state your worldview in a short paragraph, could you do it?

"Through my English teacher, I started to sense that words not only convey some thing, but are something; that words have color, depth, texture of their own, and the power to evoke vastly more than they mean; that words can be used not merely to make things clear, make things vivid, make things interesting and whatever else, but to make things happen inside the one who reads them or hears them."

WHY I LOVE THIS QUOTE:

Buechner expresses gratitude for turning points in his life when the influence and guidance of another showed him things that made a difference. Then, the idea of the power of words. Similarly, Marcus Aurelius begins in just the same way with an extended discourse on specifically each important person in his life that has made a difference or taught him something singular and important. It is important to begin with gratitude for mentors, guides, coaches, teachers, and others along life's path of self-transformation.

WHY THIS IS A TRANSFORMATIVE BOOK:

I first discovered *The Sacred Journey* by Frederick Buechner my second year of Seminary in 1995, when what I really wanted was to be a writer. Years later, I assigned it to hundreds of students when I taught at Lee University. I've read and reread it. Buechner is a wonderful, diverse writer. This memoir isn't simply a retelling of his major life moments, it is actually an attempt to explain and paint humanity and the vast array of feelings and emotions and timelessness that connects the past and the present. It weaves in three narratives. His sincerity, vulnerability, and the power of his intellect to process and interpret his specific journey, enlightens us universally on our own journeys.

QUESTIONS FOR MEDITATION:

Who are you grateful for that served you well or taught you something critical at a turning point moment in your life?

"Begin by answering this question in a single, memorable sentence: Why do you get up in the morning?"

WHY I LOVE THIS QUOTE:
A conscious sense of purpose can plant the seeds of habits and rituals that lead to unconscious positive self-regard and life satisfaction.

WHY THIS IS A TRANSFORMATIVE BOOK:
The Blue Zones: Lessons for Living Longer From the People Who've Lived the Longest by Dan Buettner is a fascinating ethnographic study. The blue zones are regions in the world where loads of people live healthy lives to very old age, often beyond 100. Dan Buettner personally goes on research expeditions to various locations around the world. He and his team's goal is to determine first whether the people claiming to be very old are, in fact, as old as they claim, and second, to interview the super-seniors to determine the factors contributing to their long and healthy lives. The in-depth studies focus on four locations: Sardinia, Loma Linda in southern California, Nicoya in Costa Rica, and Okinawa. Buettner uncovers a variety of factors that have contributed to their long lives. The lifestyles include near-vegetarian diets, daily exercise, social connections through extended families and neighbors, laughter and a sense of humor, and a sense of purpose in living.

QUESTIONS FOR MEDITATION:

Why do you get up in the morning?

"Education is thinking, and thinking is looking for yourself and seeing what's there, not what you got told was there."

WHY I LOVE THIS QUOTE:

We have heard that a true education meets knowledge with character from MLK Jr. Now we get a perspective of education with an emphasis on looking for yourself. That is the broadening and enriching experience of travel.

WHY THIS IS A TRANSFORMATIVE BOOK:

I love *Blue Highways: A Journey into America* by William Least-Heat Moon. It is a rich and rewarding journey you take with the author. I took the book with me on a long road trip from Chattanooga through St. Louis, Kansas City, Denver, all the way to Moab, Utah and then through a number of small Colorado towns like Telluride, Silverton, and Leadville. I was so inspired I had to teach it to my students when we did ethnographic field research essays, even though there is no way they read the whole thing.

Destiny Allison writes, "I loved the people he met, the rain on his windshield, the taste of fresh fish, and the holding onto history as the vehicle through which we arrive at our future. I loved more the metaphor of his small roads. We think our lives are along the big highways, our achievements and milestones the things we celebrate and commemorate. But really, it is the blue highways of our lives — the small twisted roads, the roads that end and force us to turn around, the hitchhikers and creeks we happen upon without intention that are the fabric of who we are and where we are going."

QUESTIONS FOR MEDITATION:

Where have you traveled to that surprised you by what you found compared to what you expected? How does travel educate you?

"I'd like to repeat the advice that I gave you before, in that I think you really should make a radical change in your lifestyle and begin to boldly do things which you may previously never have thought of doing, or been too hesitant to attempt. So many people live within unhappy circumstances and yet will not take the initiative to change their situation because they are conditioned to a life of security, conformity, and conservatism, all of which may appear to give one peace of mind, but in reality nothing is more damaging to the adventurous spirit within a man than a secure future."

WHY I LOVE THIS QUOTE:
Chris McCandless gave this advice to his friend Ron that he met during some of his travels before he finally went as far into the wild as he could possibly find, namely the Alaskan wilderness, where he eventually died. While McCandless's story is a cautionary tale in some respects, there is also much to be admired in his strength of character and desire for boldness and search for truth. There's always the chance that we will fail when we move boldly out and take that "leap of faith" and say yes to adventure. Certainly we should meditate and listen and think through plans to re-direct, plans for bold new adventures, and self-inventions, but there comes a time to strike.

WHY THIS IS A TRANSFORMATIVE BOOK:
I used *Into the Wild* by Jon Krakauer in one of my more interesting composition courses, the one that was supposed to be slightly less advanced — the 106 section rather than the 110. With the 106 course I had the freedom to construct readings that had a better fighting chance to get reluctant readers to read. This book never failed to elicit strong responses from students and get them to really think about their values and life choices. Some admired McCandless, some thought he was a fool. Few were on the fence.

QUESTIONS FOR MEDITATION:

What do you say are your values? If they are clear to you, are you living them boldly?

"Neuroscience research shows that the only way we can change the way we feel is by becoming aware of our inner experience and learning to befriend what is going inside ourselves."

WHY I LOVE THIS QUOTE:
First, I'm always attracted to research and science backing up what we call the "inner work" because so many want to dismiss it as subjective or just something you choose to believe in or not. No doubt, for the vast majority this type of defensiveness is a refusal (conscious or otherwise) to have the courage to self-reflect and therefore become who they are. More importantly, something is going on inside ourselves whether we want to acknowledge it or not, and it is having an impact. We can choose to be at war within ourselves or come to peace. No one said it would be easy. Life is not easy, but it is necessary for growth and what we could call renewal.

WHY THIS IS A TRANSFORMATIVE BOOK:
The Body Keeps the Score: Brain, Mind, and Body in the Healing of Trauma by Bessel A. van der Kolk features empirical, innovative research with hands-on clinical experience to explain trauma in a clear, authentic way. He emphasizes incorporating both biology and social relationships into our understanding of trauma, as awful events impact both the body as well as the overall life of a struggling individual. He clarifies many misconceptions by stressing how many victims of child abuse often go ignored when compared to war veterans, and he argues with much logic that we cannot just use drugs to treat Post-Traumatic Stress Disorder (PTSD) and other mental illnesses. We must treat the whole person.

QUESTIONS FOR MEDITATION:

If you were to track your thoughts for a few minutes, just listening to yourself having them, what are they saying?

february

"Our deepest fear is not that we are inadequate. Our deepest fear is that we are powerful beyond measure. It is our light, not our darkness, that most frightens us."

WHY I LOVE THIS QUOTE:

This quote throws the gauntlet down on our potential. If we really do possess the power to create the change we say we believe in, then why aren't we doing more about it? I find the reversal of expectation in this startling. It's actually the good we are capable of that contains the deepest fear.

WHY THIS IS A TRANSFORMATIVE BOOK:

Emotive, compelling and uplifting, *Long Walk to Freedom: Volume 1* by Nelson Mandela tells the beginnings of the story of an epic life, a story of hardship, resilience and ultimate triumph conveyed with the clarity and eloquence of the outstanding moral and political leader of the 20th century. We are left with the reassuring knowledge that one man can indeed make a difference, and that positive social change, albeit painfully slow, is always possible. Mandela's dignified stance where he refuses to use harsh, condemning words about his enemies is awe-inspiring. His restraint and humility are a lesson in human behavior and, for that matter, for successful national and international politics.

QUESTIONS FOR MEDITATION:

Take a personal inventory: On your journey of transformation, where are you right now? Would you say you're still focused on the necessary inner part? Are you ready for bringing your inner change to the outer world?

"The things that I saw, I never thought I would see and be able to live through it."

WHY I LOVE THIS QUOTE:

"I was never guilty of anything except stealing a ride on a freight train during the Depression, just as the poor whites were doing," writes Clarence Norris. But after some angry whites demanded the other blacks get off the train in the middle of nowhere, a fight broke out. The whites lost, got thrown off the train themselves, then ran to tell the nearest Sheriff. And a few stops later at Paint Rock the train was stopped, and the nine black boys were almost lynched on the spot. Instead, they were tied together and taken to jail where a lifelong struggle for justice would ensue.

WHY THIS IS A TRANSFORMATIVE BOOK:

The Last of the Scottsboro Boys: An Autobiography written by Clarence Norris, the last survivor of the Scottsboro Boys, recounts his experiences through the trials, his years imprisoned on Death Row, and his final exoneration. He also discusses his lifelong fight for vindication, freedom, and principle. Although uneducated he is an astute and intelligent man, who offers incredible insight and perspective into the systematic racism that is so distressingly real and deep and haunting in some parts of the country.

QUESTIONS FOR MEDITATION:

How can you listen and learn from those who have suffered from racism and oppression?

"When asked what gave her the strength and commitment to refuse segregation, Rosa Parks credited her mother and grandfather 'for giving me the spirit of freedom... that I should not feel because of my race or color, inferior to any person. That I should do my very best to be a respectable person, to respect myself, to expect respect from others.'"

WHY I LOVE THIS QUOTE:

What's not to love? Not unlike Marcus Aurelius, Rosa Parks, not a Roman Emperor but a seamstress who took a spontaneous stand against the injustice she was fed up with at the age of 42, credits her mom and grandad. And what is she crediting them with? Building within her a belief in her character, in her dignity as a person.

WHY THIS IS A TRANSFORMATIVE BOOK:

The Rebellious Life of Mrs. Rosa Parks by Jeanne Theoharis paints a picture of the battle against the injustice that pervaded the Jim Crow South during the civil rights era from the point of view of one very courageous woman. The book is intricately researched. Much of the text is provided through direct quotes. An exceptional scholarly work, but also one that draws the reader in and builds deep empathy. The book concludes with 57 pages of index and appendices so it is a great research resource but unlike most books of that genre it is innately readable as well.

QUESTIONS FOR MEDITATION:

How can we change ourselves by developing greater empathy?

"I had reasoned this out in my mind; there was one of two things I had a right to, liberty or death; if I could not have one, I would have the other."

WHY I LOVE THIS QUOTE:
I love the strength of character and the intelligence that shines through. Not unlike the quotation attributed to Patrick Henry from a speech he made to the Second Virginia Convention on March 23, 1775, at St. John's Church in Richmond, Virginia, "Give me liberty, or give me death!"

WHY THIS IS A TRANSFORMATIVE BOOK:
Harriet Tubman: The Road to Freedom by Catherine Clinton is the definitive biography of one of the most courageous women in American history "reveals Harriet Tubman to be even more remarkable than her legend." Celebrated for her exploits as a conductor on the Underground Railroad, Harriet Tubman has entered history as one of nineteenth-century America's most enduring and important figures. But just who was this remarkable woman? To John Brown, leader of the Harper's Ferry slave uprising, she was General Tubman. For the many slaves she led north to freedom, she was Moses. To the slaveholders who sought her capture, she was a thief and a trickster. To abolitionists, she was a prophet.

QUESTIONS FOR MEDITATION:

Do you want more freedom in your life? Tubman would tell you to keep going.

"When a new kind of 'race trouble' broke out in 1912, Forsyth was a place that had already witnessed the rapid expulsion of an entire people, and many residents, like Charlie Harris, had heard firsthand accounts from relatives who'd taken part in the Cherokee removals. So whenever someone first suggested that blacks in the county should not only be punished for the murder of Mae Crow but driven out of the county forever, the white people of Forsyth knew in their bones that such a thing was possible. After all, many families owed their land and their livelihoods to exactly such a racial cleansing in the 1830s."

WHY I LOVE THIS QUOTE:

Today we have a quote that is more of a summary. The incredible part of the history of the removal of the peaceful black citizens of Forsyth is that there was really no effort to hide the history. Much like the blatant disregard for life of Cherokee removals this was seen similarly. Until through education we can get to the root cause of the fear that racism stirs up we can hardly expect fundamental change in our culture.

WHY THIS IS A TRANSFORMATIVE BOOK:

Blood at the Root: A Racial Cleansing in America by Patrick Phillips is a harrowing testament to the deep roots of racial violence in America. In September of 1912, three young black laborers were accused of raping and murdering a white girl in Forsyth County, Georgia. One man was dragged from a jail cell and lynched on the town square, two teenagers were hung after a one-day trial, and soon bands of white "night riders" launched a coordinated campaign of arson and terror, driving all 1,098 black citizens out of the county.

QUESTIONS FOR MEDITATION:

What do you fear most when it comes to racial and cultural change in our country?

"More than five decades apart, black people in the same communities found themselves protesting the same problems."

WHY I LOVE THIS QUOTE:
Change in the United States has come slowly. Partly there are discriminatory practices that are layered upon layers so that there is always plausible deniability to social conditions. There is also this way of destroying failing institutions and simply ignoring or not talking about the past that seeks to literally "whitewash" history. During times of unrest, the same discussions resurface and we find ourselves having the same conversations. It certainly becomes a clear signal how connected we are to the past. It's not some distant thing.

WHY THIS IS A TRANSFORMATIVE BOOK:
Ghosts in the Schoolyard: Racism and School Closings on Chicago's South Side by Eve L. Ewing uses critical discourse analysis, which sees speech as a form of action — when a person speaks, they are doing something, revealing the ideologies, inequality, social relationships, and political institutions that might be backing their analyses. Ewing's careful and steady interpretations of wording, language, and presentation pick apart the debate over these school closures in a way that is ultimately powerful and convincing.

Chicago Public Schools may insist that the past has no impact on the present, but Ewing says otherwise — while the closures might not seem racist to the actors, they "were the culmination of several generations of racist policy stacked on racist policy, each one disregarding, controlling, and displacing black children and families in new ways layered upon the callousness of the last."

QUESTIONS FOR MEDITATION:

Do you see signs of collective or systemic racism where you live?

"Transformation begins in you, wherever you are, whatever has happened, however you are suffering. Transformation is always possible. We do not heal in isolation. When we reach out and connect with one another — when we tell the story, name the hurt, grant forgiveness, and renew or release the relationship — our suffering begins to transform."

WHY I LOVE THIS QUOTE:
This is an incredible summary of some of the most powerful statements about personal transformation. We have emphasized in other readings that it begins with you, the "self." We have emphasized that one of the possible doors through which healing and growth occurs is through a pain, scar, or trauma. We have discussed how hopefulness and courage can always make what doesn't seem possible, possible. We have also mentioned how helping others, serving others, is a way to greater fulfillment. This captures all of that, and also speaks to the transformation of suffering.

WHY THIS IS A TRANSFORMATIVE BOOK:
The Book of Forgiving: The Fourfold Path for Healing Ourselves and Our World by Desmond Tutu and Mpho Tutu is a remarkable guide to personal and collective transformation. Not only does the book offer solid justifications for forgiving others, and personal experiences to back up the justifications, it also includes unique rituals and meditations for readers to try if they're struggling with forgiving others. There is so much to learn from this book.

QUESTIONS FOR MEDITATION:

What current personal suffering are you holding onto?

"I revered the civil rights movement and appreciated the laws that granted us the right to ride buses, to sit at lunch counters, to cast ballots. But the slowness of real change fueled the riots' intensity, from coast to coast. Decades later, inequality still ravaged poor and black communities. Then toss in the continued international struggle to end apartheid, the skyrocketing incarceration rates that scooped up too many of black folks' cousins, and a youth poverty rate that defied the wealth of the era. I knew the truth behind their rage."

WHY I LOVE THIS QUOTE:

Just as MLK Jr. once said in a *60 Minutes* interview: "I think that riots are the language of the unheard, and what is it that America has failed to hear?" The movement afoot in the United States today is asking for change to happen now, not in some distant future. We need to see that we are all in this together.

WHY THIS IS A TRANSFORMATIVE BOOK:

Lead from the Outside: How to Build Your Future and Make Real Change by Stacey Abrams is a candid and thoughtful memoir. She speaks about her lived experience as a minority leader, and provides tools for others. Abrams uses her hard-won insights to break down how ambition, fear, money, and failure function in leadership, and she includes practical exercises to help you realize your own ambition and hone your skills. Abrams discusses what she has learned over the course of her career in politics, business, and the nonprofit world, and how differences in race, gender, and class provide vitality to organizations.

QUESTIONS FOR MEDITATION:

While we revere the words of Martin Luther King, Jr. as the words of a prophet, what would he be saying now?

"She comprehended the perversity of life, that in the struggle lies the joy."

WHY I LOVE THIS QUOTE:

It's easy to call it a paradox, it's much more interesting to call it perversity. Perversity suggests there's something wrong with the way life is in the first place. But what's interesting is that even though it is perverse, still there is this hopefulness, this joy that still surfaces. It surfaces through the long struggle. Struggle is an ongoing condition, not like a "pain" or a single "scar," but suggests a succession of injustices.

WHY THIS IS A TRANSFORMATIVE BOOK:

Before she won her multitudes of awards and honors, Maya was raised in rural Stamps, Arkansas by her grandmother and uncle during the depression. First published in 1969 and now considered a modern classic, *I Know Why the Caged Bird Sings* details Angelou's tumultuous childhood in poignant detail. This book is in part a catalogue of man's inhumanity to man, woman's inhumanity to woman. It will also, however, make you proud of what can be achieved. It is an important, defining, incredibly brave work for its time of 1969. From a relatively unknown author, a world was firmly introduced to the reality of racial tensions and prejudice in the southern United States. It was a book which would have been very hard to read without the author's strength and humor throughout the hardships.

QUESTIONS FOR MEDITATION:

As we plunge deeper into Black History Month, what themes are you hearing?

"As we drove along the road, the birds chattering among the trees, the crow was cawing, the squirrel was running through the woods – all seemed mocking me in the enjoyment of their freedom. Even the horses in the fields came galloping to the fence to take a look at me; then with head and tail up, trotted nimbly by our side till a partition fence in the meadow brought them to a stand still. I seemed to be the worst slave of them all."

WHY I LOVE THIS QUOTE:
When Henrietta Wood was kidnapped back into slavery she went on to suffer in the fields of Texas and Mississippi for another 15 years. These are her words as she was taken into bondage a second time.

WHY THIS IS A TRANSFORMATIVE BOOK:
Sweet Taste of Liberty: A True Story of Slavery and Restitution in America by W. Caleb McDaniel traces the incredible story of Henrietta Wood, born into slavery, but in 1848, taken to Cincinnati and legally freed by her owner. In 1855, a Kentucky businessman named Zebulon Ward colluded with Wood's employer, abducted her, and sold her back into bondage. She remained enslaved through the Civil War, and for two years after it had ended. In 1867, she obtained her freedom for a second time and returned to Cincinnati, where she sued Ward for damages. Astonishingly, after ten years of litigation, Wood won her case: in 1878, a Federal jury awarded her $2,500. The story, in effect, gives Henrietta Wood her identity back. She was illiterate but recognized the power of having your story told, so she spoke of her experience in the court filings and to a reporter, so we have a record of who she was. Her suffering and experiences are devastating. It is hard to read at times, hard to fathom, but necessary.

QUESTIONS FOR MEDITATION:

How can we learn about the suffering of others without obstructing the search for truth with guilt?

"To refuse to listen to someone's cries for justice and equality until the request comes in a language you feel comfortable with is a way of asserting your dominance over them in the situation."

WHY I LOVE THIS QUOTE:

It is just another level of our systemic privilege that we get to pick and choose the timing of the discourse, and the way we have the discourse in the first place. It's not comfortable to discuss racism and injustice deeply embedded in our systems if not always in our hearts. If you're here, considering the meditations and readings from this book, then you already know that. Personal transformation is hard. Seeking collective understanding and change? Daunting.

WHY THIS IS A TRANSFORMATIVE BOOK:

So You Want to Talk About Race by Ijeoma Oluo is full of so many useful ideas, tips, and strategies — particularly for white people who want to be allies to racialized people. Chapter 4 and 16 deal with privilege and "checking" it, and are both essential reminders. Even if you are a newcomer to these issues, this book is accessible. There is something for readers of every level of familiarity with the issues. If you are truly open to learning more about social justice and how to dismantle institutionalized racism, you are going to find useful ideas in clear language, and in a tone that helps you hear her frustration but also her intense empathy for humanity, and her hope for a better future. You don't have to agree with everything everyone says to be in a conversation. Developing empathy has to be done in relationship. Oluo's style is confrontational and candid — she is not trying to appease anyone — but she is also witty and incisive and the topics (in the form of questions we are all asking but in some cases may have been afraid to ask).

QUESTIONS FOR MEDITATION:

How do you determine what is about race and what is not?

"I had reached the point, at which I was not afraid to die. This spirit made me a Freeman in *fact*, while I remained a slave in *form*."

WHY I LOVE THIS QUOTE:

It embodies the challenging and disciplined Stoic concept that you can remain master of what is going on within, even when external events are calling the shots on what you can't control. His lack of fear is paradoxically laced with hope. He was freeing himself psychologically in order for the opportunity to free himself physically as well.

WHY THIS IS A TRANSFORMATIVE BOOK:

My Bondage and My Freedom by Frederick Douglass is a riveting read. Douglas is a master storyteller. This is actually the second of three autobiographies written by Douglass. The first, *Narrative of the Life of Frederick Douglass*, published in 1845, is the most famous and arguably of the three the most influential and historically important. Yet the second biography is arguably the better, more strongly written book. In the decade since the first biography Douglass spent years as editor of *The North Star*, which honed his thinking and writing. Here he has grown more mature, forceful, analytical, and complex with a deepened commitment to the fight for equal rights and liberties. Douglass helps us understand in more detail the horrors of slavery, especially the psychological. He describes the hypocrisy and evils he encountered and observed as a slave, showing us that not a single part of life was untouched by slavery. He goes into detail of how he came to learn what it meant to be a slave, especially a bright slave, whose environment clearly did not nourish him, and how he strategically tried to better himself and those around him, and eventually escape.

QUESTIONS FOR MEDITATION:

Is it possible for you to call the shots on who you are and what you believe even while under the influence and control of external events?

"It is healing simply to be heard, to be met, to be seen, to be known."

WHY I LOVE THIS QUOTE:

This is an important follow-up to Frederick Douglass' *My Bondage and My Freedom* reading from yesterday. The basic message here is about paying attention, each moment, right here and right now, a radically different way to live for most of us. Many who have suffered and want to heal simply seek validation that someone else heard them, in some way can try and understand what they have been through. It doesn't make you responsible for their suffering to listen.

WHY THIS IS A TRANSFORMATIVE BOOK:

Coming to Our Senses: Healing Ourselves and the World Through Mindfulness by Jon Kabat-Zinn is a wise book about being mindful and living life to its fullest. It is the kind of book to return to from time to time. It's length may intimidate first-time readers, particularly if you approach it like many books, consuming it in large gulps over several days. This book, similar to Pessoa's *The Book of Disquiet*, asks to be consumed in tiny bites, perhaps even reading without too much attempt being made to "understand" it. Let it sink in gradually so that it becomes a part of your own intuitive wisdom. The book asks you simply to focus on truly seeing and knowing what is going on moment by moment, not because you can necessarily change the circumstances, but so that you can respond wisely and well.

QUESTIONS FOR MEDITATION:

Can you think of a hard time in your life where you just wanted to share what you had been through with someone?

"Awareness of our problems thus does not necessarily mean that they get solved. It may just mean that we are able to perfectly anticipate where we will fail."

WHY I LOVE THIS QUOTE:

We know people who are well aware of their problems, but still don't do anything about them. They may or may not then truly know where they will fail because various forms of denial may still exist. This can happen on micro and macro scales (individual or collective). The step beyond awareness is taking practical steps.

WHY THIS IS A TRANSFORMATIVE BOOK:

Poor Economics: A Radical Rethinking of the Way to Fight Global Poverty by Abhijit V. Banerjee and Esther Duflo is a systematic examination about the economics of being poor. The authors have pioneered the use of randomized control trials in development economics. Work based on these principles, supervised by the Poverty Action Lab, is being carried out in dozens of countries. Drawing on this and their 15 years of research from Chile to India, Kenya to Indonesia, they have identified wholly new aspects of the behavior of poor people, their needs, and the way that aid or financial investment can affect their lives. Their work defies certain presumptions: that microfinance is a cure-all, that schooling equals learning, that poverty at the level of 99 cents a day is just a more extreme version of the experience any of us have when our income falls uncomfortably low. This important book illuminates how the poor live, and offers all of us an opportunity to think of a world beyond poverty.

QUESTIONS FOR MEDITATION:

What problems are you aware of within yourself that you tolerate? What problems are you aware of within someone close to you that they tolerate? Which bothers you more, your self-aware problem, or the person's close to you?

"Whatever your calling, it's already rooted within you, and those roots can be trampled or tugged at but never removed. They grow stronger only when tended, nurtured, and most important, shared with others."

WHY I LOVE THIS QUOTE:
As we explore every day the connection to our own true self, and how we live out our lives, we need to remember that whoever we are, we need others. We need others to help us deepen the roots of who we really are. We need others who will listen.

WHY THIS IS A TRANSFORMATIVE BOOK:
The Path Made Clear: Discovering Your Life's Direction and Purpose by Oprah Winfrey is an inspirational read full of the guidance of mentors and with a clear and non-controversial aim to help make a little more clear the idea of how you can lead a more meaning-filled life. Winfrey showcases multiple stories and pieces of advice from a variety of popular figures that all explore the topic of "discovering your life's direction and purpose." She shares what she sees as a guide for activating your deepest vision of yourself, offering the framework for creating not just a life of success, but one of significance. She dedicates her book to teachers, and in doing so she reminds us all that we teach one another just by living with honesty.

QUESTIONS FOR MEDITATION:

What is the most honest thing you can tell yourself right now that you may or may not want to hear?

"Sometimes you can do everything right and things will still go wrong. The key is to never stop doing right."

WHY I LOVE THIS QUOTE:
I love the stubborn optimism and commitment to integrity. Maybe not in the short term, but in the long term, what is right will win out. Maybe what is right can make bigger strides sooner than later.

WHY THIS IS A TRANSFORMATIVE BOOK:
The Hate U Give by Angie Thomas is about how Starr Carter deals with the aftermath of witnessing Khalil being shot by a cop for doing nothing wrong. Her fear is palpable as she confronts a system that she knows is working against her. She's afraid to speak out, yet angry that Khalil's murderer could escape justice. We see, through Starr's eyes, how the media presents young black men as guilty until proven innocent — and when you're poor, black, and from a rough neighborhood, it's virtually impossible to appear innocent.

Published in 2017, this book is almost prophetic in the way it looks at institutional racism and a broken criminal justice system in anticipation of the dramatic events of 2020. Police can violate the civil rights of thousands of people publicly and openly with impunity. It's about what happens when racialized and marginalized communities stand up for their rights in any visible way whatsoever. It's about how piles and piles of evidence showing sustained corruption and racism and literally hundreds of civilian deaths per year at the hands of the police is still somehow not enough to delegitimize a deeply flawed system. This book is important, timely, emotional, and extremely well-written in and of itself. Destined to be a classic similar to the likes of *The Outsiders*.

QUESTIONS FOR MEDITATION:

What righteous cause are you committed to within your own personal growth?

"Failure is a feeling long before it becomes an actual result. It's vulnerability that breeds with self-doubt and then is escalated, often deliberately, by fear."

WHY I LOVE THIS QUOTE:
We explore the concept of failure from time to time in this reader. We have considered perspectives of looking at failure as a gift in terms of the feedback it gives us. This idea encourages us to think about how fear and self-doubt lead to failure in the first place. We might consider this early feedback. Sometimes you don't have to bring things to a head, you don't have to learn every lesson the hard way. There can be warning signs ahead.

WHY THIS IS A TRANSFORMATIVE BOOK:
Becoming by Michelle Obama is the deeply personal reckoning of a woman of soul and substance who has steadily defied expectations — and whose story inspires us to do the same.

She writes, "For me, becoming isn't about arriving somewhere or achieving a certain aim. I see it instead as forward motion, a means of evolving, a way to reach continuously toward a better self. The journey doesn't end. I became a mother, but I still have a lot to learn from and give to my children. I became a wife, but I continue to adapt to and be humbled by what it means to truly love and make a life with another person. I have become, by certain measures, a person of power, and yet there are moments when I still feel insecure or unheard. It's all a process, steps along a path. Becoming requires equal parts patience and rigor. Becoming is never giving up on the idea that there's more growing to be done."

QUESTIONS FOR MEDITATION:

In what area(s) of your life are you aware of self-doubt?

"The key to moving forward is what we do with our discomfort. We can use it as a door out — blame the messenger and disregard the message. Or we can use it as a door in by asking, Why does this unsettle me? What would it mean for me if this were true?"

WHY I LOVE THIS QUOTE:
These are tough, but critically important questions for white people to ask.

WHY THIS IS A TRANSFORMATIVE TEXT:
White Fragility: Why It's So Hard for White People to Talk About Racism by Robin DiAngelo is a great conversation starter, more for white people and from a white perspective than it is for or from people of color. Critics may say that we're not all necessarily racist just because we live in a dominant culture, but the truth is there are layers and layers of individual and collective racism. DiAngelo's main concern is that people take action as a result of what they learn and not retreat in anger or befuddled silence. This, too, becomes another looping mechanism in the way things never fundamentally change.

As professional reader and GoodReads reviewer, Jenna, writes: "I think this is an incredibly important book. Though it is very basic and rudimentary and repetitive at times, this book is a crucial starting point. It demands we look honestly at ourselves. If we are against racism and truly want change, we have to first start with ourselves. I cannot change my behaviour or thoughts if I am certain I am without blame. How then can I hope to change an entire system? I need to be open to criticism without becoming defensive. Is it comfortable to do so? Nope, absolutely not. But I can deal with a bit of discomfort, especially in light of all the pain that people of colour have endured and still endure. It is imperative that I honestly examine myself; it is not going to kill me — but racism does kill people of colour."

QUESTIONS FOR MEDITATION:

Does it irritate you to be called a racist by virtue of participating in a system that promotes racist values?

"The recognition that what we have seen is the rise of an insecure narcissism – particularly among young people – rather than a rise in genuine self-esteem now seems widely accepted."

WHY I LOVE THIS QUOTE:

Narcissism is based in insecurity. It focuses on the self in comparison to others superior and does everything it can to maintain the great delusion. For those who suffer from it, and then are able to surround themselves with power and money, they keep the illusion alive with greater success. Most have to be broken again and again until they come to the truth that their value does not lie in how they are superior or inferior to others. Part of the mission of this book is helping to uncover the lies we tell ourselves, and to boldly integrate the parts of us that have been overlooked or ignored.

WHY THIS IS A TRANSFORMATIVE BOOK:

The Spirit Level: Why More Equal Societies Almost Always Do Better by Richard G. Wilkinson and Kate E. Pickett offers compelling evidence that more equal societies have better health and social outcomes, such as trust, life expectancy, violence and child well-being. These benefits affect all income levels, not only the poorest, and are unrelated to GDP. The authors point out that increasing wealth has not benefited people beyond the level where basic needs are met, but that increasing equality brings significant benefits. They also link their case to the sustainability imperative.

QUESTIONS FOR MEDITATION:

What personal anxieties have you accepted as reality in your own life?

"Self-knowledge is like lost innocence; however unsettling you find it, it can never be 'unthought' or 'unknown'."

WHY I LOVE THIS QUOTE:

You can't put the genie back in the lamp. Each day as you consider an idea expressed in a new way, as you ask yourself questions about who you are, and what kind of world you live in, you are getting closer to answering questions that will pay dividends for the rest of your life. Sometimes we're afraid of the answers. That's okay. Acknowledge the fear, but keep on going. Ignorance is only temporary bliss.

WHY THIS IS A TRANSFORMATIVE BOOK:

Justice: What's the Right Thing to Do? by Michael J. Sandel discusses what's the right thing for humans to do, whereby he explains theories around justice, morality, and human good. In order to do so, he constantly starts with a controversial, real or theoretical, case study to juxtapose different theories of justice and morality. Sandel argues that speaking of justice requires embarking on finding a framework to define the 'Telos' of life. Is it God and religion? Is it pure reasoning? He sticks to the script of philosophy in light of politics and ethics — and the result is a thrilling read. A must for thoughtful people across the political spectrum.

QUESTIONS FOR MEDITATION:

What is one small step you can take today to learn a little more about yourself?

"'When men oppress their fellow-men, the oppressor ever finds, in the character of the oppressed, a full justification for his oppression'. Douglass, amazingly, summed up the history of racist ideas in a single sentence."

WHY I LOVE THIS QUOTE:

It's like a law of human behavior, and part of the reason those committed to racism will not be persuaded by logic or history books.

WHY THIS IS A TRANSFORMATIVE TEXT:

Stamped from the Beginning: The Definitive History of Racist Ideas in America by Ibram X. Kendi is the kind of history we need when it comes to a high-level, systematic study of how and from where racism has come — and how it's positioned amongst us now. Americans like to insist that we live in a post-racial, colorblind society. Racist thought is alive and well. The need for such a work is obvious from the moment Kendi begins to trace the evolution of America's history of racist ideas, from the pre-revolutionary settlers and the sermons of Cotton Mather right through Thomas Jefferson, William Lloyd Garrison, W.E.B. DuBois, and Angela Davis. By the end we have a framework to evaluate and calmly deconstruct the words of Clarence Thomas and Bill Clinton and the voices raised in Black Lives Matter.

QUESTIONS FOR MEDITATION:

How do we play a part in our social conditions by what we don't do as much as by what we do?

"It would be easy to speculate about the impact of years of cocaine use on my father's heart, but I suspect that it will tell us less than if we could measure the cumulative effects of hatred, racism and indignity. What is the impact of years of strip searches, of being bent over, the years before that when you were a child and knew that no dream you had for yourself was taken seriously by anyone, that you were not someone who would be fully invested in by a nation that treated you as expendable?"

WHY I LOVE THIS QUOTE:

The focus, in other words, shouldn't be on how her father covered over his inner pain through addictions for years, and thereby damaged himself. The focus should be on why the intense need in the first place? How and why did that damage have to happen in the first place?

WHY THIS IS A TRANSFORMATIVE TEXT:

Patrisse Khan-Cullors, co-founder of the Black Lives Matter movement, shares her story in *When They Call You a Terrorist: A Black Lives Matter Memoir* about growing up in a poor neighborhood in Los Angeles in a loving family. We learn about the intimacies of her childhood, how her mother worked multiple jobs and still struggled to make a living wage, the development of her queer identity, her brother's unjust and devastating imprisonment, and much more. The police effectively terrorized her family. It is eye-opening even for those who consider themselves fairly knowledgeable on the topic of systemic racism and the role of the policy in black subjugation. Racial hatred is the central political and sociological fact in America. Race is not a sideshow. It is the main event. Nixon and his successors have provided political excuses and distractions in order to ignore race. Black Lives Matter makes that less possible by bringing back the rage which is the only ethical response appropriate to the situation.

QUESTIONS FOR MEDITATION:

What is the impact of not being valued? How do you measure the loss of what a human being does not receive?

"If you don't like my story, write your own."

WHY I LOVE THIS QUOTE:
It frees itself from the judgment of others while it then goes on to narrate its own story. In a sense, you could say all of our lives are both heroic and plain at the same time. But I admire the way this quote puts it right back on us (the "you"). The story, by the way, is centered on the motif of a Greek tragedy: pride (hubris) comes before the fall.

WHY THIS IS A TRANSFORMATIVE BOOK:
Things Fall Apart by Chinua Achebe was the first book I read in my postcolonial literature course at Georgia State University, and it has stuck with me ever since. I reread it and taught it in World Literature courses as well. It is a brilliant book that launched a movement, a field of literature. It is compelling in and of itself, but the themes it explores are rich.

For our purposes, we might consider the protagonist, Okonkwo. As Achebe writes, "Perhaps down in his heart Okonkwo was not a cruel man. But his whole life was dominated by fear, the fear of failure and of weakness. It was deeper and more intimate that the fear of evil and capricious gods and of magic, the fear of the forest, and of the forces of nature, malevolent, red in tooth and claw. Okonkwo's fear was greater than these. It was not external but lay deep within himself."

QUESTIONS FOR MEDITATION:

What is the story you are writing of your life?

How is it ordinary? How is it heroic?

"We could choose to be a nation that extends care, compassion, and concern to those who are locked up and locked out or headed for prison before they are old enough to vote. We could seek for them the same opportunities we seek for our own children; we could treat them like one of 'us'. We could do that. Or we can choose to be a nation that shames and blames its most vulnerable, affixes badges of dishonor upon them at young ages, and then relegates them to a permanent second-class status for life. That is the path we have chosen, and it leads to a familiar place."

WHY I LOVE THIS QUOTE:

This quote paints a picture of what we could actually do, and also tells us what we should already know. The path we continue to choose is dismal. It's dismal for some than others, but it's not good for anyone.

WHY THIS IS A TRANSFORMATIVE TEXT:

The New Jim Crow: Mass Incarceration in the Age of Colorblindness by Michelle Alexander provocatively argues that we have not ended racial caste in America: we have simply redesigned it. Alexander shows that, by targeting black men and decimating communities of color, the U.S. criminal justice system functions as a contemporary system of racial control, even as it formally adheres to the principle of color blindness. The New Jim Crow challenges the civil rights community — and all of us — to place mass incarceration at the forefront of a new movement for racial justice in America. Written during the early years of Obama's presidency, this book remains all the more relevant now.

QUESTIONS FOR MEDITATION:

What is the culture around mistakes at your job or school? What is your own view of mistakes? What is the culture around mistakes involving the criminal justice system?

"Now is the time to get serious about living your ideals. How long can you afford to put off who you really want to be? Your nobler self cannot wait any longer. Put your principles into practice – now. Stop the excuses and the procrastination. This is your life! You aren't a child anymore. The sooner you set yourself to your spiritual program, the happier you will be. The longer you wait, the more you'll be vulnerable to mediocrity and feel filled with shame and regret, because you know you are capable of better. From this instant on, vow to stop disappointing yourself. Separate yourself from the mob. Decide to be extraordinary and do what you need to do – now."

WHY I LOVE THIS QUOTE:

This was written around 2,000 years ago. I love it for its urgency. He also reminds us of Trevor Noah's quote earlier in this reader, that the biggest regrets are the things he wished he had done but didn't.

WHY THIS IS A TRANSFORMATIVE BOOK:

Epictetus was born into slavery about 55 C.E. in the eastern outreaches of the Roman Empire. Sold as a child and crippled from the beatings of his master, Epictetus was eventually freed, rising from his humble roots to establish an influential school of Stoic philosophy. Stressing that human beings cannot control life, only how they respond to it, Epictetus dedicated his life to outlining the simple way to happiness, fulfillment, and tranquility. By putting into practice the ninety-three witty, wise, and razor-sharp instructions that make up *The Art of Living*, you learn to successfully meet the challenges of everyday life and face life's inevitable losses and disappointments with grace. Epictetus's teachings rank among the greatest wisdom texts of human civilization.

QUESTIONS FOR MEDITATION:

What do you need to do to be extraordinary right now?

"I was born upon the prairie, where the wind blew free and there was nothing to break the light of the sun. I was born where there are no enclosures and where everything drew a free breath. I want to die there and not within walls. I know every stream and every wood between the Rio Grande and the Arkansas. I have hunted and lived over that country. I lived like my fathers before me, and, like them, I lived happily."

WHY I LOVE THIS QUOTE:

This was spoken by Para-Wa-Samen (Ten Bears) of the Tamparika Comanches. You hear the pride in his statement, a validation that in spite of tyranny and forces of resistance against his culture, he knows who he is. Within that courage and strength is a freedom of spirit.

WHY THIS IS A TRANSFORMATIVE BOOK:

Bury My Heart at Wounded Knee: An Indian History of the American West by Dee Brown is a masterpiece of conscientious research and organizational artistry. Brown provides a sympathetic account of the plight of many Indian tribes as the wheels of progress arrived to wipe out their lifestyle, if not their culture. This is also a book about spiritual leaders too — Sitting Bull, Crazy Horse, Geronimo, Chief Joseph. He writes, "Not all of Anthony's officers, however, were eager or even willing to join Chivington's well-planned massacre. Captain Silas Soule, Lieutenant Joseph Cramer, and Lieutenant James Connor protested that an attack on Black Kettle's peaceful camp would violate the pledge of safety given the Indians by both Wynkoop and Anthony, that it would be murder in every sense of the word, and any officer participating would dishonor the uniform of the Army."

QUESTIONS FOR MEDITATION:

Transformation is a process and requires rest. What does rest look like in your life?

"You are growing into consciousness, and my wish for you is that you feel no need to constrict yourself to make other people comfortable."

WHY I LOVE THIS QUOTE:
The honest tone, the naked authenticity of Coates writing this to his teenage son about his hopes and wishes for him in a world that others broke, but that he will be expected to fix, what strikes me the most.

WHY THIS IS A TRANSFORMATIVE TEXT:
Between the World and Me by Ta-Nehisi Coates is not a book written to explain the African American experience to white people (or as Coates likes to say, people who believe they are white.) As a middle-aged white guy, I am in no way the intended audience for this book. Perhaps that's what made it such an enlightening read for me. There was no sugar-coating, no careful racial diplomacy, no worry about mediating opinions to cater to what white people might be able to hear. It was just a heartfelt, raw, painful and honest letter from a father to a son, laying plain Coates' worry, anger, frustration, and fear for his son's future in light of Coates' own past and the world his son will grow up in. Coates' most powerful assertion: doing violence to the African American body is an American legacy and tradition. It is not a failure of the system. It is part of the system. As much as may have changed in the past decades, the past centuries, the basic fear of African American parents remains: that their children can be snatched away, brutalized, killed for the smallest of reasons or no reason at all. There is no grand vision here, just an honest accounting to his experience and understanding to his fifteen-year-old son. This is a book of timeless relevance.

QUESTIONS FOR MEDITATION:

What are your expectations for change over the next few weeks and months? Have you experienced resistance? If so, how have you handled it?

"Here's to us being afraid and doing it anyway."

WHY I LOVE THIS QUOTE:
Sometimes it feels like being courageous enough to be yourself means everyone is throwing roses at your feet and you're dancing down the halls with streamers and confetti. In fact, there's a reason why it takes courage in the first place. Not everyone is going to like you being free. Most people are not free, and most people want others to please their worldview and agendas. It may not be easy. We may face resistance. We may have reason to fear speaking up and speaking out and committing to change within ourselves and in our communities. Let's keep growing anyway.

WHY THIS IS A TRANSFORMATIVE BOOK:
We're Going to Need More Wine by Gabrielle Union touches on topics from growing up black in a predominantly white community, relationships, sex, racism, the pressure of dealing with public perception, friendships, and most importantly, the freedom one can feel when they decide to truly be themselves. Genuine and perceptive, Union bravely lays herself bare, uncovering a complex and courageous life of self-doubt and self-discovery with incredible poise and brutal honesty. Throughout, she compels us to be ethical and empathic, and reminds us of the importance of confidence, self-awareness, and the power of sharing truth, laughter, and support. A moving collection of essays connecting pivotal moments in her life.

QUESTIONS FOR MEDITATION:

What parts of you have you seen grow over the past few weeks and months?

march

"Don't surrender all your joy for an idea you used to have about yourself that isn't true anymore."

WHY I LOVE THIS QUOTE:

This quote speaks to me when it comes to early adulthood efforts I made in certain kinds of writing that didn't succeed the way I wanted them to. Simply put, I failed to become what I believed I was intended to become. My identity was wrapped up in it to such an extent that failing at it meant failing at life. When successes weren't coming, I doubled down on my efforts, but still it wasn't happening. For years, I would beat myself up about my failure. There is a lot of reframing and perception that needed work, as well as personal growth, and this is a well-framed way of saying it.

WHY THIS IS A TRANSFORMATIVE BOOK:

Cheryl Strayed played the role of "Dear Sugar" for the online magazine The Rumpus for several years. It became popular, and they arranged the best moments into *Tiny Beautiful Things: Advice on Life and Love from Dear Sugar*. Sometimes a collection is more than the sum of its parts, and that is true in this case. Turns out, it is a profound and personal book. Piece by piece, Strayed's responses win you over — even though she's speaking to someone else, and maybe on a topic you haven't even struggled with. She manages to be both loving and also challenging and seems to know instinctively how to thread the needle tonally. She is gifted at empathy, communicating it clearly, and provoking it in others.

QUESTIONS FOR MEDITATION:

How has your perception of yourself changed over the years?

"Simple people with less education, sophistication, social ties, and professional obligations seem in general to have somewhat less difficulty in facing this final crisis than people of affluence who lose a great deal more in terms of material luxuries, comfort, and number of interpersonal relationships. It appears that people who have gone through a life of suffering, hard work, and labor, who have raised their children and been gratified in their work, have shown greater ease in accepting death with peace and dignity compared to those who have been ambitiously controlling their environment, accumulating material goods, and a great number of social relationships but few meaningful interpersonal relationships which would have been available at the end of life."

WHY I LOVE THIS QUOTE:

Nobody gets out of this alive. Embrace life's struggle. Develop your inner resilience. Try things out. Don't be afraid to fail. Serve others. These things bring you fulfillment, and will give you deeper life satisfaction because, in the end, you die anyway.

WHY THIS IS A TRANSFORMATIVE BOOK:

One of the most important psychological studies of the late twentieth century, *On Death and Dying* grew out of Elisabeth Kübler-Ross's famous interdisciplinary seminar on death, life, and transition. Kübler-Ross first explored the now-famous five stages of death: denial and isolation, anger, bargaining, depression, and acceptance. Through sample interviews and conversations, she gives the reader a better understanding of how imminent death affects the patient, the professionals who serve that patient, and the patient's family, bringing hope to all who are involved.

QUESTIONS FOR MEDITATION:

Does the prospect of death mobilize you to live a life on your own terms, or does it create anxiety? Be still for a few moments and listen to what your self is saying.

"Art never responds to the wish to make it democratic; it is not for everybody; it is only for those who are willing to undergo the effort needed to understand it."

WHY I LOVE THIS QUOTE:
Much like art is the application and practice of meditation, of making time for rituals such as the one you may be committed to now. Self-discipline and patient, persistent resolve to work on yourself and your capacity to understand self and others is not for everybody. Reading and examination are there for the taking, but only those willing to make the effort are going to "get it."

WHY THIS IS A TRANSFORMATIVE BOOK:
At her death in 1964, Flannery O'Connor left behind a body of unpublished essays and lectures as well as a number of critical articles that had appeared in scattered publications during her too-short lifetime of just 38 years. The keen writings comprising *Mystery and Manners*, selected and edited by O'Connor's lifelong friends Sally and Robert Fitzgerald, are characterized by the directness and simplicity of her style, a fine-tuned wit, understated perspicacity, and profound faith. She stresses the importance of writing which is based on concrete details rather than on abstraction, unmediated emotions or even misdirected devotion. It is important to be true to one's vocation as a writer, and to write reality as it is, not as one would like it to be. One cannot and should not reduce reading to the extraction of handy themes or morals.

QUESTIONS FOR MEDITATION:

What is difficult for you to understand that you therefore have no interest in?

"Self-knowledge is no guarantee of happiness, but it is on the side of happiness and can supply the courage to fight for it."

WHY I LOVE THIS QUOTE:
Self-knowledge is a step in the direction toward greater fulfillment, but you can't stop there. If you just build up the knowledge but don't let it pour out of you, you'll end up a stagnant pool. It has to translate into action and transformation.

WHY THIS IS A TRANSFORMATIVE BOOK:
The Second Sex by Simone de Beauvoir is regarded as a major work of feminist philosophy and the starting point of second-wave feminism. De Beauvoir offers a sustained exploration of what it means to know, to be, to make, and ultimately to become a self. She starts from the perplexing situation in which she encounters her selfhood as somehow incomplete, and deeply problematic to herself.

As Judith Thurman writes: "Opportunities for women have proliferated so broadly in the past six decades, at least in the Western world, that the distance between 2010 and 1949, when *The Second Sex* was published in France, seems like an eternity (until, that is, one opens a newspaper — the victims of misogyny and sexual abuse are still with us, everywhere). While no one individual or her work is responsible for that seismic shift in laws and attitudes, the millions of young women who now confidently assume that their entitlement to work, pleasure, and autonomy is equal to that of their brothers owe a measure of their freedom to Beauvoir. *The Second Sex* was an act of Promethean audacity — a theft of Olympian fire — from which there was no turning back. It is not the last word on 'the problem of woman', which, Beauvoir wrote, 'has always been a problem of men', but it marks the place in history where an enlightenment begins.'"

QUESTIONS FOR MEDITATION:

What does it really take to know a self, our self? Does it come from stripping away our particulars or embracing them?

"The most fundamental aggression to ourselves, the most fundamental harm we can do to ourselves, is to remain ignorant by not having the courage and the respect to look at ourselves honestly and gently."

WHY I LOVE THIS QUOTE:
We continue to emphasize that this process takes courage. It is also necessary to be compassionate with yourself, but what stands out the most in this way of putting it is that to ignore what is within us is actually an aggressive, hostile stance to take.

WHY THIS IS A TRANSFORMATIVE BOOK:
Accepting the impermanence of our own worldly existence, says Pema Chödrön in *When Things Fall Apart: Heart Advice for Difficult Times*, opens our hearts to the vast beauty of the sacred. When we are on the verge of such acceptance, it seems like the world is falling apart, but in reality it is just our illusions that are facing imminent dissolution. It's easy to read these brief meditations in moments of stillness and sense the rightness they contain, but much more challenging to practice in the midst of despair or joy or distraction. But practice is exactly what they demand, and what we need.

QUESTIONS FOR MEDITATION:

What parts of yourself have you overlooked or neglected as a result of your self-belief?

"One mental habit that can wreak havoc in our lives is self-judgment. If you watch your mind for 10 minutes after something goes wrong, you'll probably notice that you're criticizing yourself. It's undoubtedly useful to know what went wrong and to correct our mistakes, but usually we go way beyond that. What can we do about self-judgment? It doesn't work to 'just stop judging yourself' because you're likely to judge yourself for judging yourself. (Remember, what we resist persists.) The best solution is simply to 'witness' judgments, letting them come and go."

WHY I LOVE THIS QUOTE:

This idea embodies much of the spirit of what meditation offers. We can free ourselves from anxieties and fear by witnessing what is in our mind without guiding the thoughts one way or another. Simply listening to them without reaction can be disarming.

WHY THIS IS A TRANSFORMATIVE BOOK:

The Mindful Path to Self-Compassion: Freeing Yourself from Destructive Thoughts and Emotions by Christopher K. Germer offers simple and effective strategies for changing our ingrained habits of resistance. Mindfulness meditation is neurological reprogramming that helps us cultivate a calmer and less reactive state. Since "neurons that fire together, wire together," we can practice paying attention to what we are doing. This allows us to be more intentional in our lives on many levels. By practicing intentional attention in formal sitting practice, we can develop habits of mindfulness that can serve us in times of stress and difficulty.

QUESTIONS FOR MEDITATION:

Does your ego tend to assert itself as needing to be superior to others? Or do you tend to belittle yourself? Are you aware of either tendency?

"Life is a drama full of tragedy and comedy. You should learn to enjoy the comic episodes a little more."

WHY I LOVE THIS QUOTE:

This speaks to me about gratitude, living more consciously and looking for the good, the lighthearted moments, the joy. During the long quarantine of 2020, I found myself more aware of the family members and moments that made me laugh, because laughing almost seemed out of place in the sober moment-to-moment quiet of the long spring and summer months especially.

WHY THIS IS A TRANSFORMATIVE BOOK:

The Glass Castle by Jeannette Walls is an incredible memoir, and not the kind in which the author roils in self-pity. What is so astonishing about Jeannette Walls is not just that she had the guts and tenacity and intelligence to get out, but that she describes her parents with such deep affection and generosity. Hers is a story of triumph against all odds, but also a tender, moving tale of unconditional love in a family that despite its profound flaws gave her the fiery determination to carve out a successful life on her own terms. In fact, the ever-returning theme of the book is exactly how resilient the family was, especially her brother and her sisters. What's also evident is the great deal of love they all shared, even toward their parents. Walls shows clear anger toward her parents, at least in spots, but there always at the same time a incredible current of love — a combination that feels very true. Walls is not a poet but a journalist, and she writes as one.

QUESTIONS FOR MEDITATION:

If you tuned in a little more to the goodness all around you, what could you say authentically you are grateful for? What brings you joy right now?

"Patients coming for consultation complain about headaches, sexual disturbances, inhibitions in work, or other symptoms; as a rule, they do not complain about having lost touch with the core of their psychic existence."

WHY I LOVE THIS QUOTE:

It's a reminder that we see the symptoms far in advance of the core issue. When you lose touch with the soulful center of your identity, your "psychic existence" suffers. It shows up in any number of ways. The efforts of a therapist, life coach, or meditation books such as these, is to point the way, however gently, back to your self.

WHY THIS IS A TRANSFORMATIVE BOOK:

Neurosis and Human Growth: The Struggle Towards Self-Realization by Karen Horney explores the neurotic process as a special form of human development, which is the antithesis of healthy growth. She unfolds the different stages of this situation, describing neurotic claims, the tyranny or inner dictates and the neurotic's solutions for relieving the tensions of conflict in such emotional attitudes as domination, self-effacement, dependency, or resignation. Throughout, she outlines with penetrating insight the forces that work for and against the person's realization of his or her potentialities. Informative, well-structured, and mind-provoking especially for those interested struggling with neurosis symptoms.

QUESTIONS FOR MEDITATION:

What inner work are you committed to within your own self?

"We find common bonds in the shared details of the human journey, not in the divergent conclusions we draw from those details."

WHY I LOVE THIS QUOTE:

Most conversation at family gatherings, church coffee hours, break and conference rooms at work, etc. tends to be of the fixing, advising, persuasion variety, with plenty of complexes tossed into the mix. Palmer gives insight into how to instead speak one's truth and engage in "deep speaks to deep" type of listening. We develop our empathy muscle, and our sense of connection, through listening without fixing.

WHY THIS IS A TRANSFORMATIVE BOOK:

"No fixing, no saving, no advising, no setting each other straight," is the main rule of the circles of trust Parker Palmer describes. With his Quaker background and worldview, Palmer has learned to place a great confidence in the inner teacher that is within each of us, otherwise known as the soul. In *A Hidden Wholeness: The Journey Toward an Undivided Life* he suggests that the only path to an undivided life in which soul and role are joined is to provide space for the soul to speak. He advises us to "let things alone" in the lives of other people. In our ego-driven attempt to instruct and advise others on how they should live their lives, we leave other people feeling diminished and disrespected.

QUESTIONS FOR MEDITATION:

How can the path be made more clear? How can we learn to listen deeply?

"This being human is a guest-house. Every morning a new arrival. A joy, a depression, a meanness, some momentary awareness comes as an unexpected visitor. Welcome and entertain them all! Even if they're a crowd of sorrows, who violently sweep your house empty of its furniture, still, treat each guest honorably."

WHY I LOVE THIS QUOTE:

I like the metaphor that we are housing various guests within our "self." The focus of this quote, and of the book, is to seek to understand all parts of who we are. A "dark" side isn't necessarily a "bad" or even unhealthy side. It's a side that we have repressed, either for others, or out of a sense of what we felt we needed to do to function among others. Repressing the shadow side, rather than listening to it, leads to neurosis.

WHY THIS IS A TRANSFORMATIVE BOOK:

Romancing the Shadow: A Guide to Soul Work for a Vital, Authentic Life by Connie Zweig and Steve Wolf is a fantastic book on dealing with our shadow (or repressed elements of our authentic selves). The point is to enjoy all of our "selves" rather than to try to suppress or repress them. We need to integrate our shadow, so that we can become whole. That is what Zweig and Wolf mean by "romancing the shadow."

QUESTIONS FOR MEDITATION:

What could help lead you to making deeper peace with yourself?

"Will we take up what we know is our moral and spiritual responsibility: to make the world a better place for all, to bring to life the fullness of Creation for all? To help bring about equality, safety, security, and compassion for all?"

WHY I LOVE THIS QUOTE:

She asks with such direct clarity. If who you think you are is a moral and spiritual person, then doesn't it make sense that you seek justice for others as well? We are asked to have compassionate respect for others. Character is a crucial component of leadership. Striving for the common good. These are the values we are challenged to consider and act on.

WHY THIS IS A TRANSFORMATIVE BOOK:

The Time Is Now: A Call to Uncommon Courage by Joan D. Chittister, a social activist nun, calls us to be brothers and sisters to each other, to love, to feed the hunger and dive into the world's pain and injustice and just to something risk taking to help the marginalized people. Pay attention to world around you and be astonished by the hurt, the pain and lack of concern. Talk about it and find little ways to help others and to solve the root of the problems. The time is now.

For the weary, the cranky, and the fearful, Sister Joan's energizing message invites us to participate in a vision for a world greater than the one we find ourselves in today. This is spirituality in action, this is practical and powerful activism for our times.

QUESTIONS FOR MEDITATION:

What excuses do we use when we think of the poor and why they are poor?

"Enthusiasm is common. Endurance is rare."

WHY I LOVE THIS QUOTE:
It is great to be enthusiastic. You do need excitement and passion in bucket-loads to succeed. The problem is what happens when the headwinds start. Also, we treat endurance and stamina like second-class citizens. Like, "Oh, anyone can just keep at it, but who really has talent or enthusiasm?"

WHY THIS IS A TRANSFORMATIVE BOOK:
Grit by Angela Duckworth is encouraging children and adults to be gritty, to follow their passion while embracing the fact that "to be gritty is to fall down seven times and rise eight" is far more important than an overemphasis on talent. Perseverance is a major part of the path to reach a goal. Natural talents exists of course, but at the end of the day the aim is not to be the next Mozart, Dickens, or Usain Bolt. Rather the idea is to learn to put significant effort in what you like so that you reach your personal potential, which is richer and wider than most of us believe.

QUESTIONS FOR MEDITATION:

What stands before you asking for your full presence and determination today?

"In the darkness and pain of the story we engage our own 'stuck' places, the blocks, the wounds, the fears, the passions, the possibilities. We learn that only anguish and disenchantment can transform us...Only in disenchantment and in lowliness will the hero become real."

WHY I LOVE THIS QUOTE:

I wish it weren't the case, but the laws of the universe are strange things. Seems that there is very little chance for transformation without struggle, or being brought low. At least we can take this truth with us when times are tough. When we rise again, if we have listened, if we have stayed close to our truth, we will emerge stronger and changed.

WHY THIS IS A TRANSFORMATIVE BOOK:

Here All Dwell Free: Stories to Heal the Wounded Feminine by Gertrud Mueller Nelson is a mesmerizing interpretation of two of Grimm's fairy tales, "The Handless Maiden," and "Briar Rose." Everyone has both masculine and feminine characteristics, but because our civilization undervalues the feminine, she hides within many. Nelson shows us how the wisdom of folk mythology offers us both the diagnosis of our ills and a healing prescription. Nelson shows us the difference between passivity and receptivity; the wounded healer and her spirituality; Earth as the wounded feminine; and the inner and outer synthesis of masculine and feminine polarities that must redeem the whole kingdom, so that all can live free.

QUESTIONS FOR MEDITATION:

Do you see vulnerability as weak?

"Most people, when directly confronted by evidence that they are wrong, do not change their point of view or course of action but justify it even more tenaciously. Even irrefutable evidence is rarely enough to pierce the mental armor of self-justification."

WHY I LOVE THIS QUOTE:

It's an amazing component to human psychology, and one that makes authentic and lasting change all the harder to achieve. It happens in every field, in every action that humans might make. When confronted even with hard facts they just dig in all the more. This quote also summarizes what many in the black community say about the majority of white people when it comes to their response to racism. There is quite often the self-exoneration, which absolves them of their participation.

WHY THIS IS A TRANSFORMATIVE TEXT:

Mistakes Were Made (But Not by Me): Why We Justify Foolish Beliefs, Bad Decisions, and Hurtful Acts by Carol Tavris, Elliot Aronson looks at the consequences that our tendencies to underrate our own culpability for mistakes and misdemeanours has and to overrate the intention and severity of the actions of others when committed against us. When we make mistakes, we must calm the cognitive dissonance that jars our feelings of self-worth. And so we create fictions that absolve us of responsibility, restoring our belief that we are smart, moral, and right — a belief that often keeps us on a course that is dumb, immoral, and wrong. Why do people dodge responsibility when things fall apart?

QUESTIONS FOR MEDITATION:

If someone else were to achieve the same accomplishment as you, do you think you would give them the same credit?

"The term *psychiatrist* means 'doctor of the soul', and in today's world, millions of individuals are seeking their own souls — to feel alive, real, and strong — *to feel like themselves.*"

WHY I LOVE THIS QUOTE:

Feeling better begins with inner work. Pills and other substances have led to so much addiction and dependency in our culture, it's hard to overstate. We are missing ourselves in all this. Here is a psychiatrist, training in the medical profession, who realizes that there are better prescriptions for people than the ones she was doling out until 2010, when she stopped.

WHY THIS IS A TRANSFORMATIVE BOOK:

Own Your Self: The Surprising Path beyond Depression, Anxiety, and Fatigue to Reclaiming Your Authenticity, Vitality, and Freedom by Kelly Brogan offers a new yet ancient path for radical health and healing that puts the individual fully in the driver's seat and she does so with intuitive insights and science. Brogan sifts through confusing messages that have us believing that we are fundamentally sick and broken and in need of big pharma to parcel out our required medicine and string us along while we become sicker and poorer. She offers a way to get off the merry-go-round and reclaim our autonomy.

QUESTIONS FOR MEDITATION:

What practice could you begin that might begin to unwind or unfold some of the negative patterns of thinking that might be holding you down or holding you back?

"May I have the courage to be who I say I am."

WHY I LOVE THIS QUOTE:
It's hard enough to know ourselves well enough to be able put it into words — to say who we are. Once we've done that, the next step is to be bold enough to live into that self. This quote is like a prayer on behalf of one's self.

WHY THIS IS A TRANSFORMATIVE BOOK:
On Being Human: A Memoir of Waking Up, Living Real, and Listening Hard by Jennifer Pastiloff is a debut memoir that explores a childhood shaped around the early loss of her beloved father, and a coming-of-age haunted by anorexia and depression is deeply personal and corporeal. It becomes universal and palpable in its telling. There are beautiful pairings of heartbreak and humor, despair and hope as Pastiloff moves through the world fighting and also often denying her grief and eating disorder and depression and hearing loss before discovering, through yoga and writing, how those very things are a part of what make her so very special — and human.

QUESTIONS FOR MEDITATION:

Who should you be listening more to right now?

Who should you be listening less to?

"But when we really delve into the reasons for why we can't let something go, there are only two: an attachment to the past or a fear for the future."

WHY I LOVE THIS QUOTE:

This is a fascinating insight. Physical objects have emotional connections, and in both cases they tend to be unhealthy. The main idea is to let go as often as possible and free yourself.

WHY THIS IS A TRANSFORMATIVE BOOK:

The Life-Changing Magic of Tidying Up: The Japanese Art of Decluttering and Organizing by Marie Kondo challenges readers to alter their relationship with the world around them. It's about altering what goes on internally, not endowing inanimate objects with agency. This little book makes you laugh, and maybe at times scratch your head. A lot of critics say it doesn't deserve its status on the bestseller lists, and that the book could be summarized in about ten pages. It's more than that, though. It's an exploration. Kondo is trying to gently — and maybe at times with some eccentricity — guide you in the journey of parting with clutter. There is an underlying Shinto philosophy guiding her suggestions, like treating your possessions with respect, and they will respond in kind. The key question to discarding is this: "Does it give you joy?" If not, chuck it. When it comes to books, though, maybe have a different approach. Not every book sparks joy that you may want to revisit.

QUESTIONS FOR MEDITATION:

What is most important to you?

"This is a moment of suffering. Suffering is part of life. May I be kind to myself in this moment. May I give myself the compassion I need."

WHY I LOVE THIS QUOTE:

Compassion is, by definition, relational. Compassion literally means 'to suffer with,' which implies a basic mutuality in the experience of suffering. The emotion of compassion springs from the recognition that the human experience is imperfect.

WHY THIS IS A TRANSFORMATIVE TEXT:

Self-Compassion: The Proven Power of Being Kind to Yourself by Kristin Neff will show you how to let go of debilitating self-criticism and finally learn to be kind to yourself. As she defines it: "Self-compassion entails three core components. First, it requires self-kindness, that we be gentle and understanding with ourselves rather than harshly critical and judgmental. Second, it requires recognition of our common humanity, feeling connected with others in the experience of life rather than feeling isolated and alienated by our suffering. Third, it requires mindfulness - that we hold our experience in balanced awareness, rather than ignoring our pain or exaggerating it. We must achieve and combine these three essential elements in order to be truly self-compassionate."

QUESTIONS FOR MEDITATION:

What are some important life experiences that you know you can't make go away, but possibly you can change the way you relate to?

"It is easier to live through someone else than to become complete yourself."

WHY I LOVE THIS QUOTE:

Friedan's whole point is this, it doesn't diminish the want of a woman to be a housewife and a mother, it just states the actual fact, that you can be all that and a thousand more things, or not. You can be a mother and a working woman, or you can be a mother, or you can be a working woman, period. You can be anything you want, so long it is your choice, not just an outdated inclination. Don't barricade yourself behind meaningless gender roles, labels or privileges, make choices.

WHY THIS IS A TRANSFORMATIVE BOOK:

The Feminine Mystique by Betty Friedan is an iconic book that relentlessly changed the way the American woman saw herself, until its first publication in 1963. Writing in a time when the average woman first married in her teens and 60 percent of women students dropped out of college to marry, Betty Friedan captured the frustrations and thwarted ambitions of a generation and showed women how they could reclaim their lives. Part social chronicle, part manifesto, it is filled with fascinating anecdotes and interviews as well as insights that continue to inspire. Relevant even now and if you don't choose to believe so, at least you can appreciate it as a historical document.

QUESTIONS FOR MEDITATION:

What or who are you living for?

"If you want to build a ship, don't drum up people to collect wood and don't assign them tasks and work, but rather teach them to long for the endless immensity of the sea."

WHY I LOVE THIS QUOTE:

In other words, empower and inspire people, which in turn engages people to work with each other for a common cause. Figuring out the mundane tasks will get done, but you have to understand the cause, which includes the challenges. Through this kind of engagement you also get people to think creatively.

WHY THIS IS A TRANSFORMATIVE BOOK:

Radical Candor: Be a Kickass Boss Without Losing Your Humanity by Kim Scott is written for managers/bosses, but is really for anyone in the workplace. Her observations have wide application, and she does a great job of prioritizing the need to treat everyone as a human being first and foremost. The title refers to the ideal quadrant on a chart with two axes: "care personally" and "challenge directly." It is important to care about the people you work with, but easy to let that care stifle the need to be honest with them: a quadrant called "ruinous empathy." Alternately, you can offer criticism without demonstrating care, and end up in the "obnoxious aggression" quadrant.

QUESTIONS FOR MEDITATION:

Why does it matter what you do?

"We search for happiness everywhere, but we are like Tolstoy's fabled beggar who spent his life sitting on a pot of gold, under him the whole time. Your treasure — your perfection — is within you already. But to claim it, you must leave the busy commotion of the mind and abandon the desires of the ego and enter into the silence of the heart."

WHY I LOVE THIS QUOTE:
There are literally hundreds of possible quotes from this book, but this one sums up a lot in a powerful space of words. We have untapped access to riches within us already. Like Flannery O'Connor suggests, it may not be for everyone. Some people refuse their inner redemption. Some people refuse the work for whatever reason. But not you. That is why you are here. You are listening. Transformation is a process, and there is both a letting go and silencing that must take place for the sake of clarity. With clarity, then, we must see what we want and ask. How can we be transformed if we don't even know what we want?

WHY THIS IS A TRANSFORMATIVE BOOK:
An intensely articulate and moving memoir of self-discovery, *Eat, Pray, Love* by Elizabeth Gilbert is about what can happen when you claim responsibility for your own contentment and stop trying to live in imitation of society's ideals. It is certain to touch anyone who has ever woken up to the unrelenting need for change.

QUESTIONS FOR MEDITATION:

I want less_____ in my life.

I want more_____ in my life.

Do I have the power to make these changes on my own?

If I don't, who can help me to make these changes?

"I don't mind losing as long as I see improvement or I feel I've done as well as I possibly could."

WHY I LOVE THIS QUOTE:
"This is something I know for a fact: You have to work hardest for the things you love most." It takes real character to keep working as hard or even harder once you're there. When you read about an athlete or team that wins over and over and over, remind yourself, 'More than ability, they have character.' "

WHY THIS IS A TRANSFORMATIVE BOOK:
We can all agree that meaningful schoolwork promotes students' learning of academic content. But why stop there? Meaningful work can also teach students to love challenges, to enjoy effort, to be resilient, and to value their own improvement. In other words, we can design and present learning tasks in a way that helps students develop a growth mindset, which leads to not just short-term achievement but also long-term success. That's what Carol Dweck's findings in *Mindset: The New Psychology of Success* demonstrate through groundbreaking research. And that's primarily what sets this book apart from just any ol' self-help book that purports that if you just "think a little more positively" you'll see what great results abound.

QUESTIONS FOR MEDITATION:

Can you think of a time when you shifted your mindset and set yourself free?

"What is clear is that meaning may not be something we find. We found no meaning in our son's death, or in the deaths of countless others. The most we could hope was that we might be able to create meaning."

WHY I LOVE THIS QUOTE:
The idea that meaning is something you have to actively put together. You probably won't stumble across life meaning, or a meaning-filled life, without trying to do work toward it on some level.

WHY THIS IS A TRANSFORMATIVE BOOK:
Why Religion?: A Personal Story by Elaine Pagels is a reminder how pain and grief can strip away the usual comforts of religious faith. "Whatever most people mean by faith was never more remote than during times of mourning, when professions of faith in God sounded only like unintelligible noise, heard from the bottom of the sea."

As Clif Hostetler writes, "This memoir, in addition to being an account of overcoming personal tragedy, adds the unique dimension of insights of a respected historian of religion. Elaine Pagels is not only knowledgeable of the historical circumstances under which early scriptures were written, she found personal solace in those ancient words by identifying with the emotions and feelings that may have motivated those early writers. This book tells the story of how her personal and academic life combined to provide a unique reservoir of spiritual wisdom when facing the death of her 6-year-old son followed a year later by the death of her husband while mountain climbing."

QUESTIONS FOR MEDITATION:

What wounds do you carry that can guide you to a larger, fuller, but even saner life?

"We have to be committed to unlearning the unhelpful, broken, unredemptive, false, or incomplete God if we want to have space to relearn the goodness, the wholeness, the joy of a loving God."

WHY I LOVE THIS QUOTE:

It is incredible that even when we authentically want to learn about God we are confronted with all the agendas, all the flawed ways that people want to tell you with authority is the "true" way to view God. Many still weaponize religion, and use it as a tool for judgment and condemnation, keeping some in and others out. This suggests much our unlearning is to free ourselves from these jaded mindsets and expect grace, love, hope, understanding, and the miraculous.

WHY THIS IS A TRANSFORMATIVE BOOK:

Miracles and Other Reasonable Things: A Story of Unlearning and Relearning God by Sarah Bessey brings her own personal story to life and allows the reader to be a living part of her own personal journey of a tragic event, and all the pain and grace and grit and truth and revival of the fallout. She encourages you to fully live right where you're at. She writes about her own miraculous healing, learning to live with chronic pain, and the ways God unexpectedly makes us whole in the midst of suffering. She invites us to a path of knowing God that is filled with ordinary miracles, hope in the face of overwhelming evidence to the contrary, surprising holiness, and other completely reasonable things.

QUESTIONS FOR MEDITATION:

What are you unlearning about yourself right now?

"Whomever you become, whatever you make yourself into, that is who you always were."

WHY I LOVE THIS QUOTE:

In other words, as you shape yourself and grow into your authentic self, you transcend the illusions of how others saw you, and perhaps even how you saw yourself. In the journey to become your true self, you begin to realize that the other parts of you that you thought were you were not authentic. They were constructs made up of the expectations of individuals and the collective culture. They separated you from yourself. This idea mirrors Alan Watts' *The Book: On the Taboo Against Knowing Who You Really Are*, and Thomas Merton's development of the True Self concept.

WHY THIS IS A TRANSFORMATIVE BOOK:

Educated by Tara Westover is a multi-layered memoir that is truly groundbreaking because she goes well beyond the personal story to write about the historical and sociological. Amazingly, she went from living an isolated, uneducated Idaho life with her family of extreme Mormon survivalists to ten years later receiving a Ph.D. from Cambridge in England. This book will make you think and hurt a bit. And also hope somehow that things can get better. It is also a tale of fierce family loyalty and of the grief that comes with severing the closest of ties. With the acute insight that distinguishes all great writers, Westover has crafted a universal coming-of-age story that gets to the heart of what an education is and what it offers: the perspective to see one's life through new eyes and the will to change it.

QUESTIONS FOR MEDITATION:

What are some of the unspoken rules we live by every day?

"To judge is to believe that a person is capable of doing better. It's to know that people can change their behavior, even quite radically in response to what is expected of them."

WHY I LOVE THIS QUOTE:

It turns the idea of judgment on its head. We tend to view judgment as labeling, categorizing, and boxing people in for the sake of certainty and usually to make ourselves feel better or more confident about our choices. This statement about judgment keeps the concept malleable. We judge because we know someone is capable of more.

WHY THIS IS A TRANSFORMATIVE TEXT:

Strangers Drowning: Grappling with Impossible Idealism, Drastic Choices, and the Overpowering Urge to Help by Larissa MacFarquhar digs deep into the psychological roots and existential dilemmas motivating those rare individuals practicing lives of extreme ethical commitment.

As David Sasaki writes: "This will likely turn out to be one of the ten books that have most shaped my worldview. I've struggled my whole life to find the right balance between duty, altruism and hedonism — the responsibil-ities we have toward others, both near and far, and to our own pursuits of pleasure. Like so many others, I suffer from the nagging guilt that I should be more altruistic, but where does that guilt come from and why do I seem to feel it more than most? *Strangers Drowning* by New Yorker staff writer Larissa MacFarquhar helped me place that guilt into a much larger picture of what it means to be human and what motivates our moral behavior."

QUESTIONS FOR MEDITATION:

Where do we draw the line between whom we love and our responsibility to those we don't know?

"Happiness comes from living as you need to, as you want to. As your inner voice tells you to. Happiness comes from being who you actually are instead of who you think you are supposed to be."

WHY I LOVE THIS QUOTE:

This quote embodies the spirit of this book. Now, some may take issue with the idea of happiness and redefine and say things like it's just a transient thing, or what we really need is fulfillment or joy, or that happiness isn't even what life is supposed to be about. This doesn't sound like the kind of happiness that comes easy, though. This sounds like earned happiness, and the kind you have to continually pursue. Being who you are is definitely more fulfilling than being who others think you should be.

WHY THIS IS A TRANSFORMATIVE BOOK:

Year of Yes by Shonda Rimes tells it like it is. She reveals her flaws, insecurities, and weaknesses all while sharing the story of the greatest challenge she made for herself. The book gives hardcore helpful advice on how you can't do it all, it's okay to admit you need help, and saying yes to yourself comes in many forms.

QUESTIONS FOR MEDITATION:

What does it mean to be a grown, fully actualized adult?

"Things and people moved around me, taking positions in obscure hierarchies, participating in systems I didn't know about and never would. A complex network of objects and concepts. You live through certain things before you understand them. You can't always take the analytical position."

WHY I LOVE THIS QUOTE:

We can't think our way or reflect our way through everything. Many experiences we have to live through to understand.

WHY THIS IS A TRANSFORMATIVE BOOK:

Conversations with Friends by Sally Rooney is a smart novel about two college students and the strange, unexpected connection they forge with a married couple ten years older than them. As Frances whirls in place, the product of an alcoholic father, an enabler mother, and her own making, the core of Frances reveals itself: she feels like a damaged person who deserves nothing, believing that those she loves are exalted and somehow special. "Suffering wouldn't make me special, and pretending not to suffer wouldn't make me special," she reflects at one point. To reveal yourself is dangerous in a world that often conspires against you. An interesting psychological profile, and with an unexpected ending.

QUESTIONS FOR MEDITATION:

If you have gone through a personal transformation, what experiences

"Your judgment is sound, your opinion is worthy to be counted."

WHY I LOVE THIS QUOTE:

This is Susan B. Anthony's final message to women everywhere. When fully understanding her dedication to the cause of universal suffrage, which she didn't live to see, but never doubted would one day come, women everywhere should be inspired to vote. We all should. The right to vote didn't come easily for anyone, but certainly it remains incredible to think it was just barely 100 years ago that women first even had this basic right.

WHY THIS IS A TRANSFORMATIVE TEXT:

Failure is Impossible: Susan B. Anthony in Her Own Words by Lynn Sherr organizes Anthony's own letters, diary entries, pamphlets, and speeches, as well as quotations and letters from fellow suffragists and enemies, into loose categories ranging from the Temperance movement that prompted Anthony's interest in social causes to slavery to the actual definition of womens' rights. Through it all we get to see a woman far ahead of her time: she remained single all through her life and considered her fellow suffragists not just her friends but as her family. Susan B. Anthony not only helped create the first women's movement in this country, she led it — for more than 50 years.

QUESTIONS FOR MEDITATION:

What or to whom are you committed? Would you say you more need to free yourself from a commitment, or make a commitment?

"There's something about sober living and sober thinking, about facing long afternoons without the numbing distraction of anesthesia, that disabuses you of the belief in externals, shows you that strength and hope come not from circumstances or the acquisition of things but from the simple accumulation of active experience, from gritting the teeth and checking the items off the list, one by one, even though it's painful and you're afraid. When you drink, you can't do that. You can't make the distinction between getting through painful feelings and getting away from them. All you can do is just sit there, numb and sipping, numb and drunk."

WHY I LOVE THIS QUOTE:
As Ade Bailey writes, "The book is a valuable contribution to narratives of addiction and recovery. It is also a mirror to all of us and the times we live in."

WHY THIS IS A TRANSFORMATIVE BOOK:
Drinking: A Love Story by Caroline Knapp is a profoundly insightful account from a skilled journalist. Honest and informative, and one of the most compelling (and useful) stories about addiction you're likely to come across. The author died at the age of 42 from lung cancer. She stopped drinking in 1995, and maintained sobriety and continued a successful career until her untimely death in 2002. Knapp, an Ivy-League educated columnist and editor, shares the story of her slide into alcoholism and her road to recovery with brutal honesty. Her down-to-earth, conversational tone pulls you in, and paints a very credible picture of someone who goes beyond the singular, self-serving notion of merely writing a memoir. Recovery has brought out the best in her, and her writing is filled with gratitude and a deep sense of caring for the health of all those around her with or without addiction issues.

QUESTIONS FOR MEDITATION:

How do you tune out? Does it desensitize you from yourself and others?

Is there someone with whom you can share your struggle?

"What is the meaning of life? That was all — a simple question; one that tended to close in on one with years, the great revelation had never come. The great revelation perhaps never did come. Instead, there were little daily miracles, illuminations, matches struck unexpectedly in the dark; here was one."

WHY I LOVE THIS QUOTE:
It's just a beautiful expression of how life is often experienced.

WHY THIS IS A TRANSFORMATIVE BOOK:
To the Lighthouse by Virginia Woolf is a beautiful book about the slowly changing nature of time. In some ways, the quote above summarizes the book. The serene and maternal Mrs. Ramsay, the tragic yet absurd Mr. Ramsay, and their children and assorted guests are on holiday on the Isle of Skye. From the seemingly trivial postponement of a visit to a nearby lighthouse, Woolf constructs a remarkable, moving examination of the complex tensions and allegiances of family life and the conflict between men and women. As time winds its way through their lives, the Ramsays face, alone and simultaneously, the greatest of human challenges and its greatest triumph — the human capacity for change.

As Elizabeth Kadetsky writes, "The shifts in point of view, often mid paragraph, and the blatant disregard for that rule that a pronoun refers to what came immediately before, are not disorienting as they would be (and are) in less able writers' hands...Woolf is a master of clarity and simplicity. The story of *To the Lighthouse* is a very simple rise and fall narrative driven by surprise. What you believed to be true in part I is revealed in part III to be merely what was held in one character's point of view...What a gift this book is."

QUESTIONS FOR MEDITATION:

How do you experience meaning in your life?

april

"We don't read and write poetry because it's cute. We read and write poetry because we are members of the human race. And the human race is filled with passion. So medicine, law, business, engineering...these are noble pursuits and necessary to sustain life. But poetry, beauty, romance, love...these are what we stay alive for."

WHY I LOVE THIS QUOTE:

"Do anything, but let it produce joy," Whitman also writes. I love the way he distinguishes between both what is noble and what is necessary to do to make a living, but strikes a contrast with what is soulful, with what makes life worth living.

WHY THIS IS A TRANSFORMATIVE BOOK:

The United States should be eternally grateful for *Leaves of Grass* by Walt Whitman. What a contribution to our early literature in a time when we were still very in the shadows of the colonial empires. The democratic spirit, and effusive and innovative poetry of Whitman was genius.

As for the quality of the work the words speak for themselves: "This is what you shall do: Love the earth and sun and the animals, despise riches, give alms to every one that asks, stand up for the stupid and crazy, devote your income and labor to others, hate tyrants, argue not concerning god, have patience and indulgence toward the people, take off your hat to nothing known or unknown or to any man or number of men, go freely with powerful uneducated persons and with the young and with the mothers of families, read these leaves in the open air every season of every year of your life, re-examine all you have been told at school or church or in any book, dismiss whatever insults your own soul, and your very flesh shall be a great poem and have the richest fluency not only in its words but in the silent lines of its lips and face and between the lashes of your eyes and in every motion and joint of your body."

QUESTIONS FOR MEDITATION:

Where do you seek your deep learning?

"That it will never come again / Is what makes life so sweet."

WHY I LOVE THIS QUOTE:

As a reminder that whatever may have happened before, and whatever is to come, this life, these passing moments right now, will never be here again. That is what makes life beautiful even in the longing and sadness that may also accompany the knowledge.

WHY THIS IS A TRANSFORMATIVE BOOK:

Dickinson's poetry is remarkable for its tightly controlled emotional and intellectual energy. Dickinson's brevity makes her work accessible even to readers who typically dislike poetry. Still, the complexity of her thought, as well as her engagement with the major issues of her time, invites careful readings of her poems, be they focused on form or history or both. A true innovator, Dickinson experimented freely with conventional rhythm and meter, and often used dashes, off rhymes, and unusual metaphors — techniques that strongly influenced modern poetry. Dickinson's idiosyncratic style, along with her deep resonance of thought and her observations about life and death, love and nature, and solitude and society, have firmly established her as one of America's true poetic geniuses.

QUESTION FOR MEDITATION:

If you had to say right now what is your deepest desire, what is it? How would you go about possessing it? What is stopping you?

"Be patient and tough; one day this pain will be useful to you."

WHY I LOVE THIS QUOTE:

Being patient doesn't mean being passive. In fact, it can very well mean you're being strong. Also, the idea of how the suffering or pain or struggle you may be enduring right now is a teacher that informs you for life experiences ahead. It reminds me of Rumi's statement: "These pains you feel are messengers. Listen to them."

WHY THIS IS A TRANSFORMATIVE BOOK:

The Metamorphoses by Ovid is a massive undertaking, but a worthwhile journey should you be willing to accept the mission.

As Man Martin writes, "*The Metamorphoses* is no slim volume, in fifteen books it comprises a virtual encyclopedia of mythology from creation to the apotheosis of Julius Caesar...Yesterday, as I reached the final words, 'I will live', and put the book aside, I felt as if I'd incompletely awoken from a long and vivid afternoon dream. The title is apt because over and over Ovid returns to the story of some transformation or other — men changing into birds, women into trees...he loves to catch a character in the very midst of transformation: a young girl who tries to scream but realizes the tree bark that is now her skin has grown up over her throat, a man fleeing in terror who realizes he is no longer running but flying because he has turned into a bird, a woman piteously reaches for her husband while she still has arms to reach because her lower body has turned into a coiling snake. This same device — what we might call the poetic use of transformation — appears in *The Odyssey*; in a few swift words, Homer accomplished the transformation of men into swine on Circe's Island. We are reading about men at the beginning of a line, and the insertion of one tale-tell word 'bristles' gives us a warning, and by the end of the line, the crew are men no longer, but pigs. As for Ovid, the one thing that will not change is his immortality through these words."

QUESTIONS FOR MEDITATION:

How would you describe your personal transformation? At what stage would you describe yourself?

"Before you know kindness as the deepest thing inside, / you must know sorrow as the other deepest thing. / You must wake up with sorrow. / You must speak to it till your voice / catches the thread of all sorrows / and you see the size of the cloth."

WHY I LOVE THIS QUOTE:

The idea that kindness, synonymous in many respects to compassion, is the "deepest thing." And also that in order to come to it, you need to be able to understand another deep thing, which is sorrow, or sadness, or grief. We experience empathy by having shared feelings and experiences that we can access when putting ourselves in another's shoes.

WHY THIS IS A TRANSFORMATIVE BOOK:

Words Under the Words: Selected Poems by Naomi Shihab Nye was published in 1994 and already shows an accomplished and brilliant poet. I have always found Nye's poems to be accessible and moving. Her poems are flooded with honesty. For the majority of readers who don't get poetry — modern or otherwise — I would venture to guess this is a collection that would resonate. She has the rare gift of being "easy" to understand, but also remaining long in the memory.

QUESTIONS FOR MEDITATION:

Do you feel helpless or hopeful when it comes to the issue of poverty in our communities?

"Yesterday I was clever, so I wanted to change the world. Today I am wise, so I am changing myself."

WHY I LOVE THIS QUOTE:

Back in the 2010s you'd hear a lot of the startup scene language about how their company was going to do nothing less than change the world. It's good to have ambition, but then again, maybe you should start with a healthy and diverse culture. Same with the "self." Wisdom teaches us that one of the best ways to "change the world" is to begin with our self. This includes the way we interact with our own family. Want to change the dysfunctional behavior of others? Great, start with yourself.

WHY THIS IS A TRANSFORMATIVE BOOK:

The Essential Rumi by Rumi, translated Coleman Barks is a beautiful collection. Barks' lyrical translations have been instrumental in bringing this exquisite literature to a wide range of readers, making the ecstatic, spiritual poetry of thirteenth-century Sufi Mystic Rumi more popular than ever. Essential is a good word for the title of this anthology. The verses are organized into playful groupings that refer to one another subtlety but completely. This particular collection is brimming with gems. Rumi speaks to everyone. These are devotional poems.

QUESTIONS FOR MEDITATION:

In what ways do you still need to grow yourself up?

"Every angel is terrifying."

WHY I LOVE THIS QUOTE:
This famous opening line to this book is fascinating. We are reminded of Isaiah's terror and awe in the face of the seraphim. Why? We realize how small we are when in their presence. "Who, if I cried out, would hear me among the angels' / hierarchies? and even if one of them / pressed me against his heart: I would be consumed / in that overwhelming existence. For beauty is nothing / but the beginning of terror, which we still are just able to endure, / and we are so awed because it serenely disdains / to annihilate us."

WHY THIS IS A TRANSFORMATIVE BOOK:
The Duino Elegies by Rainer Maria Rilke came about from a marvelous, almost legendary set of circumstances. Rilke was staying at Duino Castle, on a rocky headland of the Adriatic Sea near Trieste. One morning he walked out onto the battlements and climbed down to where the cliffs dropped sharply to the sea. From out of the fierce wind, Rilke seemed to hear a voice: "If I cried out, who would hear me up there, among the angelic orders?" He wrote these words, the opening of the first Duino Elegy, in his notebook, then went inside to continue what was to be his major opus — completely only after another ten, tormented years of effort — and one of the literary masterpieces of the century. *Duino Elegies* speaks in a voice that is both intimate and majestic on the mysteries of human life and our attempt, in the words of the translator David Young, "to use our self-consciousness to some advantage: to transcend, through art and the imagination, our self-deception and our fear."

QUESTIONS FOR MEDITATION:

What inspires awe and transcendence in your life? Do you long for more of it?

"When we let go of insisting that we are who we think we are and that the world should give us exactly and only what we want, all things shine forth."

WHY I LOVE THIS QUOTE:

A reminder that things become lighter when we unburden ourselves from others' expectations and live out of who we are. It's a theme we return to again over the course of the year, as it's not always straightforward or easy.

WHY THIS IS A TRANSFORMATIVE BOOK:

The Poetry of Impermanence, Mindfulness, and Joy by John Brehm is a collection where East meets West. Ancient poets like Chuang-Tzu, Tu Fu, Han Shan and Li Po meet their modern-counterparts in Fernando Pessoa, Yannis Ritsos, Szymborska, Anna Swir, Philip Larkin, Ellen Bass, William Carlos Williams, James Wright and many others. Chinese and Japanese poems ranging from the 4th century BCE to the 19th century (like three of the four haiku masters) are placed alongside contemporaneous European and American poetry, of Buddhist and non-Buddhist inspiration, finding each other in the unifying premise that mindfulness of impermanence leads to joy. Joy can be found in the present moment. According to the editor of this anthology, the poet John Brehm, living in the full knowledge that everything changes changes everything and so we can see the world as what it truly is: a source of amazement and delight. It's a fun, unique assemblage of poets in line with some of the themes and concepts within this assemblage of books, quotations, and meditation questions.

QUESTIONS FOR MEDITATION:

Have you ever tried meditation? Even if it's not meditation, how can you develop your own mindfulness, developing more consciousness of your moment-by-moment passage through each day?

If you long for it, ask yourself how you can create the conditions to make it happen.

"The ultimate touchstone of friendship is not improvement, neither of the other nor of the self, the ultimate touchstone is witness, the privilege of having been seen by someone and the equal privilege of being granted the sight of the essence of another, to have walked with them and to have believed in them, and sometimes just to have accompanied them for however brief a span, on a journey impossible to accomplish alone."

WHY I LOVE THIS QUOTE:

This is not only an eloquent statement of what friendship is, it's also full of grace for ourselves and for the others. Friends often come and go, and sometimes that makes us feel less like trusting in the next friendship. We want loyalty, but that's not always what friendship is or needs to be. Sometimes — more often than not, in fact — friendships are there for a certain season in your life and theirs.

WHY THIS IS A TRANSFORMATIVE BOOK:

Consolations: The Solace, Nourishment and Underlying Meaning of Everyday Words by David Whyte uses a compact, lyrical style to explore the depths of meaning for each "everyday" word. And because the author manages to capture so many angles of insight in a short space, one can easily return to a chapter for rereading and the further reward this offers. This is the kind of book that you keep coming back to. It too can be used for deep thinking and meditation.

QUESTIONS FOR MEDITATION:

What is a friendship that you valued having, that has faded away?

Have you had a friendship that has stood the test of time?

"That want to be known, governs us all."

WHY I LOVE THIS QUOTE:
It's not that he's saying we all want to be famous. Being known is like being heard. We all want to be heard, to be understood, to feel like we matter, that we are counted. To know and be known. This is what constructing a meaningful life is all about.

WHY THIS IS A TRANSFORMATIVE TEXT:
Felon: Poems by Reginald Dwayne Betts is a powerful, lyrical look at incarceration — the poems tackle the subject from many angles, through many forms. The language is informed by the streets, prisons and jails, newspapers, classical, and biblical works, in vocabulary, allusion, and rhythm. Betts himself is evidence of the wide range of potential outcomes for any individual. He served eight years for carjacking. He has subsequently written and taught poetry, been active in juvenile justice programs, and graduated from Yale Law School. His work speaks to the complex realities of race, gender, and mass incarceration. The Redaction Poems are an absolute highlight in this collection.

QUESTIONS FOR MEDITATION:

In what ways are you known? In what ways would you still like to be known?

"How confidently the desires / of God are spoken of! / Perhaps God wants / something quite different. / Or nothing, nothing at all."

WHY I LOVE THIS QUOTE:
I have often had a similar thought. It used to be shocking how many people seemed so certain of "God's will." Then, I became used to it as I came to understand human psychology and behavior. People speak with certitudes (and in platitudes) about what they believe is God's will, and that's fine, that's really all we have, our belief based upon the best of our reasoning and interpretation. It is a belief, not a fact. People with such apparent certainty would do well to try to understand God better.

WHY THIS IS A TRANSFORMATIVE TEXT:
In her poetry collection, *Evening Train*, Denise Levertov is moving, meditative, and musical (alliteration not intended). The collection explores the nature of faith and love, the imperiled beauty of the natural world, as well as the horrors of the Gulf War. Levertov died in 1997, but was always a favorite modern poet of mine, straddling the ability to talk about spirituality in a way that opened up the mystery, rather than boxed it in. As a child, she wrote about the strangeness she felt growing up part Jewish, German, Welsh, and English, but not fully belonging to any of these identities. She notes that it lent her a sense of being special rather than excluded: "[I knew] before I was ten that I was an artist-person and I had a destiny."

As Larry Smith writes, "Levertov kept her spirit open and free and yet deeply reflective. She moves so smoothly along trails and streets and opens eye and heart."

As Caroliena Cabada writes, "Precise images and an array of concerns, from war to environmental destruction, that all feel timely and timeless. Personal without feeling exclusive, universal without being too presumptuous."

QUESTIONS FOR MEDITATION:
How confident of your own desires are you? Do you have a destiny?

"Tell me, what is it you plan to do / with your one wild and precious life?"

WHY I LOVE THIS QUOTE:

Having just died in 2019 at the age of 83, it's clear that Mary Oliver knew what she wanted to do with her "one wild and precious life," and it's easy for us to see many successful people who seem to have found "their thing" go at it year after year. Meanwhile, the great majority of us feel like we're floundering for purpose. We don't often know what we should do, or even what we want to do. That doesn't stop the fact that life is short and we can make choices. There are doors to knock on yet.

WHY THIS IS A TRANSFORMATIVE TEXT:

Devotions: The Selected Poems by Mary Oliver features over 200 poems, starting from her very first book of poetry, *No Voyage and Other Poems*, published in 1963 at the age of 28, through *Felicity*, published in 2015. Arranged by Oliver herself, the volume provides us with an extraordinary and invaluable collection of her passionate, perceptive, and much-treasured observations of the natural world.

As Ali Nuri writes, "*Devotions* provides a fitting culmination of her life philosophy, her core tenets bound together in one vulnerable place. Ultimately, her work divulges with astute observation the crux of what we are: at once human and animal, at once selfish and full of gratitude, at once perfect and profoundly flawed. The paradoxical balancing act between shameless desire and overwhelming selflessness is deftly traversed through her lush turns of phrase."

QUESTIONS FOR MEDITATION:

Let's ask it again: What is it you plan to do with your one wild and precious life?

"The truth is that life will break us and burn us at some point on the journey. This is not pessimistic or cynical but descriptive of the geography of being alive. It is part of how we are transformed by the journey. Yet when we're broken or burned by events, we feel betrayed by God. When we're broken or burned by people, we feel betrayed by other souls."

WHY I LOVE THIS QUOTE:

The point is to live in expectation, not only in the hope of more goodness to come, but also in the reality check that hard things are very much on their way. We need to be alive to navigating all parts of life's geography.

WHY THIS IS A TRANSFORMATIVE TEXT:

Seven Thousand Ways to Listen: Staying Close to What Is Sacred by Mark Nepo offers ancient and contemporary practices to help us stay close to what is sacred. In this spiritual memoir, Nepo explores the transformational journey with insight and grace. He unfolds the many gifts and challenges of deep listening as we are asked to reflect on the life we are given. Nepo decided to write this when he learned that he was losing his hearing. He thought of all the thousands of ways there are to talk, and then asked himself if there were just as many ways to listen. A moving exploration of self and our relationship to others and the world around us, the book unpacks the many ways we are called to redefine ourselves and to name what is meaningful as we move through the changes that come from experience and aging and the challenge of surviving loss.

QUESTIONS FOR MEDITATION:

Have you experienced much grief, loss, or hardship in your life? Did you navigate it in healthy or unhealthy ways? What did the struggles teach you about yourself?

"In these dark times, will there also be singing? / Yes, there will be singing. / About the dark times."

WHY I LOVE THIS QUOTE:

It may be easy to forget that poetry isn't all frolicking among the daylilies, triumphant odes, or calming meditations. There are lamentations. There is the singing in good times and, perhaps especially, in bad times as well. The most important takeaway, however, isn't about what poetry does or doesn't do, it's about what we do in response to life's challenges, sufferings, and atrocities.

WHY THIS IS A TRANSFORMATIVE TEXT:

Against Forgetting: Twentieth-Century Poetry of Witness by Carolyn Forché is an anthology that attempts to bear testament to the extreme of human experience and endurance. The heavy volume draws from other noted poets throughout the former century, across a broad spectrum of tumultuous human rights events — war, torture, exile, repression — from the Armenian genocide to World War II to Tiananmen Square.

Forche's own poem "The Colonel" from *The Country Between Us* begins, "This really happened..." Likewise, the poems she chose as editor for this historical anthology remind us that war, genocide, and oppression really happened. Bearing witness to extremity — whether of war, torture, exile, or repression — this collection of poems from more than 140 poets from five continents, over the span of the 20th century, refuses silence. The poets will sing still. An incredible, essential, and rare collection of modern poetry.

QUESTIONS FOR MEDITATION:

How can you bear witness to the dark parts of human experience while maintaining a sense of courage and hopefulness?

"The paradox of vengefulness is that it makes men dependent upon those who have harmed them, believing that their
release from pain will come only when their tormentors suffer."

WHY I LOVE THIS QUOTE:
Most of us carry at least the seeds of anger and hostility toward those who
have wronged us, and it's hard — so hard — to forgive or forget, especially
when those people don't want either. But it's also important. If not for moral
or virtuous reasons, then at least for the pragmatic ones of taking care of
yourself: You will be released when you are able to forgive, even if you will
never forget.

WHY THIS IS A TRANSFORMATIVE BOOK:
Unbroken: A World War II Story of Survival, Resilience and Redemption by
Laura Hillenbrand is about Louie Zamperini who went from being a reckless
youth to a member of the 1936 Olympic track team to a bombardier on a
B-24 in the Pacific theatre to being stranded on the ocean for 47 days to
being rescued by the Japanese, where things only got worse. He and fellow
prisoners were given little food or water, and were expected to perform
hard labor until eventually Japan surrendered, and he came back to his
family and became an instant celebrity, but also struggled with PTSD and
suffered from addiction. It was at his lowest point that he attended a revival
by Billy Graham that changed his life. He was able to overcome his night-
mares and thirst for revenge and became a spiritual speaker that finally
started a camp for boys with problems.

As Paul Pessalano writes: "Sometimes you come across a book that is heads
and tails above just about everything you have read during the past year.
Unbroken is that book...It is a tribute to the human mind, body, and spirit."

QUESTIONS FOR MEDITATION:

Who do you need to forgive?

"All goes back to the earth, / and so I do not desire / pride of excess or power / but the contentments made / by men who have had little"

WHY I LOVE THIS QUOTE:

I love this quote because for all the talk of taking ownership of oneself and how to have power in relationships, and how to have difficult conversations, and develop relationships with others if we are to be anything or anyone in the world, there is also the constant reminder that "all goes back to the earth." And it is for that very reason that the speaker of the poem, or Wendell Berry, is saying he doesn't care about having material goods "in excess" or "power." We might begin to take his inclination as despair if not for the immediate next thought of just wanting to be modest, content, and humble as — well — most of the rest of humankind.

WHY THIS IS A TRANSFORMATIVE BOOK:

The poem comes from Wendell Berry's third book of poems *Openings*, but for a current volume overview of a lot of his wonderful verse *The Selected Poems of Wendell Berry* is the best choice.

QUESTIONS FOR MEDITATION:

At the end of my life, how would I like to feel about myself?

How can I have less anxiety in my life right now?

"Time will say nothing but I told you so, / Time only knows the price we have to pay; / If I could tell you I would let you know."

WHY I LOVE THIS QUOTE:

This quote is the opening of a beautiful villanelle called "If I Could Tell You." The sentiment is similar to Bob Dylan's "the answer, my friend, is blowin' in the wind." It speaks to life's mysteries, and certainties. We don't know where the wind comes from, or where it goes. We don't know why time is passing and that there is a "price we have to pay," only that there is, only that we do.

WHY THIS IS A TRANSFORMATIVE TEXT:

Selected Poems by W.H. Auden makes available the preferred original versions of some thirty poems that Auden revised later in life, making it the best source for enjoying the many facets of Auden's art in one volume. More and more over the years Auden continues to grow on me. He may not be as imminently quotable as Frost or as monumental as Yeats and T.S. Eliot. He's more like a friend who's not always steady on his feet, occasionally overreaching, a bit heartbroken, a bit bitter, a bit sweet. Overall, Auden's poetry was noted for its stylistic and technical achievement, its engagement with politics, morals, love, and religion, and its variety in tone, form and content. Since his death in 1973 there has been ongoing critical debate as to his stature among the greats. Many have argued that he is the greatest of the 20th century. Among my very favorites are "Musee des Beaux Arts," and "In Memory of W.B. Yeats."

QUESTIONS FOR MEDITATION:

What does it mean to give the "power" over to time?

"I love things with a wild passion, extravagantly."

WHY I LOVE THIS QUOTE:

We love Neruda for his passion, his intensity. We love him for his direct-ness, his authenticity. His perceptions are held in the body. He is, in his own words, "A poet closer to death than to philosophy, closer to pain than to intelligence, closer to blood than to ink." Neruda is not a distanced observer of life, it has his full attention. He is engaged, and wants to pull you along with him in his enthusiasm.

WHY THIS IS A TRANSFORMATIVE TEXT:

The Poetry of Pablo Neruda is the most comprehensive single volume available in English, presents nearly six hundred poems. Scores of them are in new and sometimes multiple translations, and many accompanied by the Spanish original. In his introduction, Ilan Stavans situates Neruda in his native milieu as well as in a contemporary English-language one, and a group of new translations by leading poets testifies to Neruda's enduring, vibrant legacy among English-speaking writers and readers today. mixed in with this earthy prose is an appreciation for the subtle, fleeting moments that last only in quick impressions and memories of wanting and desire. This is a large and representative collection covering sonnets, odes, cantos and free verse drawn from across Neruda's entire career.

QUESTIONS FOR MEDITATION:

What gets you really excited? What obsesses you? What ignites your pas-sion?

"Lucky you can be purified over and over again. / Lucky there is the same cleanliness for everyone."

WHY I LOVE THIS QUOTE:

I love the tender enthusiasm, the hope, the democratic grace available to everyone, not to mention that you get more than a second chance. You can be purified again and again. Luck is a fascinating theological concept.

WHY THIS IS A TRANSFORMATIVE TEXT:

Lucky Life by Gerald Stern takes the reader on a journey, pausing everywhere from the streets of New York to post-Holocaust Germany to the soil of a lobelia plant. In an intimate and mature voice, although this was only his second book, he shares with us the lineage of his ancestors; his personal relationships; and bits of art, music, history — even the neighbors he chats with on the beach. His style is Whitmanesque, urging us to "listen a little for the spongy world" after it has rained, and reminding us how to "understand the power of maples."

As Jessica Freeman writes, "It's not hyperbole to say this book completely changed my life, and my belief in poetry as an avenue to relate to the world. Poems of place, poems about work, economical language and images that have almost a muscularity to them. I will always return to these poems for solace and comfort in place and the world around me. So thankful for Gerald Stern."

QUESTIONS FOR MEDITATION:

How are you lucky? Are you lucky because you earned it, or are you just purely lucky?

"When I leave this body, Woman, / I want to be pure flame. I want to be your song."

WHY I LOVE THIS QUOTE:

He wants to be the light that lives on what the flames devour, as Lorca said. He doesn't want to be the yellowing photograph in some stale book. He wants to live within her. He wants to light the way. He wants to live with such brilliant intensity that even when he is gone he lives on through her. There is this constant tension through the poem (and the poems from this book) between freedom and constraint. As the last line of the poem, this is how he wants it to end, with a freedom marked by passion and purity.

WHY THIS IS A TRANSFORMATIVE TEXT:

Wind in a Box by Terrance Hayes has an impressive scope and range. The struggle for freedom (the wind) within containment (the box) is the unifying motif as Hayes explores identity through race, heritage, masculinity, and spirituality, and often where least expected. Experiments with structure, rhyme and sound add to the appeal.

As Craig Werner writes, "Terrance Hayes at his best triangulates Langston Hughes' vernacular smarts, Lorca's duende lyricism, and a determination to move past racial categories without abandoning the grounding of his specific experience."

QUESTIONS FOR MEDITATION:

How can you "be" in your thinking mind? Are you comfortable there? Does it come at the expense of cutting yourself off from your feelings?

"I would live forever if I could, but not like this."

WHY I LOVE THIS QUOTE:

When I first read this I laughed out loud. It starts off with this longing we all feel, and then hits you with this plainspoken reality check. It also strikes me that this is similar to how our imaginations are always way ahead of what our bodies are actually capable of. The spirit is willing, but the flesh is weak.

WHY THIS IS A TRANSFORMATIVE TEXT:

No Other Life by Gary Young are lean prose poems that bring together three books of Young's trilogy in one volume. A great introduction into Young's work. Some will bring tears, some will bring smiles, most will bring both. Young's work reveals modesty and restraint. He could be more effusive, but he is saying it with le mot juste. Lean, sometimes spare, as if saying the exact right thing doesn't always come easily, but when it does, it counts. These prose poems are distinct and spiritual in nature.

QUESTIONS FOR MEDITATION:

What one small adjustment could you make to the way you're living now that would pay the biggest dividends?

"I will die in Paris with a rainstorm, / on a day I already remember"

WHY I LOVE THIS QUOTE:
He begins to specifically predict the day of his death. It is here with him now in the present. He holds it dear. It is happening and is as real as the moment is now.

WHY THIS IS A TRANSFORMATIVE TEXT:
The Complete Poetry by César Vallejo is a comprehensive and well-translated edition. Vallejo is admired among poets, but not broadly known.

As Richard Jackson writes, "Cesar Vallejo's poetry changed me. When I was in my 20s, I was especially moved by the agonizing poems Vallejo wrote in Paris, which I discovered in *Poemas Humanos*. I put myself to school on his deeply compassionate poetry. In "A Walk with Vallejo in Paris," a poem of poetic apprenticeship, I imagined myself walking with the master learning about poetry — and life — from him."

As Christopher Buckley writes from an anthology he put together, *Homage to Vallejo*, in 2006, "I think it is difficult to match Vallejo's intensity, for it is hard to divide his life from his poetry. He is the poor, and so when he writes of poverty, the grinding effect on the soul, he is speaking from immediate experience — his daily poverty in the world, the poverty of the human spirit abandoned by God."

As Philip Levine writes, "In 1965, living in Barcelona, I read César Vallejo's poems in Spanish for the first time...Before that year was over, I knew I'd unearthed one of the great American visionaries, a man in possession of a biblical imagination and a terrifying tenderness...anyone who writes can be inspired by his daring and his capacity for invention."

QUESTIONS FOR MEDITATION:

Should art and poetry be democratic and accessible to everyone, or should it be difficult and challenging and only for those willing to work at it?

"Forgive me. This is my favorite sin: despair — / whose love I celebrate with wine and prayer."

WHY I LOVE THIS QUOTE:

This poem, "Praying Drunk," which as it says "lurches from metaphor to metaphor," yearns to be a form of prayer. In fact, it is. On the superficial level, it follows the script of what is expected: confession, intercession, supplication, even requests. But it is a prayer by any definition. It is also funny in its very humanness as it "lurches" between the sacred and the profane.

WHY THIS IS A TRANSFORMATIVE TEXT:

The Never-Ending by Andrew Hudgins was his third book in a row nominated for a major American prize (the National Book Award, this time); it was also his third book overall. That's a track record that's pretty hard to miss, and yet, much lauded, he is little known, and one of modern America's finest poetic voices. After reading *The Never-Ending*, I found a copy of his second book, *After the Lost War*, and couldn't believe how different and how good it is too, although very different. The latter is a sustained narrative unlike any you'll read in contemporary poetry. The former is a series of lyric meditations which delights and appalls all at the same time.

QUESTIONS FOR MEDITATION:

What actions do you take over the course of a day that you could call a form of prayer? If you don't pray in a traditional sense, can you expand your definition of prayer? Is there a way to live mindfully or with a sense of each passing moment as sacred?

"When the war is over / We will be proud of course the air will be / Good for breathing at last / The water will have been improved the salmon / And the silence of heaven will migrate more perfectly / The dead will think the living are worth it we will know / Who we are / And we will all enlist again"

WHY I LOVE THIS QUOTE:

The context of this poem from *The Lice* was 1968, so it's Vietnam-era, but it can also mean "war" universally. Under the conditions of the COVID-19 pandemic of 2020, the air being "good for breathing at last" resonates in a whole new context. There are several great lines in this quote, but one I especially like is, "And the silence of heaven will migrate more perfectly." Then, of course, for all the good news about the war finally being over, the last line hits us with the circuitous nature of it all: we're going to do it all over again. We always have a reason.

WHY THIS IS A TRANSFORMATIVE TEXT:

The Second Four Books of Poems by W.S. Merwin includes some of the most startlingly original and influential poetry of the second half of this century, a poetry that has moved, as Richard Howard writes, "from preterition to presence to prophecy."

ANOTHER GREAT QUOTE:

"Your absence has gone through me / Like thread through a needle. / Everything I do is stitched with its color."

QUESTIONS FOR MEDITATION:

"The dead will think the living are worth it." Are we the living worthy of the dead?

"Suddenly I realize / That if I stepped out of my body I would break / Into blossom."

WHY I LOVE THIS QUOTE:

The last lines of "The Blessing," where he's been spending a moment with two "Indian ponies." Then, the unexpected and beautiful turn. Let the line speak for itself.

WHY THIS IS A TRANSFORMATIVE TEXT:

Above the River: The Complete Poems by James Wright is an astounding array of lush descriptions, celebration of the socially forgotten, and killer ending lines. In the forward, Donald Hall says that Wright's poems are weaker when they try to be pretty but masterful when they are beautiful. Basically, if you were to have five books of poems to keep on your shelf for whatever reason, give this one strong consideration. Each of the volumes contained within it are private, humble masterpieces. The trace an intuitive master through formal stages, through theological inquiry and lament, through his so-called "deep imagist" work, through carefully wrought translations of Neruda, Trakl, and Vallejo, through gospel-like hallelujah's and travel way beyond the scope and context of Ohio. While he's most anthologized for work from his 1963 and '68 collections, I find myself most often wanting to revisit the work from his 1982 collection, *The Journey*.

As Sheila Dane writes, "Lyrical, gritty, moving. Wright's poetry is deeply personal, yet universal, a sort of every man's struggle to find himself. We follow him from his Ohio blue collar roots all the way to Italy where he for the first time, finds a sort of peace (having much to do with his marriage to Anne Wright) that had eluded him for the greater part of his life. This collection was put together by his wife, Anne Wright and contains a thoughtful foreword by Donald Hall."

QUESTIONS FOR MEDITATION:

Have you ever noticed how you can feel intense longing and desire as much when things are sad and lonely as when you're quiet and peaceful?

"I say that one must be a visionary — that one must make oneself a visionary."

WHY I LOVE THIS QUOTE:

Well, this is National Poetry month. We would be remiss not to talk about how you must be a visionary. Okay, not everyone can put words to their visions like poets. That's part of what makes them so rare. But perhaps we can all be bothered to spend a little more time reflecting on the nature of our reality. We all have visions when we dream. It's about how we pay attention. Poetry calls us to listen and pay closer attention.

WHY THIS IS A TRANSFORMATIVE TEXT:

A Season in Hell, The Drunken Boat, and Illuminations by Arthur Rimbaud is all you need to see the breadth of his work: which he stopped at age 19. *A Season in Hell*, has been referred to as a pioneering example of modern symbolism, along with *The Drunken Boat*, a fragmented first-person narrative which vividly describes the drifting and sinking of a boat lost at sea, probably the best known work. Also included in this edition is what is arguably Rimbaud's masterpiece, *Illuminations*. A collection of forty-two poems almost all of which are in a prose format.

Albert Camus hailed Rimbaud as "the poet of revolt, and the greatest."

QUESTIONS FOR MEDITATION:

What would happen if you practiced mindful listening with each person that you spoke with?

"We find out the heart only by dismantling what / the heart knows."

WHY I LOVE THIS QUOTE:
So begins the poem "Tear it Down." By dismantling the heart, you get to know it from outside in and not only the inside out. By breaking it down you get to rebuild it. It's a painful process, but you are made new again by the reconstruction. Also, by breaking down the heart's structures, you break down the ego's structure. It's only a good thing to live more from the heart and less from the ego. Sometimes in the process of rebuilding and transforming we have to break things down to their constituent parts before we can begin again.

WHY THIS IS A TRANSFORMATIVE TEXT:
The Great Fires by Jack Gilbert is a late 20th century masterpiece. Many of the poems are elegiac. They are spare and exacting. They are precise in their clarity of thought, and moving in their intensity, and memorable for both qualities.

As James Dickey writes, "He takes himself away to a place more inward than is safe to go; from that awful silence and tightening, he returns to us poems savage compassion. Gilbert is the rarest of beings: a necessary poet, who teaches us not only how to live but to die creatively, and with all meaning."

QUESTIONS FOR MEDITATION:

What part of yourself could stand to be broken down so you can build it back over again?

"What can you expect, in a world that blooms / and freezes all at once?"

WHY I LOVE THIS QUOTE:
The world does some crazy things. It contains seemingly limitless para-doxes, contrasts, and inconsistencies. It's beautiful even when you're looking at it through a lens of grief and melancholy.

WHY THIS IS A TRANSFORMATIVE TEXT:
Atlantis by Mark Doty draws connections between things ordinary and rapturous which has a strange effect of making you feel sad, but also grateful to be alive. He finds consolation for death in the ocean's cast offs. Rows of frozen mackerels on ice suddenly become "like seams of lead / in a Tiffany window. / Iridescent, watery / prismatics: think abalone, / the wildly rainbowed / mirror of a soapbubble sphere, / think sun on gaso-line. / Splendor, and splendor, / and not a one in any way / distinguished from the other / —nothing about them / of individuality."

As Diann Blakely writes, "Mark Doty's third collection, *My Alexandria*, won the 1993 National Book Critics Circle Award, and his new volume of poems, *Atlantis* crowns its predecessor's substantial achievements. Its mythical title notwithstanding, the realm of *Atlantis* is fully human, subject to forces that make most things seem 'fallen down, broken apart, carried away.'"

QUESTIONS FOR MEDITATION:

What are you aware that you're grateful for even in times of uncertainty and stress?

"Count it the greatest of all sins to prefer life to honor, and to lose, for the sake of living, all that makes life worth having."

WHY I LOVE THIS QUOTE:

I take this to mean that if you compromise living a life of character or virtue to some idea you have of power, status, or money, so that you can supposedly live a larger life, removes the very reason for the pursuit of those things. You won't be happy when you get there because you won't be who you are — or at least who you are has become someone that you weren't intended to be.

WHY THIS IS A TRANSFORMATIVE TEXT:

The Sixteen Satires by Juvenal captures the splendour, the squalor, and the sheer energy of everyday Roman life. He evokes a fascinating world of prostitutes, fortune tellers, alcoholic politicians, slick lawyers, shameless sycophants, ageing flirts, and downtrodden teachers. A member of the traditional land-owning class that was rapidly seeing power slip into the hands of outsiders, Juvenal also creates savage portraits of decadent aristocrats — male and female — seeking excitement among the lower orders of actors and gladiators, and of the jumped-up sons of newly-rich former slaves. Constantly comparing the corruption of his own generation with its stern and upright forebears, Juvenal's powers of irony and invective make his work a stunningly satirical and bitter denunciation of the degeneracy of Roman society.

QUESTIONS FOR MEDITATION:

What are you strongest core values and are you consistent in sticking to them?

"They cannot scare me with their empty spaces / Between stars — on stars where no human race is. / I have it in me so much nearer home / To scare myself with my own desert places."

WHY I LOVE THIS QUOTE:

First, I think we can all appreciate the clever rhyme of "race is" with "places." Beyond that, what a fantastic contrast. Yes, the conceptual distance between stars is beyond comprehension and that can make us feel incredibly small, but it is also literally beyond us. It leaves us cold and abstract. There are already terrible distances within ourselves, huge untamed wildernesses barely recognizable within ourselves if only we would strike out into them and have the courage to slay the beasts we encounter. Those places within are scary enough.

WHY THIS IS A TRANSFORMATIVE TEXT:

The Poetry of Robert Frost is a comprehensive gathering of Frost's published poetry, this affordable volume offers the entire contents of his eleven books of verse, from *A Boy's Will* (1913) to *In the Clearing* (1962). Frost scholar Lathem, who was also a close friend of the four-time Pulitzer Prize-winner, scrupulously annotated the 350-plus poems in this collection, which has been the standard edition of Frost's work since it first appeared in 1969. There's not much that needs to be said about the poetry of Frost, except that, unlike most things in life, it's as good as it's supposed to be. If you are just getting into poetry, Frost is especially to be recommended. This is one of those anthologies that if you had to pick a top five for your shelves, is one to strongly consider. Many readers will find his poems more accessible than most modern poets.

QUESTIONS FOR MEDITATION:

Why are so many people scared or defensive about developing more self-knowledge? What's to be scared about? It's just you you're getting to know.

"For whatever we lose (like a you or a me), / It's always our self we find in the sea."

WHY I LOVE THIS QUOTE:

We may lose parts ourselves along the journey, but in the end, we return to ourselves. How could we not?

WHY THIS IS A TRANSFORMATIVE TEXT:

100 Selected Poems by E.E. Cummings first published in 1959, is a smart collection to consider. It's an unusual concision, harvesting 100 poems from a thirty-five-year period, but one in which we appreciate the content all the more. These poems exhibit all the extraordinary lyricism, playfulness, technical ingenuity, and compassion for which Cummings is famous. They will challenge you intellectually, emotionally, and at many levels of language. They ask you deep philosophical questions, and then they shift gears into stunning emotional moves. They beg you to parse them one way, then cleverly show you another way to read each sentence even as you try to mark out your thoughts. The poems lend themselves to conversation, to analysis, and they will reward you again and again.

QUESTIONS FOR MEDITATION:

What are the emotional or philosophical questions you've been working on during National Poetry Month? Any favorite books to take with you along your journey? Are you sad or excited to conclude?

_____

may

_____

"When parents don't take responsibility for their own unfinished business, they miss an opportunity not only to become better parents but also to continue their own development. People who remain in the dark about the origins of their behaviors and intense emotional responses are unaware of their unresolved issues and the parental ambivalence they create."

WHY I LOVE THIS QUOTE:

So many parents sideline their own growth for so many reasons. Sometimes we feel that we don't have time because we're simply too busy providing and tending and maintaining. Other times we feel that we are now living for our children and we lose our personal identity as merely being "super" mom or dad. That does a disservice to ourselves and our children.

WHY THIS IS A TRANSFORMATIVE BOOK:

Parenting From the Inside Out by Daniel J. Siegel and Mary Hartzell point out that most parents want to be good parents and even have a lot of the knowledge of how to do it "right," but find themselves unable to access and apply their knowledge in the moment when things are intense. The authors draw on psychobiology, attachment theory, and Bowenian concepts to illustrate how greater self-knowledge can get you to a point where you can parent optimally as opposed to going with your knee-jerk reaction and simply putting out fires. A great book whether you have children or not. This book explains how our childhood experiences shape our reactions, feelings, and the way we perceive parenthood — and we've all had parents.

QUESTIONS FOR MEDITATION:

Reflecting opens the door to conscious awareness, which brings with it the possibility of change. Conscious change means growth, and that's usually where we need to begin to change unhealthy systems. How often do you take the time to reflect?

"Human nature dictates that it is virtually impossible to accept advice from someone unless you feel that that person understands you."

WHY I LOVE THIS QUOTE:
Which is why it's so important to have close relationships, even though all long-term relationships are fraught with challenges. It also explains why advice is rarely taken, and we would do well to consider more listening in our relationships, and less prescribing.

WHY THIS IS A TRANSFORMATIVE BOOK:
The Seven Principles for Making Marriage Work: A Practical Guide from the Country's Foremost Relationship Expert by John M. Gottman and Nan Silver assimilate a longitudinal study of marriages for over twenty years, following the same couples. They observed how the couples talked to each other from the everyday chit chat, to the serious conversations and even the fights. Fighting is not what breaks marriages up. In fact, fighting can be good for marriages in some ways. What they did find is that in the couples who remained married and reported being happily married, there were elements of behavior present that aided in getting through disagreements and fights. In the marriages that ended or were unhappy, there were elements that were also present that contributed to the breakdown of the relationship. Their research uncovers a number of potent relationship myths, All the satisfied couples practiced their seven principles, even if they didn't know it, which helped them navigate their way through all the difficulties and keep their marriages happy and stable.

QUESTIONS FOR MEDITATION:

In what ways can you do more listening and accepting of the other person in your long-term relationship?

Could that lead to you getting more of what you want or less?

"A self is not something static, tied up in a pretty parcel and handed to the child, finished and complete. A self is always becoming."

WHY I LOVE THIS QUOTE:
Because in some sense that is why the need for this very book exists. We are always in process, always growing, always becoming. Unless of course we're not, which would mean we're foreclosed and we're already unconscious and dead to ourselves.

WHY THIS IS A TRANSFORMATIVE BOOK:
A Circle of Quiet by Madeleine L'Engle is the memoir of a woman — an amazing writer with a successful career — who has reflected deeply about her life, her family, her writing, teaching, and her place in the world. And there is careful thought here, about not only her family, her writing, her life, but also about the major questions of all life: good and evil, the presence or absence of God, how should children be taught meaningfully, how should one try to live a meaningful life. L'Engle lived many existences but appears to have remained her same true self throughout. This was an exciting, delightful and inspiring book, especially for those interested in writing, teaching and in the art of self-discovery.

QUESTIONS FOR MEDITATION:

Do you think it's necessary — or inevitable — to have a little self-delusion? Would you like to see yourself more clearly if you could?

"He allowed himself to be swayed by his conviction that human beings are not born once and for all on the day their mothers give birth to them, but that life obliges them over and over again to give birth to themselves."

WHY I LOVE THIS QUOTE:

The simple, but profound way that this idea is about transformation and renewal. It's an interesting thought. We aren't even reborn just once or twice, but that throughout the changes necessary to keep ourselves alive as it were, we must continually rebirth ourselves. It also suggests that we need to be our own best parent, our own best mentor. Sometimes even when we're in a close, loving relationship, we still need to care for ourselves better than anyone else.

WHY THIS IS A TRANSFORMATIVE BOOK:

Love in the Time of Cholera by Gabriel García Márquez is an unusual love story for an unusual time. In their youth, Florentino Ariza and Fermina Daza fall passionately in love. When Fermina eventually chooses to marry a wealthy, well-born doctor, Florentino is heartbroken, but remains a romantic. As he rises in his business career he whiles away the years in 622 affairs — yet he reserves his heart for Fermina. When her husband dies at last, Florentino attends the funeral. Fifty years, nine months, and four days after he first declared his love for Fermina, he will do so again. Marquez details his characters and their emotions with incredible intensity and subtlety. The extended essay on love is what matters most here. Love in all its forms, sacred and profane, and the conclusion that no matter how it comes to you it is never to be denied.

QUESTIONS FOR MEDITATION:

What are ways you've already succeeded in learning about yourself? Name and claim your successes.

"Self-doubt in moderation is animating and motivating, not paralyzing. Leaders who have purged themselves of all self-doubt will not be leaders for long and, in my view, are dangerous while in command. I learned, over time, that self-doubt is my friend, and arrogance my enemy."

WHY I LOVE THIS QUOTE:

This also reminds me of the famous quote by Lord Acton from the 19th century, "Power corrupts, and absolute power corrupts absolutely." Self-doubt keeps us honest to ourselves. No one has all the answers. Humility is, ironically enough, what the greatest humans possess. Arrogance is always a form of insecurity.

WHY THIS IS A TRANSFORMATIVE BOOK:

Doing Justice: A Prosecutor's Thoughts on Crime, Punishment, and the Rule of Law by Preet Bharara is inspiring — it gives us hope that rational and objective fact-based thinking, combined with compassion, can truly lead us on a path toward truth and justice. Some of what he writes about is controversial, but ultimately it is a thought-provoking, entertaining book about the need to find the humanity in our legal system — and in our society. As Tom Matthews writes, "More than anything, this is a book about what it takes to be a good prosecutor, a good attorney, and also, to a large degree, what it takes to be a good person. I regularly listen to his Stay Tuned With Preet podcast and have constantly been impressed with his level-headed approach to the issues of the day. In a world where it is all but impossible to be unbiased, Preet constantly strives to treat everyone fairly, regardless of what side of the law they may be on. This 'do-the-right-thing' attitude is readily apparent in the book as well, making it a very refreshing read in a world that appears to grow more vituperative by the day."

QUESTIONS FOR MEDITATION:

If you aren't aware of self-doubt within yourself, would you say by contrast that you are over-confident?

"Early on in my tenure, I was given a cartoon that circulated widely at the UN. The cartoon showed dozens of people listening to a speech. In the first panel, the speaker asks, 'Who wants change?' and all audience members enthusiastically raise their hands. In the second panel, the speaker refines his question, asking, 'Who wants to change?' This time, each audience member looks toward the ground, demurring."

WHY I LOVE THIS QUOTE:

It's human nature to want things to be better, to ask for more of this and less of that. It's also human nature to expect someone else to do the work. Sometimes we feel resigned that we are too small, and the things we want changed too big. Sometimes we simply feel entitled. Change within ourselves takes hard work, and so does collective change. Especially in democratic societies, we need to take ownership for where things are. We need to engage and ask what can be done.

WHY THIS IS A TRANSFORMATIVE BOOK:

The Education of an Idealist by Samantha Power traces Power's distinctly American journey from immigrant to war correspondent to presidential Cabinet official. In 2005, her critiques of U.S. foreign policy caught the eye of newly-elected senator Barack Obama, who invited her to work with him on Capitol Hill and then on his presidential campaign. After Obama was elected president, Power went from being an activist outsider to a government insider, trying to put her ideals into practice. She served for four years as Obama's human rights adviser, and in 2013, he named her U.S. Ambassador to the United Nations, the youngest American to assume the role. She transports us from her childhood in Dublin to the streets of war-torn Bosnia to the White House Situation Room and the world of high-stakes diplomacy, all while raising two young children.

QUESTIONS FOR MEDITATION:

What should the collective moral conscience of America be asking itself about justice right now? Does it feel different this time with the events of 2020 in our rearview?

"Women who love themselves are threatening; but men who love real women, more so."

WHY I LOVE THIS QUOTE:
Genuine people are threatening to the people who are committed to keeping the fantasy and ensuing power and privilege alive. The men who love real women are perhaps more threatening because men are still generally in positions of power, though this is slowly changing. Change could happen faster with recognition of the subtle and overt power exchanges, but that cuts to the very core of why people are threatened.

WHY THIS IS A TRANSFORMATIVE BOOK:
The Beauty Myth by Naomi Wolf argues that the cultural myth of feminine beauty is a political and economic weapon used by the male-dominated world to undermine women's advancement in society. It is about the atmosphere women negotiate daily, and from an early age — one in which women intuit the importance of their looks, and are apprehensive about our beauty as an indication of status, competence, wealth, power, and credibility — one in which they are manipulated by powerful corporate advertisers to feel insecure, so they will remain the largest underpaid labor pool, and simultaneously the largest consumers of unnecessary products, in the world. Without this dichotomy, created by the beauty myth, the world's economy would — if not collapse — certainly have to be reconfigured. First published in 1990, it is a bestselling classic that redefines your view of the relationship between beauty and female identity.

QUESTIONS FOR MEDITATION:

Do you feel resistance to possible changes in our culture? Do you feel hope for possible changes? What beliefs do you have that keep change from happening?

"When we donate to a good cause, it 'says' to our associates, 'Look, I'm willing to spend my resources for the benefit of others. I'm playing a positive-sum, cooperative game with society.' This helps explain why generosity is so important for those who aspire to leadership. No one wants leaders who play zero-sum, competitive games with the rest of society. If their wins are our losses, why should we support them? Instead we want leaders with a prosocial orientation, people who will look out for us because we're all in it together."

WHY I LOVE THIS QUOTE:

What I take from this quote is that even the most basic animal-like instincts want to see others playing cooperatively as leaders. In a strange sense, it is a hopeful statement because we can expect idealism to generally come from our leaders since it's what we want to see from them.

WHY THIS IS A TRANSFORMATIVE BOOK:

The Elephant in the Brain: Hidden Motives in Everyday Life by Kevin Simler and Robin Hanson explores some of the real reasons behind many of our decisions. Using evolutionary psychology, cognitive science, and observation, the authors deconstruct our lofty pretensions in education, medicine, politics, and religion. The seemingly special behavior of humans, which is supposed to set us apart from the animal kingdom turns out to be merely subconscious scheming behavior of social primates. Most of the behavior such as education and medical consumption is mostly signaling behavior on our value as an ally in a social coalition. We all spend large amounts of time and energy signaling how valuable we would be to have on one's side. The book knocks us off our idyllic perch with a dose of biosocial realism, but the work is ultimately to realize our foibles and accept them and work with them to improve our behavior. We may never truly exorcise the social chimp in us, but we can work with it on the road to human improvement.

QUESTIONS FOR MEDITATION:

Do you see authenticity as something you shouldn't have to do so long as you're surrounded by your power?

"True humility, we believe, consists of two things. The first is knowing our limitations. And the second is getting the help we need."

WHY I LOVE THIS QUOTE:

Not everyone necessarily wants humility, but humility is ultimately about maturity. Why? Because like knowledge, the more you know, the more you realize you don't know. Many men who still act like boys in grown up clothes, certainly don't want to know or accept their limitations. Even when it is painfully clear what some of these limitations are, the idea of getting help for them is a huge leap. The ones who need help the very most are likely the ones who will never pursue it.

WHY THIS IS A TRANSFORMATIVE BOOK:

King, Warrior, Magician, Lover: Rediscovering the Archetypes of the Mature Masculine by Robert L. Moore and Douglas Gillette explores the four basic archetypes that make up the male psyche: the King, the Warrior, the Magician, and the Lover. This includes what each looks like in childhood, what a poorly formed version looks like, and what a fully mature, hero-material version looks like. It also has a fascinating section on the rite-of-passage rituals that have traditionally ushered men from boyhood into manhood, which could be very helpful in designing a hero's inner journey throughout the course of a book. The book has power for self-guided transformation through practices it lays out in Jungian psychology and meditation.

QUESTIONS FOR MEDITATION:

What are the opportunities for growth within yourself right now?

How could you use a little more humility?

"And here comes in the question whether it is better to be loved rather than feared, or feared rather than loved. It might perhaps be answered that we should wish to be both; but since love and fear can hardly exist together, if we must choose between them, it is far safer to be feared than loved."

WHY I LOVE THIS QUOTE:

This famous quote is powerful at face value. It's also powerful to consider why then we still often choose to be loved over being feared even though it is in fact less safe. So, in the world of power, it is safer to be feared. Although in the end it is silly to lead with fear only. To be loved is less safe, but we are willing to risk it with the ones whom we love. For the thematic purposes of this book, I also like this quote: "Everyone sees what you appear to be, few experience what you really are."

WHY THIS IS A TRANSFORMATIVE BOOK:

The Prince by Niccolò Machiavelli was ground-breaking and brilliantly insightful, for its time and really for all time. So much of what Machiavelli says is now an ingrained part of political thinking that it comes across as obvious by today's standards. These concepts have become the dogma and foundation of modern political thought. The contribution Machiavelli made to political theory can be overstated. It was *The Prince* that called out the distinction between what men "say" and what they "do." He did not invent political immorality, but he did recognize it as an effective, and at time crucial, aspect of rule. Something the famous rulers of history have always known and practiced. Machiavelli includes dozens of vignettes about world history in supporting his ideas and keeps the reader engaged with colorful descriptions of past events.

QUESTIONS FOR MEDITATION:

Would an observer of your life — someone who knew nothing about you — see your values through your actions?

"The biggest enemies of willpower: temptation, self-criticism, and stress. These three skills — self-awareness, self-care, and remembering what matter most — are the foundation for self-control."

WHY I LOVE THIS QUOTE:

We clearly live with the first three enemies more than we do with the latter three. This quote is helpful in laying bare the foundations of what you need to ground yourself. Often, part of transformation isn't about taking big, bold leaps, it's about being able to assess what we want less of and controlling the parts of ourselves that want to override the system and function on autopilot. The three skills for self-control, however, are all about processes.

WHY THIS IS A TRANSFORMATIVE BOOK:

The Willpower Instinct: How Self-Control Works, Why It Matters, and What You Can Do to Get More of It by Kelly McGonigal shows us how willpower is a mind-body response, not a virtue. It is a biological function that can be improved through mindfulness, exercise, nutrition, and sleep. Willpower is not an unlimited resource. Too much self-control can actually be bad for your health. Temptation and stress hijack the brain's systems of self-control, and that the brain can be trained for greater willpower. Willpower is centered in a specific region of the brain (within the prefrontal cortex). It uses more energy than almost any other brain region, and therefore it gets tired after prolonged use each day. It's also like a muscle, in that training it through specific meditations, and breathing exercises increases its strength and endurance. Interestingly, over time, it is paradoxically far easier to resist temptations if you don't try to repress them, but instead actually focus on them. Many studies have proven this counterintuitive finding.

QUESTIONS FOR MEDITATION:

What is a habit you'd like most to establish, and what is keeping you from it? By contrast, what is a habit you'd most like to stop, and what is keeping you from it?

"The best bridge between despair and hope is a good night's sleep."

WHY I LOVE THIS QUOTE:

While there is a certain wit to this statement, it's all the more powerful because it's true. So much of our literal suffering comes from inadequate sleep. Some people glibly say, "I'll sleep when I die," but the truth is you're going to die a lot sooner if you don't sleep adequately and you won't let your brain repair appropriately along the way.

He also notes, "Inadequate sleep — even moderate reductions for just one week — disrupts blood sugar levels so profoundly that you would be classified as pre-diabetic."

WHY THIS IS A TRANSFORMATIVE BOOK:

Why We Sleep: Unlocking the Power of Sleep and Dreams by Matthew Walker explains how neglecting sleep undercuts your creativity, problem solving, decision-making, learning, memory, heart health, brain health, mental health, emotional well-being, immune system, and even your life span. Sleep is so critical. Maybe things shifted during the pandemic of 2020, but it's unlikely our culture will shift fundamentally to a calmer mindset any time soon. We should listen to the evidence, though, and make changes when we can and books like this shine a bright light on the vital importance of sleep in our lives.

QUESTIONS FOR MEDITATION:

What gets in the way of solid, restorative sleep for you? Does new information like this help encourage you to shift unhealthy behaviors?

"You have a substance to your life if you've felt pain. You've got understanding, that's where compassion is. It makes you a deeper, richer human being."

WHY I LOVE THIS QUOTE:
The novelist Iris Murdoch once wrote that paying attention is a moral act. Paying close attention to tragedies can feel like staring at the sun. It scares you, yet you want to see what happens if you don't look away. It's not that it is ever easy to endure suffering of any kind, but at least you can come out the other side enriched if you can endure it mindfully. At least there is restoration and hope that transcends the suffering, and that not only can you learn from it, but you can now have deeper empathy, and possibly even compassion (which some define as empathy combined with action) for others.

WHY THIS IS A TRANSFORMATIVE BOOK:
Any Ordinary Day: Blindsides, Resilience and What Happens After the Worst Day of Your Life by Leigh Sales brilliantly condenses the cutting-edge research on the way the human brain processes fear and grief, and poses the questions we too often ignore out of awkwardness. Along the way, she offers an unguarded account of her own challenges and what she's learned about coping with life's unexpected blows. Early on, she reveals her own life-and-death terror when she was in the late stages of pregnancy with her second child. It was hair-raising, as was a particularly horrifying dream she had. So she decided to "stare into the sun" and talk to people. Warm, candid and empathic, this book is about what happens when ordinary people, on ordinary days, are forced to suddenly find the resilience most of us don't know we have.

QUESTIONS FOR MEDITATION:

When the unthinkable does happen, what comes next? How does a person go on?

"Playing big doesn't come from working more, pushing harder, or finding confidence. It comes from listening to the most powerful and secure part of you, not the voice of self-doubt."

WHY I LOVE THIS QUOTE:

I also believe that listening to that powerful and secure part of you does increase confidence. Playing big — for women and men — means finding that inner wisdom, and that feedback from others tells us at least as much if not more about the person giving the feedback as it does about the content we've put out there.

WHY THIS IS A TRANSFORMATIVE BOOK:

Playing Big: Find Your Voice, Your Mission, Your Message by Tara Mohr is a wonderful book that invites not only women but also men to share leadership, and to aspire to greater equilibrium in the roles we play. When women are shaping the world as much as men — when women are playing big — the world we are creating for our sons and our daughters will be so much better. Some argue they don't "believe" in work-life balance, that you have to grind if you're passionate about something, if you're driven to compete. Mohr argues that you can work hard, and play big, and also work smart and achieve balance. Of course, it all depends on your priorities, but Mohr presents a compelling case.

QUESTIONS FOR MEDITATION:

When someone praises you can you separate yourself from the positivity and think about how it informs you about their own taste?

When someone criticizes you or your work, what is the information telling you about their taste? Is there good information to learn from?

"Depression demands that we reject simplistic answers, both 'religious' and 'scientific', and learn to embrace mystery, something our culture resists. Mystery surrounds every deep experience of the human heart: the deeper we go into the heart's darkness or its light, the closer we get to the ultimate mystery of God. But our culture wants to turn mysteries into puzzles to be explained or problems to be solved, because maintaining the illusion that we can 'straighten things out' makes us feel powerful. Yet mysteries never yield to solutions or fixes — and when we pretend that they do, life becomes not only more banal but also more hopeless, because the fixes never work."

WHY I LOVE THIS QUOTE:

Parker Palmer can identify strongly with those who have undergone (or are going through) clinical depression. He went through a long period of it in his 40s, and even long after he had come out of it — and he isn't sure why he was able to climb out of it while many are not — he wasn't able or willing to share his experience. Depression is the "ultimate state of disconnection." While Palmer doesn't wish the experience on anyone, he does believe that it now marks a pivotal passage on his pilgrimage toward self-hood and vocation.

WHY THIS IS A TRANSFORMATIVE BOOK:

Let Your Life Speak is Parker Palmer's masterpiece. This short book shares with us the main idea that our strongest gifts are usually those we are barely aware we possess. They are a part of our nature, with us from the moment we draw our first breath, and we are all too often no more conscious of having them than we are of breathing.

QUESTIONS FOR MEDITATION:

If you are depressed — or even just "down," whether you understand why or not, are you willing to move into the deepest part of yourself and embrace the mystery?

"We can understand why one of the titles given to Jesus is that of 'prophet'. Jesus is the last and greatest of the prophets, the one who sums them up and goes further than all of them. He is the prophet of the last, but also of the best, chance. With him there takes place a shift that is both tiny and gigantic – a shift that follows on directly from the Old Testament but constitutes a decisive break as well. This is the complete elimination of the sacrificial for the first time – the end of divine violence and the explicit revelation of all that has gone before. It calls for a complete change of emphasis and a spiritual metamorphosis without precedent in the whole history of mankind."

WHY I LOVE THIS QUOTE:
I find it an incredible summary of Jesus the human, as well as Jesus as a divine prophet standing in the gap, showing all of humankind a way forward.

WHY THIS IS A TRANSFORMATIVE BOOK:
Things Hidden Since the Foundation of the World is a profound, but also very challenging text. Girard is trying to do nothing less than create a Copernican revolution that merges historical agency, metaphysics, psychology, and anthropology into a combined construct. *'Things Hidden'* is Girard's most famous work on Mimetic Theory. Mimetic Theory's key insight is that human desire is not an autonomous process, but a collective one. We want things because other people want them. As more and more people want something and when that "thing" remains scarce, there is conflict. Most conflict then is not because humans want different things, but because they want the same thing. An astonishing work of cultural criticism, this book is widely recognized as a brilliant and devastating challenge to conventional views of literature, anthropology, religion, and psychoanalysis.

QUESTIONS FOR MEDITATION:

What are the right questions to ask about your community?

How do we know when we are asking better questions?

"In this way, moral formation is not individual; it is relational. Character is not something you build sitting in a room thinking about the difference between right and wrong and about your own willpower. Character emerges from our commitments. If you want to inculcate character in someone else, teach them how to form commitments — temporary ones in childhood, provisional ones in youth, permanent ones in adulthood. Commitments are the school for moral formation. When your life is defined by fervent commitments, you are on the second mountain."

WHY I LOVE THIS QUOTE:
Brooks is taking an idea about the two halves of life, one defined more by the ego and individualism, and the second being defined often through failure or hardship as more communal and outwardly focused. The idea here is powerful that we build our character from commitments. To a certain extent, it may not even matter what the commitment is to. We learn about ourselves from our experience of commitment.

WHY THIS IS A TRANSFORMATIVE BOOK:
The Second Mountain: The Quest for a Moral Life by David Brooks is part philosophy, part personal disclosure, part research. It is a complex book, but also an excellent reader to challenge your thinking about a variety of subjects including religion, marriage, social responsibility and personal growth. We have seen the idea of the richness of the second half of life popularized in recent times in books such as Richard Rohr's *Falling Upward*. This is Brooks' take and it offers an incredible variety of sources and perspectives.

QUESTIONS FOR MEDITATION:

Are you focused on things more of the ego and gaining attention and material possessions and outward accomplishments? If so, you are still on the first mountain.

"Where id is, there shall ego be."

WHY I LOVE THIS QUOTE:
The ego is not only the ally of the id. It is also a submissive slave who courts the love of his master. The ego has to mediate the desires of the id but, at the same time, it sits between the superego and the events of the external world. When people argue that the ego should be killed, and that we'd be better off free from ego, we may be arguing semantics, but in the end, what you need is a healthy ego. You need it in its place, but you can't rid yourself of it. It's part of your consciousness, and always will be.

WHY THIS IS A TRANSFORMATIVE BOOK:
The Ego and the Id by Sigmund Freud is required reading if for nothing else than to get an understanding of Freud's Id-Ego-Superego typology from the original, and how it relates to all of depth psychology. The Id is the unconscious part, the pleasure principle that dictates our urges, needs and instant gratification. This section is also the reservoir of the libido, a major biological component that affects our personality. Meanwhile, Ego is the reality principle, our own self that works in a realistic manner to obtain pleasure and avoid pain. The Ego is moulded by the external world. It mediates your self's needs and pleasures according to other people's needs. Freud also develops the idea of an ideal ego, the Superego. This part is tied to morals and ethics. The Ego is the strongest force. However, it's in constant conflict with the Id and entangled in an interplayed position against the Superego.

QUESTIONS FOR MEDITATION:

What would wholeness look like for you?

"Studies by Andrew Newberg and others have shown that long-term practice of meditation produces significant alterations in cerebral blood flow in parts of the brain related to attention, emotion, and some autonomic functions."

WHY I LOVE THIS QUOTE:
Changes do occur in the brain through meditation, and also through gratitude practice. We don't yet know all the effects, but we do see the changes. Similarly, there is increasing evidence that transcendent experiences can also be chemically-induced and performed in a safe environment. Humans need to transcend, transport, escape; we need meaning, understanding, and explanation; we need to see overall patterns in our lives. We need hope, the sense of a future. And we need freedom (or at least the illusion of freedom) to get beyond ourselves. We need detachment and engagement.

WHY THIS IS A TRANSFORMATIVE BOOK:
Hallucinations by Oliver Sacks anatomizes the species of hallucinations humans experience: we hallucinate when we suffer Charles Bonnet Syndrome, when we are in drug withdrawal, when we are about to die, when we have lost a limb, when we have suffered post-traumatic stress disorder, when we have consumed hallucinogenic drugs, and when we have conditioned ourselves to be susceptible to visions, voices, and the presence of others, sometimes an "other" self, who is passive or relatively autonomous. With curiosity and compassion, Sacks weaves together stories of his patients and of his own mind-altering experiences to illuminate what hallucinations tell us about the organization and structure of our brains, how they have influenced every culture's folklore and art, and why the potential for hallucination is present in us all, a vital part of the human condition.

QUESTIONS FOR MEDITATION:

What kinds of transcendent experiences have you experienced before? What would be the right conditions for creating a transcendent experience now?

"It is facile to imply that smoking, alcoholism, overeating, or other ingrained patterns can be upended without real effort. Genuine change requires work and self-understanding of the cravings driving behaviors."

WHY I LOVE THIS QUOTE:
There are no quick fixes. Let's quit chasing them in case we are. There is only one way out of bad habits, and the way is through. Yes, one day at a time, and yes habits are micro-efforts that over time lead to big results, and yes it is all a process. The hard truth: it doesn't just take work, the outer results begin from the inner work.

WHY THIS IS A TRANSFORMATIVE BOOK:
The Power of Habit: Why We Do What We Do in Life and Business by Charles Duhigg focuses on learning to change behavior by identifying the routine, and figuring out the cue that triggers the routine and craving underlying that cue by experimenting with different rewards. If you can figure out what you really want and substitute a better routine to satisfy that craving, you will be well on your way toward changing that habit. The book contains another compelling argument: The key to exercising regularly, losing weight, raising exceptional children, becoming more productive, building revolutionary companies and social movements, and achieving success is understanding how habits work. There are a lot of books on establishing habits and sticking with them. This one is slightly different in its approach to understanding our relationship to them.

QUESTIONS FOR MEDITATION:

In terms of a habit you want to stop: Do you think there could be a way to substitute the habit with something else? Have you ever given it a try?

In terms of forming a habit: How can you better understand what would motivate you to develop it and stick with it?

"The empirical fact is that self-actualizing people, our best experiencers, are also our most compassionate, our great improvers and reformers of society, our most effective fighters against injustice, inequality, slavery, cruelty, exploitation (and also are best fighters for excellence, effectiveness, competence). And it also becomes clearer and clearer that our best 'helpers' are the most fully human persons. What I may call the bodhisattvic path is an integration of self-improvement and social zeal, i.e., the best way to become a better 'helper' is to become a better person. But one necessary aspect of becoming a better person is via helping other people. So one must and can do both simultaneously."

WHY I LOVE THIS QUOTE:
It's a powerful summary of what makes for an actualized and good human.

WHY THIS IS A TRANSFORMATIVE BOOK:
In *Religions, Values, and Peak-Experiences* by Abraham H. Maslow he writes: "To sum it up, from this point of view, the two religions of mankind tend to be the peakers and the non-peakers, that is to say, those who have private, personal, transcendent, core-religious experiences easily and often and who accept them and make use of them, and, on the other hand, those who have never had them or who repress or suppress them and who, therefore, cannot make use of them for their personal therapy, personal growth, or personal fulfillment." Maslow's book argues that the overarching goal of education — as of psychotherapy, of family life, of work, of society, of life itself — is to aid the person to grow to fullest humanness, to the greatest fulfillment and actualization of his highest potentials, this his greatest possible stature.

QUESTIONS FOR MEDITATION:

How can curiosity about others lead us to become better ourselves?

"Gratitude is an antidote to negative emotions, a neutralizer of envy, hostility, worry, and irritation. It is savoring; it is not taking things for granted; it is present oriented."

WHY I LOVE THIS QUOTE:
Gratitude is actually a radical act. It is bold, not passive. There is also loads of research that shows the brain works different when active gratitude is practiced, and that it leads to deeper fulfillment. Gratitude is potent, and we're only just beginning to truly explore what it can mean for our lives.

WHY THIS IS A TRANSFORMATIVE BOOK:
The How of Happiness: A Scientific Approach to Getting the Life You Want by Sonja Lyubomirsky is an excellent book on tangible ways to increase happiness in your life. According to her theory, we have a genetic happiness set point that accounts for 50% of our happiness. Ten-percent of our happiness comes from our life's circumstances, like where we live, what car we drive, how much money we make, etc. And the remaining 40% rests in how we choose to be happy on a daily basis. The focus is on refining that 40%, based on empirical evidence. Study after study has been compiled into this book to come up with helpful tools for how to become happier. As it turns out, about 50% of our happiness is already predetermined by our genetics, while 10% is based on our social conditions, whether we're rich or poor, married or divorced, have achieved success or not, and the remaining 40% of our happiness is our attitude towards life. It's a compelling case with a lot of hope attached to that large slice of the pie.

QUESTIONS FOR MEDITATION:

List three things you're grateful for. Be specific. If you want to start a small but intentional habit, experiment with doing this on a daily basis for six weeks straight and see what happens.

"She would've been a good woman," said The Misfit, "if it had been somebody there to shoot her every minute of her life."

WHY I LOVE THIS QUOTE:
First, it's ironic enough that the one who murders the grandmother is the one to make this statement. Of course the strange truth is that it speaks to the human condition. We'd all be better if we felt pressured to be, if we were literally under the gun.

WHY THIS IS A TRANSFORMATIVE BOOK:
Collected Works by Flannery O'Connor is the book to turn to when it comes to this famous author who only lived to be 38.

As Steven Hart writes: "Volumes like this are the glory of the Library of America. All the Flannery O'Connor you need in one well-edited, perfectly-sized edition. And you do need to read Flannery O'Connor. As a devout Catholic living in the gaudy sectarian carnival of the Protestant South, O'Connor had a unique perspective on religion and its unpredictable power. Though I will always be fond of *Wise Blood* and Hazel Motes ("I preach the Church Without Christ where the blind don't see, the lame don't walk, and what's dead stays that way.") I think the real greatness is in the short stories. "A Good Man Is Hard to Find" is an acknowledged classic, but I often return to "The River," in which a neglected boy's baptism leads to a catastrophic accident, or the doctor's office from hell in "Revelation." O'Connor is one of the greats, and this volume is a great way to study her work."

QUESTIONS FOR MEDITATION:

If you wanted to change the world for the better in one way, what would it be?

"To be yourself in a world that is constantly trying to make you something else is the greatest accomplishment."

WHY I LOVE THIS QUOTE:
America's most eloquent champion of individualism, Emerson acknowledges at the same time the pressures of society in American life. How do you remain true to yourself even when virtually everyone you know wants you to be, to do, to believe, something? What does it mean to be yourself? Well, that's part of the journey and part of the reason for this book and all the readings and meditations.

WHY THIS IS A TRANSFORMATIVE BOOK:
Essays and Lectures by Ralph Waldo Emerson is a classic worth having on your shelf. Emerson is the quintessential American. At his peak, which he hits here often, his every sentence falls like a fiery brand imprinting itself forever on my mind. Stylistically, he is an absolutely incredible writer, and his content burns. Emerson's enduring power is apparent everywhere in American literature: in those, like Whitman and some of the major twentieth-century poets, who seek to corroborate his vision, and among those, like Hawthorne and Melville, who questioned, qualified, and struggled with it. Emerson's vision reverberates also in the tradition of American philosophy, notably in the writings of William James and John Dewey, in the works of his European admirers, such as Nietzsche, and in the avant-garde theorists of our own day who write on the nature and function of language.

QUESTIONS FOR MEDITATION:

What are the most powerful ideas to shape how you see the world?

"Expect change. Accept death. Enjoy life. As Marcus Aurelius explained, the brains that got you through the troubles you have had so far will get you through any troubles yet to come."

WHY I LOVE THIS QUOTE:

I like the direct way she states each considerable and challenging idea. All this is easier said than done, but it is worth saying, and it is worth striving for, all of it. Don't worry about what's to come. Meantime, enjoy yourself. You got this.

WHY THIS IS A TRANSFORMATIVE BOOK:

Doubt: A History by Jennifer Michael Hecht is a powerful discourse on the concept of doubt. Many faith traditions speak of doubt, many in moderate forms suggesting a healthy faith depends on doubt, yet it is viewed as suspect when you have a "dark night of the soul." In the tradition of grand sweeping histories such as *From Dawn To Decadence*, *The Structure of Scientific Revolutions*, and *A History of God,* Hecht champions doubt and questioning as one of the great and noble, if unheralded, intellectual traditions that distinguish the Western mind, especially from Socrates to Galileo and Darwin, to Wittgenstein and Hawking. This is an account of the world's greatest "intellectual virtuosos," who are also humanity's greatest doubters and disbelievers, from the ancient Greek philosophers, Jesus, and the Eastern religions, to modern secular equivalents Marx, Freud and Darwin — and their attempts to reconcile the seeming meaninglessness of the universe with the human need for meaning. It looks at doubt both from within and external to belief. It examines the motives and believers and gives each its appropriate doubting due.

QUESTIONS FOR MEDITATION:

Why do people hold rigidly to beliefs without examining them? Are they truly people of faith? Why or why not?

"If, with a warm heart and patience, we can consider the views of others and exchange ideas in calm discussion, we will find points of agreement. It is our responsibility — out of love and compassion for humankind — to seek harmony among nations, ideologies, cultures, ethnic groups, and economic and political systems."

WHY I LOVE THIS QUOTE:

You would think these aspirational thoughts would be entirely possible. It sounds so easy, yet when faced with reality feels so discouragingly impossible. The least we can do is try. We can hitch up our pants and realize it is our responsibility to have compassion for others. It always begins with ourselves. Who do we think we are?

WHY THIS IS A TRANSFORMATIVE BOOK:

The Heart of Meditation: Discovering Innermost Awareness by the Dalaia Lama XIV provides intimate details on an advanced meditation practice called Dzogchen using a visionary poem by the 19th-century saint Patrul Rinpoche, author of the Buddhist classic *Words of My Perfect Teacher*. Most of the books in this reader on meditation practices to date are highly accessible. The insights here are probably hard to understand if you're not already well along the path. If you've come to know a huge commonality between all the practices, shamata, vipassana, zen, prayer, etc, then this may be the book you're looking for. He talks about the substratum of consciousness, and clear light awareness. Dzogchen discards various meditation objects in favor of pure awareness. No more pushing thoughts away, just let them be and see them as all other manifestations, waves on the surface of awareness. Challenging stuff, but powerful when you practice and experience.

QUESTIONS FOR MEDITATION:

When was a time you genuinely sought to make others happy, and how did it make you feel?

"Courage is not simply one of the virtues but the form of every virtue at the testing point, which means at the point of highest reality. "

WHY I LOVE THIS QUOTE:

The demon, Screwtape, is speaking to the demon, Wormwood, who is on his first mission. He is observing how powerful courage is in whatever virtue his "patient" possesses, and isn't just a virtue in itself. It's an interesting point to consider. Whatever healthy habits or actions we're taking in our lives — whether the work is inward or outward or both — we should consider the place of courage within what we are doing.

WHY THIS IS A TRANSFORMATIVE BOOK:

The Screwtape Letters is an intense rumination on good and evil, as told through the letters of one demon to another, a work everyone should read, if to do nothing but understand the insidious nature of evil. The experience is fully engrossing. It does what the best books always do; it expands your understanding of the world. It gives you something to keep with you, which is in this case is a valuable, and somewhat terrible knowledge. C.S. Lewis writes in his Preface that he had to recover from writing it. After reading and processing the work, you can understand why. Interestingly enough, David Foster Wallace ranked it as his favorite book.

QUESTIONS FOR MEDITATION:

What is keeping you from being not only a healthy self, but a big, bold, courageous self?

"Change the language in the tribe, and you have changed the tribe itself."

WHY I LOVE THIS QUOTE:
It's similar to changing the story, or changing the script you've been follow-ing or telling yourself. It applies to groups every bit as much as to individuals. The application here for Big Self is to realize that while so much of the work of transformation and growth begins with you — the self — we are also always in relationship with others. The next step beyond the self is the "other" and we know ourselves through others and how we present ourselves to others, as well as our awareness of how others present themselves to us. Many of us are in, or have been in, professional organizations at a variety of degrees of health.

WHY THIS IS A TRANSFORMATIVE BOOK:
Tribal Leadership: Leveraging Natural Groups to Build a Thriving Organiza-tion by Dave Logan, John King, and Halee Fischer-Wright reminds me of Jim Collins book *Good to Great* in that both are presenting findings from lengthy research studies. While Collins' book talked more about their underlying methodology, *Tribal Leadership* shows five cultural levels and describes the transition from one to the next.

QUESTIONS FOR MEDITATION:

Is it possible that the tribe you're working in aspires to victories that are col-lective and not merely personal?

If you are a Stage 3 person (only in it for yourself), have you come to a point where you begin to realize that power is a zero-sum game (the more you have, the less others do)? In Stage 4 power is abundant: the more you give, the more you get back.

"Success, in the words of Winston Churchill, 'consists of going from failure to failure without loss of enthusiasm'. The greatest barriers to success so far have been the fear of failure and the failure to learn from mistakes."

WHY I LOVE THIS QUOTE:
It would seem it is time to make some dramatic changes to our archaic financial systems. Where there is a will there's a way.

WHY THIS IS A TRANSFORMATIVE BOOK:
Rethinking Money: How New Currencies Turn Scarcity into Prosperity by Bernard A. Lietaer and Jacqui Dunne explores the origins of our current monetary system — built on bank debt and scarcity — revealing the surprising and sometimes shocking ways its unconscious limitations give rise to so many serious problems. But there is hope. The authors present stories of ordinary people and their communities using new money, working in cooperation with national currencies, to strengthen local economies, create work, beautify cities, and provide education — and so much more is possible. These real-world examples are just the tip of the iceberg — over 4,000 cooperative currencies are already in existence. Just like monocultures in agriculture, monocultures in money increase risk. The manufacturing of scarcity by banks creates a society that privileges competition over cooperation. The current system has not served us well, and fortunately, as the authors explain, we can design other systems. Indeed, many are already flourishing today.

QUESTIONS FOR MEDITATION:

How do your beliefs about money impact your own sense of self-worth?

"Stepping out of a normal routine, finding novelty, being open to serendipity, enjoying the unexpected, embracing a little risk, and finding pleasure in the heightened vividness of life. These are all qualities of a state of play."

WHY I LOVE THIS QUOTE:
We have understood how fundamentally important play is to our fulfilment and to "becoming who we are" from the likes of D.W. Winnicott. Now, much more recent research is proving why. This quote suggests the "how" we are to achieve it.

WHY THIS IS A TRANSFORMATIVE BOOK:
Play: How It Shapes the Brain, Opens the Imagination, and Invigorates the Soul by Stuart M. Brown Jr. and Christopher Vaughan presents a fresh look at the everyday world. The author boils it down pretty simply: make sure to do the things you truly love as often as you can. This may seem obvious, but often as we get older we get so tied up with the little things and with our work that we tend to forget to play. Brown has spent his career studying animal behavior and conducting more than six thousand "play histories" of humans from all walks of life — from serial murderers to Nobel Prize winners. Backed by the latest research, *Play* explains why play is essential to our social skills, adaptability, intelligence, creativity, ability to problem solve, and more. *Play* is hardwired into our brains — it is the mechanism by which we become resilient, smart, and adaptable people. Beyond play's role in our personal fulfillment, its benefits have profound implications for child development and the way we parent, education and social policy, business innovation, productivity, and even the future of our society.

QUESTIONS FOR MEDITATION:

What creative acts do you engage in that help you evoke a sense of unconscious selflessness?

"By judging others we blind ourselves to our own evil and to the grace which others are just as entitled to as we are."

WHY I LOVE THIS QUOTE:
It reminds me of the idea that an eye for an eye leaves the whole world blind. It's also a statement directed at those practitioners of religion who do nothing to advance humanity, but only divide us further. The truth behind religion, what Jesus preached and practiced, was a compassion based on empathy and grace.

WHY THIS IS A TRANSFORMATIVE BOOK:
The Cost of Discipleship by Dietrich Bonhoeffer puts forth a number of radical ideas here. The book is a compelling statement of the demands of sacrifice and ethical consistency from a man whose life and thought were exemplary articulations of a new type of leadership inspired by the Gospel, and imbued with the spirit of Christian humanism and a creative sense of civic duty.

As Dwight Davis writes, "The idea of the Church being the physical manifestation of Christ, and therefore vicariously representing Christ on earth is brilliant. Bonhoeffer redefines ontology (metaphysics dealing with the nature of being) and personhood. He argues, 'The new human being is not the single individual who has been justified and sanctified; rather, the new human being is the church-community, the body of Christ, or Christ himself.' The implications of this train of thought on philosophy, theology, ontology, ethics, race issues, ecclesiology, etc. are staggering. And yet evangelicals skip over these ideas and only talk about Bonhoeffer's concept of cheap and costly grace. While that is a great meditation on the role of grace in our lives, there's so much more to this book."

QUESTIONS FOR MEDITATION:

How could you be more courageous on behalf of others?

How could you be more courageous on behalf of your beliefs?

june

"According to Buddhism, the root of suffering is neither the feeling of pain nor of sadness nor even of meaninglessness. Rather, the real root of suffering is this never-ending and pointless pursuit of ephemeral feelings, which causes us to be in a constant state of tension, restlessness and dissatisfaction."

WHY I LOVE THIS QUOTE:

Due to this pursuit, the mind is never satisfied. Even when experiencing pleasure, it is not content, because it fears this feeling might soon disappear, and craves that this feeling should stay and intensify. People are liberated from suffering not when they experience this or that fleeting pleasure, but rather when they understand the impermanent nature of all their feelings, and stop craving them. This is the aim of Buddhist meditation practices.

WHY THIS IS A TRANSFORMATIVE BOOK:

Sapiens: A Brief History of Humankind by Yuval Noah Harari takes us through the history of human development and migration, through the Cognitive Revolution and Agricultural Revolution. He looks at how currency and coinage developed, the creation of religions, the arrival of imperialism and capitalism, and the history of inequalities and injustices. He presents a relatively unbiased view of events. He focuses on what we know, and is quick to say when something remains a mystery to biologists and anthropologists. When there are conflicting theories, he outlines all the main ones. Hariri seems driven by a desire to present the most accurate view of humanity's history.

QUESTIONS FOR MEDITATION:

What is a situation that is keeping you blocked? What can you learn from the situation?

How can you make it smaller and take the power back?

"Everyone has a supremely low moment somewhere along the AT, usually when the urge to quit the trail becomes almost overpowering. The irony of my moment was that I wanted to get back on the trail and didn't know how. I hadn't lost just Katz, my boon companion, but my whole sense of connectedness to the trail. I had lost my momentum, my feeling of purpose. In the most literal way I needed to find my feet again."

WHY I LOVE THIS QUOTE:
It's a great metaphor for regaining your purpose.

WHY THIS IS A TRANSFORMATIVE BOOK:
A Walk in the Woods: Rediscovering America on the Appalachian Trail by Bill Bryson has a way of maintaining three difficult things at once: (1) getting to the heart of a hiker, (2) the history of the Appalachian Trail, and (3) doing it with laugh-out-loud humor. His writing is affable and encouraging. It's also a beautiful, surprisingly complex story.

The trail itself is complex. At over 2,000 miles long, it extends from Georgia into Maine, which is a lot of topography. Along the way, Bryson discourses on subjects that range from the history of the Appalachian Trail, the neglect and incompetence of the Forestry and Park services, pre-Colonial botanists, the potential flame ball that is Centralia, PA, the temperature extremes of Mount Washington (in New Hampshire), trees, the constant threat of getting eaten by bears or hogtied by hillbillies and, of course, the hike itself. The long, long hike. It's one of those books that everyone you know who's read it praises it.

QUESTIONS FOR MEDITATION:

Where is your next destination?

"But those things aren't you. They are just things about you, not the real, the core you. Look at the center of you. What do you want to change there?"

WHY I LOVE THIS QUOTE:

It's not easy to just "look at the center of you," much less to see yourself so clearly without blindspots so that you can answer the question of what you would change once you do. That is why this quote is a challenge. It's implied that it's hard to do, but it's also implied that it is essential that you perform the necessary tasks to in fact look at yourself for who you are. It's essential that we can continue to ask ourselves what we'd like to change.

WHY THIS IS A TRANSFORMATIVE BOOK:

Momma and the Meaning of Life: Tales of Psychotherapy by Irvin D. Yalom goes through a series of cases, as they would unfold. It seeks to help patients view aging and death as part of living. This is a varied collection of stories dealing with psychotherapy, all touching on existential themes of everyday life. Grief and loss are major themes, coming to terms with loss, death, relationships, mortality, both for Yalom and his patients. The anecdotal case studies are wise and moving, and he demonstrates vulnerability and insights into the thinking of a therapist.

QUESTIONS FOR MEDITATION:

Today's question refers back directly to the quote: "Look at the center of you. What do you want to change there?"

"If you care about something you have to protect it – If you're lucky enough to find a way of life you love, you have to find the courage to live it."

WHY I LOVE THIS QUOTE:

Owen Meaning has so many wise sayings, and all in that irritating but endearing voice in ALL CAPS throughout the entire book. One of the more memorable characters in modern literature. He says this to the book's narrator, John Wheelwright. I love the quote in and of itself for the threefold wisdom it offers. First, if you care about something you have to defend it, care for it, keep it safe. Basically, it's the same way as saying the second part, "if you're lucky enough to find a way of life you love." Yes, it doesn't just come from willing it, there's some grace involved, some parts that are outside yourself that come into play, which we could call luck. Finally, though, it takes courage. From first realization, to defense, to gratitude, to courage.

WHY THIS IS A TRANSFORMATIVE BOOK:

A Prayer for Owen Meany by John Irving is my favorite John Irving novel. Owen himself stands out in so many ways – he's wise, loyal, challenging, outspoken and kind. He's the kind of friend we all wish we'd had when we were growing up. Among many aspects of this novel, one of the things that stands out is that the now mature Wheelwright, who has gone on to become an episcopal priest, continues to reflect on the wisdom and insight of the late Owen Meany and how he challenges him to this day to act on his beliefs with greater courage.

QUESTIONS FOR MEDITATION:

Can you imagine someone from your life that you've overlooked, forgotten about, or never gave credit to who really was important?

"So much of the pain of loneliness is to do with concealment, with feeling compelled to hide vulnerability, to tuck ugliness away, to cover up scars as if they are literally repulsive. But why hide? What's so shameful about wanting, about desire, about having failed to achieve satisfaction, about experiencing unhappiness? Why this need to constantly inhabit peak states, or to be comfortably sealed inside a unit of two, turned inward from the world at large?"

WHY I LOVE THIS QUOTE:

I love the directness of these questions, and I love the questions themselves. I sometimes wonder these things too. What are we so afraid of? Why are we always performing impression management? Why the constant need of so many to portray only their smiling, happy selves on Facebook?

WHY THIS IS A TRANSFORMATIVE BOOK:

The Lonely City: Adventures in the Art of Being Alone by Olivia Laing reflects on a period of intense loneliness which she endured in New York after a break-up. During this difficult time she turned to art for answers and explored the interpretations of urban isolation created by some notable and other lesser known artists. They saw themselves as outsiders amid the city's multitudes and channeled their piercing, deep loneliness into their work.

QUESTIONS FOR MEDITATION:

Do you fear making yourself vulnerable to others, and if so, why?

Why do we equate loneliness with shame?

"Emotional intelligence is your ability to recognize and understand emotions in yourself and others, and your ability to use this awareness to manage your behavior and relationships."

WHY I LOVE THIS QUOTE:

Research has been showing for quite some time now how important emotional intelligence is in the workplace. Really, it's important in all social aspects of our lives, which means in all aspects of our lives. Managing ourselves through increased self-awareness, leads to better interpersonal skills, and that leads to better management and leadership. It also makes you a better team player, which helps all the more as the best teams become increasingly diverse.

WHY THIS IS A TRANSFORMATIVE BOOK:

Emotional Intelligence 2.0 by Travis Bradberry and Jean Greaves have created a useful book based on loads of research. They offer very pragmatic tools and strategies in self-awareness, self-management, social awareness, and relationship-management. While some say there is nothing earthshaking in the book, it is however succinct in expressing the importance of the 4 facets of Emotional Intelligence. And the fact that you get an opportunity to take an online assessment twice through the use of special code is a real bonus. Not all the transformative or recommended books in this reader are for everyone, but this one is.

QUESTIONS FOR MEDITATION:

Do you treat your feelings as good or bad?

"Dissatisfaction and discomfort dominate our brain's default state, but we can use them to motivate us instead of defeat us."

WHY I LOVE THIS QUOTE:
That's the very challenge, though, isn't it? We can choose to make this default state of our brain's into something motivating. Step one is a mindset shift, which tends to be a process, and is a skill that can be developed. The second part of choosing is simply to understand our brains and feelings. If we expect nothing less than dissatisfaction and discomfort, we can learn when and how to identify the experience and figure out our own methods and approaches for keeping focused and motivated anyway.

WHY THIS IS A TRANSFORMATIVE BOOK:
Indistractable: How to Control Your Attention and Choose Your Life by Nir Eyal tells us how to be more productive and how to get more done with plenty of technical detail. It focuses on social media, which is no doubt guilty of stealing our attention away from important issues. Then again, part of the very allure is that we feel like it is keeping us tuned in to what is going on, and of course we all want big platforms. Time, however, is a finite resource and that means we should spend it wisely. Eyal discusses how to implement the solutions to make use of habits in everyday life with extensively researched case studies throughout. Overall, a refreshingly different approach to time management than other books on the subject.

QUESTIONS FOR MEDITATION:

What distracts you the most? How can you give more focused attention on the things you value?

"We are unknown to ourselves, we men of knowledge — and with good reason. We have never sought ourselves — how could it happen that we should ever find ourselves? It has rightly been said: 'Where your treasure is, there will your heart be also'; our treasure is where the beehives of our knowledge are."

WHY I LOVE THIS QUOTE:

Merely knowing a lot does not help you to know yourself. We can see that through many people of higher learning who are still petty and foolish, arrogant and vain. I like the sentiment here because he puts it forth very clearly as to why: You don't value it and therefore you don't pursue it, and moreover, you never will until you do. He also would seem to include himself among their number.

WHY THIS IS A TRANSFORMATIVE BOOK:

On the Genealogy of Morals by Friedrich Nietzsche is challenging because he demands we overturn or suspend many of our assumptions. He is one of the Western tradition's great thinkers precisely because he calls so much into question. If we can come to understand Nietzsche's genealogical method, his doctrine of the will to power, and his perspectivism as all linked, his arguments become easier to follow. In a book which is meant to sketch the evolution of morals over the centuries, we also look at how science and religion have no special claim to truth, and also how we can make the most of our lives. The versatility of topics makes the Genealogy the most forcible, ambitious and amazingly accessible work of Nietzsche's. Nietzsche is a brilliant writer who expresses his complex philosophical ideas in constantly creative ways.

QUESTIONS FOR MEDITATION:

How does your self-knowledge inform your knowledge?

"Isn't it important for your friends close by and far away to know the high cost of these insights? Wouldn't they find it a source of consolation to see that light and darkness, hope and despair, love and fear are never very far from each other, and that spiritual freedom often requires a fierce spiritual battle?"

WHY I LOVE THIS QUOTE:

I think that's the motivation behind the book, to serve as an example for others who may not have the platform, privilege, or courage to put his struggles on display. We have explored faith's tenuous relationship to doubt in previous readings. This puts the paradoxical battle and the intensity of the inner work in a different light. It is in fact necessary to have the struggle if what you've achieved afterwards is to have any value or depth.

WHY THIS IS A TRANSFORMATIVE BOOK:

The Inner Voice of Love by Henri J.M. Nouwen may not be his best book (The Wounded Healer is a tough one to beat), but it is certainly the most vulnerable. He puts himself out there on public display to listen to and persevere with his private struggle.

As Brad Syverson writes, "This is a book to be read and absorbed in small doses. It is a deeply personal and very honest book written during a time of great pain. But it is a hopeful book...As is the case with all truths, there is no chronological to do list that gets you there. Instead, there are markers, guideposts, lodestars. By careful reading and thoughtful discernment, we can benefit from these markers, guideposts and lodestarts to find our own path to wholeness."

QUESTIONS FOR MEDITATION:

What is your greatest spiritual fear?

"We know, if only vaguely and inchoately, that our finest and most memorable experiences may never, and indeed, ultimately will never, happen again. That is why we cherish them so."

WHY I LOVE THIS QUOTE:

Emily Dickinson said the same thing in her distinctive way. We focus on death like we should focus on any reality in our life, with clarity. It doesn't mean you have a "morbid fascination" with death to think about death. No one gets out of this alive. We're all in this together. As a matter of fact, by calmly recognizing the finitude of life we will reduce our anxiety in our day-to-day living. It is what the authors of The Worm at the Core articulate so clearly and with great depth.

WHY THIS IS A TRANSFORMATIVE BOOK:

The Worm at the Core: On the Role of Death in Life by Sheldon Solomon, Jeff Greenberg, and Tom Pyszczynski is a restatement, confirmation, refinement, and elaboration of Ernest Becker's 1973 classic *The Denial of Death*. As John Kaufman writes, "The authors committed thirty years to conducting experiments and collecting evidence to confirm Becker's thesis...We combat mortality by striving for significance. What to do? We need to come to terms with death. We need to seek enduring significance through our own 'combination of meanings and values, social connections, spirituality, personal accomplishments, identifications with nature, and momentary experiences of transcendence'. We also should 'promote cultural worldviews that provide such paths while encouraging tolerance of uncertainty and others who harbor different beliefs.'"

QUESTIONS FOR MEDITATION:

How often would you say you consciously think about death? How often would you say you unconsciously think about death, or at least how life will move on without you one day?

"People who have recently lost someone have a certain look, recognizable maybe only to those who have seen that look on their own faces. I have noticed it on my face and I notice it now on others. The look is one of extreme vulnerability, nakedness, openness. It is the look of someone who walks from the ophthalmologist's office into the bright daylight with dilated eyes, or of someone who wears glasses and is suddenly made to take them off. These people who have lost someone look naked because they think themselves invisible. I myself felt invisible for a period of time, incorporeal."

WHY I LOVE THIS QUOTE:
As she also writes, "A single person is missing for you, and the whole world is empty."

WHY THIS IS A TRANSFORMATIVE BOOK:
The Year of Magical Thinking by Joan Didion is a profound statement on grief. As John Jeffire writes, "Sometimes you just need to read something that is well-written. This book is beautifully accessible, clear and moving. The subject matter is tough: Didion writes of her husband John Dunne's death and its aftermath. How to come to grips with such a loss, move on and yet never move too far away? How to cope with magical thinking, such as what to do with the loved one's shoes still in the closet — won't he need a pair if he were to suddenly return? If you've experienced the death of a loved one, you'll recognize yourself and your own hurt, confusion, and poignant thinking."

QUESTIONS FOR MEDITATION:

How do you move on yet honor the memory of a loved one?

"Rarely in our life is money a place of genuine freedom, joy, or clarity, yet we routinely allow it to dictate the terms of our lives and often to be the single most important factor in the decisions we make about work, love, family, and friendship."

WHY I LOVE THIS QUOTE:

There are a lot of unconscious obligations we experience as a result of money. Rarely do people feel they have enough of it regardless of their wealth. We often give it the highest status in our lives. Often we are enslaved by the dictates of money. But why? Time is also something we don't have much of, and you could say is always a declining balance.

WHY THIS IS A TRANSFORMATIVE BOOK:

The Soul of Money: Transforming Your Relationship with Money and Life by Lynne Twist and Teresa Barker is a different take on prosperity. It's not merely about prosperity and how to get it, it's also how to be good stewards of what we already have. The authors deal with the scarcity model that has created a world of "you or me." By changing our mindset to sufficiency (when is enough enough?), we co-create a world of "you and me." There are enough resources to create a world that works for everyone. A great book for anyone who has a fear of money and not having enough, as well as how to be good stewards of money, and of our personal resources and the earth's resources.

QUESTIONS FOR MEDITATION:

Would you say you spend your time working more out of love for what you do, or out of love for making money? How would you define your relationship with money?

"One of the most surprising things I've noticed during my experiments in productive disagreement is how quickly things go off the rails precisely when people stop speaking from their own perspective and try to speculate about other people's perspectives."

WHY I LOVE THIS QUOTE:

There are some interesting takeaways from this research. It seems a large part of disagreements are the formed assumptions we have of other people's thinking. We seek certainty, so we seek to categorize, so we can evaluate and ultimately, judge. And we judge the "other" as wrong, and, therefore, especially when it comes to trying to get things done, as our adversary. Partly, this is why empathy is so important, and that only comes from lots of listening and in relationship.

WHY THIS IS A TRANSFORMATIVE BOOK:

Why Are We Yelling?: The Art of Productive Disagreement by Buster Benson helps you overcome the challenge of dealing with difficult people that can leave you brimming with repressed emotions. Conflict doesn't have to be unpleasant. Properly channeled, conflict can be the most powerful tool we have at our disposal for deepening relationships, solving problems, and coming up with new ideas. As the mastermind behind some of the highest-performing teams at Amazon, Twitter, and Slack, Benson spent decades facilitating hard conversations in stressful environments. Slowly, patterns began to emerge. If you're challenged with how to have hard conversations, this book is especially for you.

QUESTIONS FOR MEDITATION:

Have you ever walked away from an argument and suddenly thought of all the brilliant things you wish you'd said?

Do you avoid certain family members and colleagues because of bitter, festering tension that you can't figure out how to address?

"Mindful breathing is the vehicle that you use to go back to your true home."

WHY I LOVE THIS QUOTE:
Mindful breathing is a meditation technique that seeks to reduce the size of the emotion or thought in the brain. The idea is to get perspective, to listen to your body, and to let the experience of conscious breathwork do its work to calm. In a calm state you can make better decisions. You also achieve greater control over yourself and your responses to things that you can't control.

WHY THIS IS A TRANSFORMATIVE BOOK:
Taming the Tiger Within: Meditations on Transforming Difficult Emotions by Thich Nhat Hanh is a collection of meditations about anger and fear, and what to do when they arise. Many pages have only one or two sentences, but this brevity is effective for the subject matter. It allows the reader to reflect and meditate on the words, have insights, and experience relief. A key concept in Buddhism is dukkha, which means "suffering." Much of what the Buddha taught concerned dukkha, and how to deal with it. Anger can be a form of suffering, especially when you keep rehashing the event that triggered the emotion. It can be like your anger is a fire, and your brain keeps adding more wood. If you ever have problems with persistent anger or fear, give this book a try. The book can help one learn how to experience these emotions in a healthy way, and then move on. It is designed to revisit.

QUESTIONS FOR MEDITATION:

Think about a person or situation that currently upsets you and practice mindful breathing while focusing on the subject for at least five minutes. See if it helps bring at least a small degree of calm and clarity in your thinking.

"One of the things that you realize when you see the nature of the self is that what you do and what happens to you are the same thing. Realizing that you do not exist separately from everything else, you realize responsibility."

WHY I LOVE THIS QUOTE:

If we do not recognize our role in our misfortune, we are unable to change the conduct that led to it, which almost guarantees that it will happen again. Part of why we emphasize focusing on your "self" first and foremost — to be the change you want to see in the world — is for the very reason stated in this quote. What you do and what happens to you is essentially the same thing. This should help you take a little more responsibility in how you treat yourself and others.

WHY THIS IS A TRANSFORMATIVE BOOK:

The Cow in the Parking Lot: A Zen Approach to Overcoming Anger by Leonard Scheff and Susan Edmiston shows the price we pay for anger and provides many techniques and ideas for dealing with anger in creative and healthy ways. The book investigates through personal queries and will ask you to examine your behavior and the motives behind your reactions. Especially helpful for those trying to figure out how to have less impulsive confrontations. The techniques bring up issues you may have thought you'd gotten over or had forgotten about. In other words, if you invest in the exercises they can work much like the guidance and good questions from a therapist. Holding onto anger is more dangerous to the angry person and has far-reaching effects on others, totally unrelated to the original incident causing the feeling. Per the title of the book, the idea is also to learn how to have a sense of humor about ourselves and circumstances. In that sense, so much is simply about perspective.

QUESTIONS FOR MEDITATION:

What is my current relationship with anger? Where does the anger come from? Does it feel like a necessary and healthy response to the situation?

"I have no idea what's awaiting me, or what will happen when this all ends. For the moment I know this: there are sick people and they need curing."

WHY I LOVE THIS QUOTE:

This is a quote from the protagonist doctor in the novel, and it sounds almost exactly like so many of the healthcare workers we hear from today regarding the COVID-19 pandemic. No one knows how long it will last, or how long the hospitals will be filled, or when an effective and mass-produced vaccine will be available, and yet day after day they doctors and nurses and other healthcare professionals go in on the front lines and tend to the sick and dying. It is courageous work.

WHY THIS IS A TRANSFORMATIVE BOOK:

The Plague by Albert Camus is an incredible and somewhat overlooked novel that traces the collective psychology of people's responses to a pandemic. The parallels to this city caught in time in the 1940s to people's responses to COVID-19 are striking. The plague has no relationship to religion. The innocent die as much as the guilty. The plague is the great equalizer: everyone can die. There nothing is no rhyme or reason and blaming it on fate or an angry god or questioning why the deities have ignored the supplicants' increasing praises, appeals and desperate petitions is all futile. Even they see it is pointless and in the end the comforting rituals of death and consignment of the remains have mostly been abandoned. The plague strikes almost all and those whom it leaves, aren't special in any way. The pacing is outstanding. It is something like a descent into hell, and then recovery into sunlight in a brisk sea air. It is a strange, unsettling novel that somehow manages to end in a kind of relief.

QUESTIONS FOR MEDITATION:

What can we learn from pandemic responses from the past? What can you do to protect your own health? What can you do to protect and assist the lives of those around you?

"It is as reasonable to represent one kind of imprisonment by another as it is to represent anything that really exists by that which exists not."

WHY I LOVE THIS QUOTE:

I read this as there are lots of ways to be imprisoned. It's also a matter of perspective. You can be imprisoned by the beliefs you are chained to, as well as by fear and anger. Any recurring pain or emotion that you are controlled by (and not in control of) is imprisoning. Some things that we cannot see are real and some are imagined, and what's hard about a plague is that it is devastatingly real and cannot be seen.

WHY THIS IS A TRANSFORMATIVE BOOK:

In 1665, the Great Plague swept through London, claiming nearly 100,000 lives. In *A Journal of the Plague Year*, Daniel Defoe chronicles the progress of the epidemic. He didn't actually live through it, but he had researched it and wrote about it several decades later. His narrator lives in a city transformed — the streets and alleyways deserted, the houses of death with crosses daubed on their doors, the dead-carts on their way to the pits — and encounter the horrified citizens of the city, as fear, isolation, and hysteria take hold. The shocking immediacy of plague-racked London makes this one of the most convincing accounts of the Great Plague ever written. Defoe is a master of detail.

QUESTIONS FOR MEDITATION:

How do you resist falling into the thought traps of others? Are you aware when you're being manipulated one way or another?

"I see no good reasons why the views given in this volume should shock the religious views of anyone."

WHY I LOVE THIS QUOTE:
Darwin amended his original 1859 text in a previous edition in response to religious critics who believed that the Creator had an intentional and guided hand in the development of all creation. He turned to a famous author and clergyman, Charles Kingsley, and said: "I have gradually learnt to see that it is just as noble a conception of Deity, to believe that he created primal forms capable of self development into all forms."

WHY THIS IS A TRANSFORMATIVE BOOK:
The Origin of Species by Charles Darwin is effectively one of the founding documents of the modern age. Darwin was a genius led on by his curiosity and his refusal to accept orthodox conclusions just because it was threatening to those in power. From his theory of natural selection to glacier theory, to hybrid plants, to fossil theory and a dozen other biological and geological theories that he developed or contributed to, it is remarkable to me how very little Darwin got wrong in a book 600 pages long. It is the scientific method at its best, one part rigorous logic, one part observation, and one part intuition. This work has had a profound effect not just on science, but the culture at large. Arguably this book had as much influence on the literature and politics of the next century as Freud or Marx. There is historical value in reading this classic.

QUESTIONS FOR MEDITATION:

What would you risk to say exactly what you believe and think?

"If you've never done anything wrong it's probably because you have never tried anything new."

WHY I LOVE THIS QUOTE:

You learn to walk by falling. You become a better mountain biker by crashing (within reason). You could even go so far as to say you literally learn by failing. It is the curious minds who pursue answers for themselves that come back with valuable findings.

WHY THIS IS A TRANSFORMATIVE BOOK:

Relativity: The Special and the General Theory by Albert Einstein, is intended "to give an exact insight into the theory of Relativity to those readers who, from a general scientific and philosophical point of view, are interested in the theory, but who are not conversant with the mathematical apparatus of theoretical physics." When he wrote the book in 1916, he was barely known outside the physics institutes. But he had just completed his masterpiece, The General Theory of Relativity — which provided a brand-new theory of gravity and promised a new perspective on the cosmos as a whole, and he set out to share his excitement with as wide a public as possible in this popular and accessible book. It features an Appendix V, which is a 20-page essay, written 36 years after the rest of the book and just three years before Einstein died. It is a tour de force on the history, philosophy, and psychology of the scientific understanding of empty space. It is shocking, thrilling, and amazing. Overall, this is an excellent introduction to special relativity, and at least the conceptual underpinnings of general relativity.

QUESTIONS FOR MEDITATION:

What risks are you taking right now?

"The great affair, we always find, is to get money."

WHY I LOVE THIS QUOTE:

We've explored this concept before in our readings, but it bears a point of return from time to time. There is the self-interested part of our lives that is focused on what we can get for ourselves and our families. To some extent, of course, it's required. We have to earn our way, and to some extent this self-interested participation in the open market is good for the collective whole. At least in theory.

WHY THIS IS A TRANSFORMATIVE BOOK:

An Inquiry into the Nature and Causes of the Wealth of Nations by Adam Smith published in 1776 is the magnum opus of the Scottish economist and moral philosopher. Reading the work from the primary source (and not having it filtered through the lens of another's interpretation) is always a rewarding experience. Adam Smith is known as the "father" of modern capitalism. Smith was a free market economist who wanted to diversify the players involved in trade. In Smith's view, humans are inherently self-interested, but by allowing them to make their own economic decisions a metaphysical force, the Invisible Hand, steers production toward industry which helps the greatest number of people.

As Robert Reich writes, "Smith's mind ranged over issues as fresh and topical today as they were in the late eighteenth century — jobs, wages, politics, government, trade, education, business, and ethics."

QUESTIONS FOR MEDITATION:

Do you have a limit in mind for what would be enough when it comes to money? How soon do you think you'll get there? Will you ever get there? Would you say you are intrinsically or extrinsically motivated by money?

"The praise of the wise few is more important than the mockery of the foolish many."

WHY I LOVE THIS QUOTE:

I suppose also the praise of the wise few is more important than the praise of the foolish many. The mockery of the foolish many would still hurt, even if we knew they were foolish. The thing about the foolish is they don't usually understand that they're foolish, and they're validated by each other in their collective misunderstanding. Plus, it can feel like they're gaslighting when they start telling you that you are actually the fool. But the point is, don't worry about them if you are pursuing higher ideals and bolder thinking.

WHY THIS IS A TRANSFORMATIVE BOOK:

Don Quixote by Miguel de Cervantes is playful and experimental, 400-years old, and is often called the first modern novel, although that becomes a subjective criteria. The book has been enormously influential on a host of major writers ever since. Faulkner reread it once a year, "just as some people read the Bible." My Spanish professor at Georgia State did the same thing. As Robert Sheppard writes, "Crucially, for Don Quixote one of his principal motivations and objects is shared with Hamlet: the quest after that which is 'nobler in the mind'. Shared equally with Hamlet as well is the cutting point of the dilemma 'To be, or not to be?' For Don Quixote's 'taking up arms' to embark on his knightly quest is never defined by any material reward, such as Sancho Panza's fixation on ruling his island, or even simply the higher concern with worldly or knightly reputation. In a sense his decision to embark on his quest is an existential one — he can only "be" in any sense commensurate with his ideal self by the willful act of throwing down the gauntlet of challenge to the entire world and its existing order of fallen values, come what may... Had he remained in his armchair as 'the good Alonso Quixano', with his nose buried in diverting books, it could be said that Don Quixote had never been."

QUESTIONS FOR MEDITATION:

Why is what you do important?

"The man who moves a mountain begins by carrying away small stones."

WHY I LOVE THIS QUOTE:

I especially love this quote because it captures so much in such an aphoristic statement. To move a mountain may be a miracle, but it's a miracle that comes through incredibly hard and persistent labor and (self) belief. It's a lesson on habits. It's a lesson in persistence.

WHY THIS IS A TRANSFORMATIVE BOOK:

The Analects by Confucius may be the most influential book of all time. As Leys states in his introduction to the Penguin edition, "No book in the entire history of the world has exerted, over a longer period of time, a greater influence on a larger number of people than this slim volume."

As the philosophy of Plato and Aristotle emerged during a period of conflict between Greek and Persian power so too did Confucius (and Sun Tzu) emerge during the "Warring States" period of Chinese history from roughly 475-221 BCE which overlaps with the emergence of the Greek philosophers. Confucius lived and taught in the 6th century BCE. To put things in perspective, that's when Buddha and Zoroaster were active, and 10 years after Confucius dies, Socrates is born. One of Confucius' most revolutionary ideas was redefining the term junzi, meaning noble person or person of status, as anyone who was educated and moral.

QUESTIONS FOR MEDITATION:

What mountain are you moving today?

"The happiness which comes from long practice, which leads to the end of suffering, which at first is like poison, but at last like nectar — this kind of happiness arises from the serenity of one's own mind."

WHY I LOVE THIS QUOTE:

While we're tackling one buried treasure after another, here is more ancient wisdom. For as much disdain as we have for the past, the past has a lot to tell us. It's like on a surface level we realize there were great thinkers, but another part of our brain tells us that we are collectively superior. We're bigger. We have electricity and planes and the combustible engine. We have bombs. We can talk with people across the globe in real time at any time. But that has nothing to do with our wisdom, our knowledge, or self-knowledge, or our ability to morally reason. This quote has much to tell us.

WHY THIS IS A TRANSFORMATIVE BOOK:

The Bhagavad Gita by Krishna-Dwaipayana Vyasa aspires to offer not just a story, but a total account of a culture: "Whatever is found here may well be found elsewhere; what is not here is nowhere." Bhagavad Gita is Sanskrit for "Song of the Lord (or Blessed One)" and is India's best known scripture. Mahatma Gandhi used it as his spiritual guidebook. It is a 700-verse Hindu scripture that is part of the epic Mahabharata (chapters 23–40 of Bhishma Parva). The setting is a battlefield that has been interpreted as an allegory for the ethical and moral struggles of human life.

QUESTIONS FOR MEDITATION:

As you meditate and grow in mindfulness, in what ways do you find it easy and natural and sustainable? In what ways do you, by contrast, find it hard and challenging?

"Like lost children we live our unfinished adventures."

WHY I LOVE THIS QUOTE:
In the ways that we don't know ourselves, you could say we haven't grown up. We haven't grown into the mature self we can be, who we, in fact, are. And so we are like children, and in that way we relive and reenact the parts of ourselves that are unfinished. When our unconscious minds go unexplored and unpursued, they end up dictating much of the terms of our behavior.

WHY THIS IS A TRANSFORMATIVE BOOK:
Few works of political and cultural theory have been as enduringly provocative as Guy Debord's *The Society of the Spectacle*. From its publication amid the social upheavals of the 1960s up to the present, the theses of this book have shaped debates on modernity, capitalism, and everyday life in the late twentieth century and on.

As Benoit Lelièvre writes, "Everybody acknowledges we live in the society of spectacle, but either don't believe its rules apply to them or adopt a defeatist attitude towards it. What is the spectacle, then? Debord has a great way of summarizing it: the colonization of human life by commodities. It's people arguing over iPhones vs Androids. People crafting their identity around fictional characters and shunning their relationship to their real environment. It's people thinking hard work alone will lead them anywhere they want because they've been told by people who haven't necessarily worked harder than them in order to become successful and who are very self-conscious about protecting the social order they prosper in. You get the gist. We live in a neoliberalism economy where the most important thing we can do is buy, so the best way we can turn the system around is by starting to think critically about your own consumerism."

QUESTIONS FOR MEDITATION:

Are you a pawn in someone's game, or do you call the shots? How free are you to decide who you really are?

"Perhaps the biggest tragedy of our lives is that freedom is possible, yet we can pass our years trapped in the same old patterns...We may want to love other people without holding back, to feel authentic, to breathe in the beauty around us, to dance and sing. Yet each day we listen to inner voices that keep our life small."

WHY I LOVE THIS QUOTE:

The biggest regrets the dying often report were the chances they didn't take, the things they wish they hadn't lived enslaved to but felt they had no other choice. We do have choices. We do have opportunities for greater freedom and fulfillment. We need to slow down and begin reflecting. We need to know who we are. Then we need to get out there and do something about it.

WHY THIS IS A TRANSFORMATIVE BOOK:

Radical Acceptance: Embracing Your Life With the Heart of a Buddha by Tara Brach begins by introducing the Buddhist practice of mindfulness as applied to difficult experiences. It progresses to practices of radical compassion for oneself and others, and practicing radical lovingkindness. Brach begins by teaching a new way of approaching emotionally intolerable situations, such as feeling overwhelmed by physical manifestations of anxiety, fear, desire, melancholy, depression, anger, embarrassment, as well as unworthiness, guilt, or shame. She delves into challenging situations of interpersonal conflict, loss, grief, and learning to forgive when forgiveness seems impossible. It is a radical book, which asks for a steady commitment.

QUESTIONS FOR MEDITATION:

Why do we remain stuck in the same old patterns when the world awaits us? What are we waiting for?

"The wonderful paradox about the truth of suffering is that the more we open to it and understand it, the lighter and freer our mind becomes. Our mind becomes more spacious, more open, and happier as we move past our avoidance and denial to see what is true. We become less driven by compulsive desires and addictions, because we see clearly the nature of things as they are."

WHY I LOVE THIS QUOTE:

You hear about this approach a lot when it comes to compulsions and ingrained bad habits, even anxieties. Look them in the eye and stay with them. Mirror back to them an acknowledgment that you see them. You are aware of them. Neutrally. You aren't afraid, but neither are you trying too hard. You're not hunting them down. You're letting them know you know they're already there, and you're not running.

WHY THIS IS A TRANSFORMATIVE BOOK:

Insight Meditation: A Psychology of Freedom by Joseph Goldstein explores the question "Why meditate?" at length and in depth. Issues such as morality, karma, and the relationship between self and emotion are addressed beautifully. Goldstein's writing is flowing and affable — it calms you down. When we observe our emotions in meditation we don't over-identify with them. If we experience anger, we don't say "my anger." If we experience grief we don't say "my grief." We simply say "anger" or "grief." This is the path of meditation in the beginning — to identify what is going on, then let it go. We get wrapped up in negative emotions when we over-identify with them, instead of just letting them go.

QUESTIONS FOR MEDITATION:

What anxieties, addictions, or unacknowledged compulsions need your attention?

"Are you paralyzed with fear? That's a good sign. Fear is good. Like self-doubt, fear is an indicator. Fear tells us what we have to do. Remember one rule of thumb: the more scared we are of a work or calling, the more sure we can be that we have to do it."

WHY I LOVE THIS QUOTE:

When you come across this quote at the right time it can be such an encouragement. It's true, for all the assistance and encouragement you're like to find when you first strike out into the wild frontier of trying to learn more about who you are, it starts to get scary when you start taking action. But much like the idea of the "obstacle is the way," so is that fear resistance we're almost certain to have. Push through it, and know you are on the right path.

WHY THIS IS A TRANSFORMATIVE BOOK:

The War of Art: Break Through the Blocks & Win Your Inner Creative Battles by Steven Pressfield delivers a guide to inspire and support those who struggle to express their creativity. As Steve Turtell writes, "It is the kick in the ass every artist needs, sometimes daily. Because we all face the same enemy, fight the same battle every day: Resistance. According to Pressman, this is the whole story. Every day you either win or lose your battle with resistance. All the rest is talk. Why you lost it doesn't matter. Maybe your mother didn't love you enough. Maybe you don't believe in yourself enough. Maybe you think you're not as talented as you wish you were. Well, so what? No one's mother loved them enough, all of us suffer from self-doubt (If you don't, you're a sociopath and I don't want to know you), and even Shakespeare wrote about 'Desiring this man's art, and that man's scope'. If Shakespeare sometimes thought he wasn't good enough, I think that lets the rest of us off the hook. The only answer is to get up every day and do your work to the best of your ability."

QUESTIONS FOR MEDITATION:

Are you paralyzed with fear?

"A stationary body will stay stationary unless an external force is applied to it."

WHY I LOVE THIS QUOTE:

Force is equal to mass times acceleration, and a change in motion (change in speed) is proportional to the force applied. For every action, there is an equal and opposite reaction. Think about these laws in relation to your own life.

WHY THIS IS A TRANSFORMATIVE BOOK:

It is impossible to overstate the importance of the *Philosophiae Naturalis Principia Mathematica* (known widely as the *Principia*) in the history of science, the history of ideas, and indeed in the history of Western civilization. It is one of the crowning glories of humankind's ability to observe and explain the natural world. In his monumental 1687 work Isaac Newton laid out in mathematical terms the principles of time, force, and motion that have guided the development of modern physical science. Even after more than three centuries and the revolutions of Einsteinian relativity and quantum mechanics, Newtonian physics continues to account for many of the phenomena of the observed world, and Newtonian celestial dynamics is used to determine the orbits of our space vehicles. Paging through the *Principia* and stopping to read anything that looks interesting is a way to begin. The Prefaces that Newton wrote to the first three editions should not be missed.

QUESTIONS FOR MEDITATION:

What is the external force being applied to your life?

"Whereas the truth is that fullness of soul can sometimes overflow in utter vapidity of language, for none of us can ever express the exact measure of his needs or his thoughts or his sorrows; and human speech is like a cracked kettle on which we tap crude rhythms for bears to dance to, while we long to make music that will melt the stars."

WHY I LOVE THIS QUOTE:
This quote says something to me about longing. We long to express the intensity of our experience. There are things we want to say that we can't put words to, feelings without descriptions. Our spirits and imaginations want magic, want many lives, yearn for thousands of experiences, but our time is limited, our language is limited, and we come down to earth as it were, faced with the realism of one ordinary moment turning into the next.

WHY THIS IS A TRANSFORMATIVE BOOK:
Flaubert's erotically charged and psychologically acute portrayal of Emma Bovary caused a moral outcry on its publication in 1857. It was deemed so lifelike that many women claimed they were the model for his heroine; but Flaubert insisted: "Madame Bovary, c'est moi." The narration is actually quite modern in that the perspective changes quite often from a mysterious first person in the beginning (a schoolmate of Charles Bovary?) to the interior monologues of Charles, Emma, Léon, and Rodolphe. The descriptions of the various locations in the book are always surprising with tiny references to the principle characters. Often called the first "modern novel," you can see it as a precursor for so much literature that followed over the 19th and 20th century.

QUESTIONS FOR MEDITATION:

What do you desire? How would it make you feel if you attained it?

"If you celebrate your differentness, the world will, too. It believes exactly what you tell it — through the words you use to describe yourself, the actions you take to care for yourself, and the choices you make to express yourself. Tell the world you are a one-of-a-kind creation who came here to experience wonder and spread joy. Expect to be accommodated."

WHY I LOVE THIS QUOTE:

By contrast to a lot of the resistance and fear that we can experience when moving into ourselves, this quote is saying tell the world who you are and the world will respond in kind. Just like overcoming fear, this takes courage. It's a mindset shift, and I don't think it's necessarily "a law of attraction" type of thinking. Live out who you are freely and in expectation.

WHY THIS IS A TRANSFORMATIVE BOOK:

In *Lit From Within: Tending Your Soul For Lifelong Beauty*, Victoria Moran shares the wisdom and experience from her own search for inner and outer beauty. Her thoughtful observations and advice show how anyone can transform their thinking about what makes us beautiful, while providing simple guidance for creating a radiance that comes from within. Each essay offers a tool to develop more self-awareness. She illustrates how "true beauty" comes from a sense of wholeness. She combines tips for taking care of your spirit and your body. It is a sane, sensible approach to a strong self-image grounded in the integration of body and soul.

QUESTIONS FOR MEDITATION:

How do you celebrate what is different about you?

july

"Addictive behavior is often a search for safety rather than an attempt to rebel or a selfish turn inward."

WHY I LOVE THIS QUOTE:

This is a good reminder, especially when we see it manifesting in our children's behaviors. Of course, it doesn't take long for addiction to manifest in rebellion or a self-interested turn inward, but that often has as much to do with the punitive responses to the addictive behavior.

WHY THIS IS A TRANSFORMATIVE TEXT:

Unbroken Brain: A Revolutionary New Way of Understanding Addiction by Maia Szalavitz is the result of thirty years spent researching and writing about addiction. Woven into this distillation of addiction and treatment is the author's own experience with heroin and cocaine abuse as a young woman in the 1980s that nearly ended her life more than once. The central premise to *Unbroken Brain* is that we're in the middle of an epidemic of addiction and we are stuck in treating it ineffectively when there are better methods available. One in ten Americans are in the throes of some type of substance use disorder. That doesn't even count tobacco addiction and the myriad millions who have behavioral addictions to sex, gambling, shopping. Nor, one third of Americans who overeat and are said to be addicted to food.

QUESTIONS FOR MEDITATION:

How can we begin to focus on the causes, not the symptoms of addictive behavior? Can we advocate for humane, empathic treatment that allows people with addictions to find new ways to cope?

"With every breath, the old moment is lost; a new moment arrives. We exhale and we let go of the old moment. It is lost to us. In doing so, we let go of the person we used to be. We inhale and breathe in the moment that is becoming. In doing so, we welcome the person we are becoming. We repeat the process. This is meditation. This is renewal. This is life."

WHY I LOVE THIS QUOTE:
This is a summary of the simplicity and process — and beauty — of meditation. It induces calm, acceptance, and compassion.

WHY THIS IS A TRANSFORMATIVE BOOK:
Letting Go of the Person You Used to Be: Lessons on Change, Loss, and Spiritual Transformation by Surya Das simply points out the Buddhist mindset, and allows you to apply these views and values in your own life. It is designed for every person for everyday living. Starting to understand and accept impermanence today is going to help you through all of life's planned and unplanned changes, regardless of where your life is at in this moment. From this essential insight Surya Das has crafted a fulfilling and important path to understanding and healing ourselves and finding peace. Full of personal stories, anecdotes, practical exercises, guided meditations and reflections, this book addresses universal difficulties in an accessible way.

QUESTIONS FOR MEDITATION:

As you breathe in, bring to consciousness what is bothering you, and as you breathe out, let it go. Do this several times until your body begins to feel your mind letting go.

After a few minutes, ask yourself:

What are you most hopeful for? What can you do to make it happen?

"Grief is the conflicting feelings caused by the end of or change in a familiar pattern of behavior."

WHY I LOVE THIS QUOTE:

The emphasis is on feelings. Grief involves emotions, however intense the grief may be.

Six common responses to loss that completely ignore emotional needs: (1) Don't feel bad; (2) Replace the loss; (3) Grieve alone; (4) Just give it time; (5) Be strong for others; (6) Keep busy. Each of the misconceptions is examined in the book where this quote comes from and revealed for the damage it does.

WHY THIS IS A TRANSFORMATIVE BOOK:

The Grief Recovery Handbook by John W. James, and Russell Friedman is a classic handbook that everyone should have in their library. A clear presentation of their method to grief recovery makes this book work. Rather than academic research, the writers present a straightforward approach based on hard-won personal knowledge and years of presenting their method at workshops. The book makes it possible to find "completion" for grief in a way that is carefully explained and outlined. Society prefers intellect to emotion and so emotions — what gets so stirred up in grief — are muffled and marginalized. There are wrong ways to mourn. Most do it wrong, leading to years of mental anguish.

QUESTIONS FOR MEDITATION:

Have you allowed yourself to grieve the end of a recent loss or forced change in your patterns of behavior?

Has what you've been doing to heal been helping or hurting you?

"It is by tracing things to their origin, that we learn to understand them; and it is by keeping that line and that origin always in view, that we never forget them."

WHY I LOVE THIS QUOTE:

Paine had a provocative and idealistic sense of what we often should see as "self-evident" truths. It seems he was already tracing things to their origins, such as the basic rights of a peasant child compared with one of royal pedigree. If only these ideals had become reality through the Founders in the first place. For our purposes, too, we should think about how this quote applies to the self. Keep sourcing yourself for the core questions and you will get somewhere.

WHY THIS IS A TRANSFORMATIVE BOOK:

Common Sense, The Rights of Man and Other Essential Writings by Thomas Paine paved the way for the Declaration of Independence and the Revolutionary War. It might even be said that while Jefferson's abstract diction justified rebellion, Paine's explosive words got rebel men and muskets into the field. Paine despised monarchies and desired a greater role for the multitude.

"Society is produced by our wants, and the government by our wickedness," he wrote. In the first part of *Common Sense*, Paine describes the basic purpose of the government as the one of protector of Human Rights and establishment of a welfare state that exercises its authority with the general consent of the public. He describes all the human beings as equals, any discrimination on the basis of race, religion, caste or creed is atrocious and petrifying to the very essence of a civilized society.

QUESTIONS FOR MEDITATION:

What are your values, and are you living in alignment with them?

"Totally without hope one cannot live. To live without hope is to cease to live. Hell is hopelessness. It is no accident that above the entrance to Dante's hell is the inscription: 'Leave behind all hope, you who enter here.'"

WHY I LOVE THIS QUOTE:

There is a lot of darkness in our current historical moment, but there remains tremendous goodness. We live with the hope of a more just and equitable culture. Hope brings us to life. There are scientifically-based studies that investigate the concept of hope in people's lives. It is also helpful to know theologians have done their own systematic research into the concept of hope. To hope is to want a better outcome. It makes the present situation more bearable, and motivates us to create the conditions for a better future.

WHY THIS IS A TRANSFORMATIVE BOOK:

A Theology of Hope put Jurgen Moltmann on the theological map and started his career as among the most influential Protestant theologians of the last 70 years. Moltmann argues that all of theology is centered on eschatology. Not the doom and gloom eschatology prevalent in so much of evangelicalism, but a hopeful Christian eschatology which "speaks of Jesus Christ and his future. It recognizes the reality of the raising of Jesus and proclaims the future of the risen Lord." Theology of Hope is one of the most important and influential works of twentieth century Christian theology. It is a dense academic theological work, but well worth the read.

QUESTIONS FOR MEDITATION:

What are you most grateful for right now in your personal life?

"If you are distressed by anything external, the pain is not due to the thing itself, but to your estimate of it; and this you have the power to revoke at any moment."

WHY I LOVE THIS QUOTE:
This book teaches the powerful and resonating lesson that our perceptions create our reality. There are external events outside of our control that happen all the time. We can do nothing about that part of life, but the part we have complete control over is how we respond to circumstances. It is a mindset approach to all of life, and can lead us to how we respond to and handle failure, amongst other things.

WHY THIS IS A TRANSFORMATIVE BOOK:
The Meditations by Marcus Aurelius are without parallel in our literature. Written in Greek by the only Roman emperor who was also a philosopher, without any intention of publication, they offer a remarkable series of challenging spiritual reflections and exercises developed as the emperor struggled to understand himself and make sense of the constant chaos he was perpetually surrounded by during the 19 years that he ruled.

As Ryan Holiday writes, "While the Meditations were composed to provide personal consolation and encouragement, Marcus Aurelius also created one of the greatest of all works of philosophy: a timeless collection that has been consulted and admired by statesmen, thinkers and readers throughout the centuries."

QUESTIONS FOR MEDITATION:

What is outside of your control that you are frustrated by, blocked, or feel like you're at an impasse?

"We are triggered not by their behavior, but by our own unresolved emotional issues."

WHY I LOVE THIS QUOTE:

"Do you see me?" This is the big question your child is asking every day. "Can you recognize me for who I am, different from your dreams and expectations for me, separate from your agenda for me?"

WHY THIS IS A TRANSFORMATIVE BOOK:

The Awakened Family: A Revolution in Parenting by Shefali Tsabary is a gamechanger in parenting literature. If you are a parent, or even someone who was once a kid, this book contains the potential to change you. The premise is mindfulness for the parent, and being mindful that at the core of all of us is a need to be seen.

QUESTIONS FOR MEDITATION:

If you're really honest with yourself for a moment, what would you say is your top unresolved emotional issue? How does it impact your relationships with others?

"You can't know where you're going until you know where you are."

WHY I LOVE THIS QUOTE:
Pretend this book is a map, and you are looking at the point that says: You are here. That's where you're starting really all the time, from where you are. It doesn't matter where you come from, where you think you are going, what job or career you have had or think you should have. You are not too late, and you're not too early. But where are you? Strategic thinking can help you build your way forward from wherever you are, regardless of the life problem you are facing. But before you can figure out which direction to head in, you need to know where you are and what problems you are trying to solve.

WHY THIS IS A TRANSFORMATIVE BOOK:
Designing Your Life: Build a Life that Works for You by Bill Burnett and Dave Evans is ultimately a way to redefine the way you live. It can be transformative in how you look at your life and how you live, especially from a vocational perspective. The end result could very well be a well-designed life and therefore a life "well lived." The book is aimed more through the lens of jobs and vocation, and actively promotes ideas that at worst can keep you from taking a job that sucks the soul out of you, and at best can actually aid in creating a dream designed life.

QUESTIONS FOR MEDITATION:

These are the beginning points for building a compass to know where you are. You want the answers to these questions to align in wholeness and authenticity.

Who are you? What do you believe? What are you doing?

"The technocratic illusion is that poverty results from a shortage of expertise, whereas poverty is really about a shortage of rights. The emphasis on the problem of expertise makes the problem of rights worse. The technical problems of the poor (and the absence of technical solutions for those problems) are a symptom of poverty, not a cause of poverty.

WHY I LOVE THIS QUOTE:
In some ways it states the obvious, but it is an argument you rarely hear in today's discourse on systemic racism, whether or not it exists, and why various impoverished communities remain with so few resources, opportunities, or people who rise from such conditions.

WHY THIS IS A TRANSFORMATIVE BOOK:
The Tyranny of Experts: Economists, Dictators, and the Forgotten Rights of the Poor by William Easterly argues that the cause of poverty is the absence of political and economic rights, the absence of a free political and economic system that would find the technical solutions to the poor's problems.

As Daniel Clausen writes, "Largely, Easterly makes a great argument for 'rights-based' development and bottom-up forms of development based on the economic theory of Friedrich Hayek. Some reviewers have argued against the structure of the book. But I actually found its approach refreshing. I found the early use of the 'debate that never happened' to be excellent. I like when authors interrogate the historical genesis of ideas. It highlights that ideas are never innocent — they are always for something (and usually for someone)."

QUESTIONS FOR MEDITATION:

What do you think causes poverty? What are your assumptions about how it happens?

"I cannot make you understand. I cannot make anyone under-stand what is happening inside me. I cannot even explain it to myself."

WHY I LOVE THIS QUOTE:
Sometimes our struggles transcend words, or our ability to articulate what is going on inside ourselves, whether or not we're having a good day.

WHY THIS IS A TRANSFORMATIVE BOOK:
With it's startling, bizarre, yet also funny opening, Franz Kafka begins his masterpiece, *The Metamorphosis.* It is the story of a young man who, transformed overnight into a giant beetle-like insect, becomes an object of disgrace to his family, an outsider in his own home, a quintessentially alien-ated man. A harrowing — though absurdly comic — meditation on human feelings of inadequacy, guilt, and isolation. It has become one of the most widely read and influential works of twentieth-century fiction. It's a story of turning mute, being unable to communicate with the world, your own family first and foremost. It's a depiction of what it's like to be alien, foreign, liminal. *The Metamorphosis* is as poignant and relevant today as it was when it was first published.

As W.H. Auden wrote, "Kafka is important to us because his predicament is the predicament of modern man."

QUESTIONS FOR MEDITATION:

What are the fragmented parts of your identity?

Can you explain yourself to yourself?

"Being human is not hard because you're doing it wrong, it's hard because you're doing it right. You will never change the fact that being human is hard, so you must change your idea that it was ever supposed to be easy."

WHY I LOVE THIS QUOTE:

The mindset that life is supposed to be easy gets a lot of us in trouble. We want to avoid pain and struggle and as a result (perhaps ironically), we suffer. It may not be easy to embrace the struggle of being true to yourself, but in the end you will live a more fulfilled, joyful life.

WHY THIS IS A TRANSFORMATIVE BOOK:

Untamed by Glennon Doyle is a stunning collection of essays on feminism, spirituality, and intersectionality, just to name a few. Doyle is untaming and unlearning western society's expectations of how a person should look and act accordingly, and uncovering the reason (or lack thereof) that we have been conditioned to think this way, the cages we unconsciously live in. The Knowing inside of her guides her away from the boxes of religion and sexuality, and in turn she finds her true self, as well as the truest love she's ever experienced. Through her self reflection of our cultural norms, readers will have the concepts to re-evaluate their own views and values on what we expect of ourselves and others. *Untamed* opens the eyes, the heart, and the soul.

She writes, "It's the story of how I learned, through my relationship with Tish, that a responsible mother is not one who slowly dies for her children, but one who shows her children how to bravely live. It's about how I stopped being a martyr and started being a model."

QUESTIONS FOR MEDITATION:

If you believe you are living as a sacrifice for someone, or some ideal, but you aren't living out who you really are, have you paused to consider there might be a better way? Is there a way for you to live for someone else while showing them how you live for yourself?

"What I know now is that when we derive our worth from the relationships in our lives — the intimate ones, the social circles we belong to, the companies we work for — we give away our power and become dependent upon external validation. When that is taken away, our sense of value, and identity, goes with it."

WHY I LOVE THIS QUOTE:

This reaffirms a theme we explore from a variety of angles throughout this reader. The idea that you are good enough for who you are, regardless of the relationships outside yourself, is important. It's all the more impactful when it comes from someone who is achieving great success within those relationships and as an African American woman. It's a message for everyone.

WHY THIS IS A TRANSFORMATIVE BOOK:

More Than Enough: Claiming Space for Who You Are (No Matter What They Say) by Elaine Welteroth is an inspiring, honest, humorous and authentic look at the life of the author as she navigates her early years to her journey to becoming the first African American editor of a *Conde Nast* magazine. She takes a detailed look into her family history — how her parents met and their struggles — to navigating her own enthusiastic pursuits and interests, stepping stones and setbacks. Along the way, she gives many insightful life lessons that include building self worth, making room for self-discovery, navigating self-identity (with an emphasis on navigating her own biracial background), and finding relationships and opportunities that work.

QUESTIONS FOR MEDITATION:

How can you keep and maintain your power even while navigating an array of relationships whether intimate, social, or professional?

"Hope is not a lottery ticket you can sit on the sofa and clutch, feeling lucky. It is an axe you break down doors with in an emergency."

WHY I LOVE THIS QUOTE:
We explore hope as optimism, as necessity, as beacon shining a light forward. One thing it should not function as is an "opiate for the masses." Hope, like love and faith, is not a passive condition. I love the idea of how it can be a call to action in a time that should be viewed as an emergency. It asks us to look at situations with urgency rather than bland acceptance and resignation.

WHY THIS IS A TRANSFORMATIVE BOOK:
Hope in the Dark by Rebecca Solnit was first written in response to the Bush administration's invasion of Iraq, but rereleased in early 2016 in the wake of America's deteriorating political climate. *Hope in the Dark* puts forth a lucid thesis: hope is "an embrace of the unknown and the unknowable," and in "the spaciousness of uncertainty is room to act."

The book consists of several short essays that survey overlooked environmental, cultural, and political victories over the past five decades. Stressing that change rarely is absolute, immediate, or straightforward, she convincingly argues for approaching civic engagement as a way of life, fueled by the belief that a more just world is always possible. The speed at which Solnit synthesizes disparate ideas is astounding, and her hopefulness is as inspiring and moving as it ever has been.

QUESTIONS FOR MEDITATION:

What doors are you breaking down with your axe?

"With lovingkindness for myself I allow all the feelings of the irrational, perplexing, agonizing relationship to wash over me. Suddenly, I see it clearly: my whining, my sense that I'm trapped by this relationship, my seeming powerlessness over the irrationality of the Other are reenactments. And with that observation I'm suddenly free from the burden, the trap of trying to make the irrational rational. Not only is it completely irrationational to argue with the Irrational Other, it's irrational to try to alter them so that they make sense to me."

WHY I LOVE THIS QUOTE:
We all have an "Irrationational Other" in our lives. We have a choice to make when it comes to how we experience that person. We can remain stuck and let that person continue to provoke us or keep us locked up, or with love and self-understanding, we can wake up to the repetition, we can move past the pain or fear or shame and take a step on the path to awakening.

WHY THIS IS A TRANSFORMATIVE BOOK:
Reboot: Leadership and the Art of Growing Up by Jerry Colonna is a journey of radical self-inquiry, helping you to reset your life by sorting through the emotional baggage that is holding you back professionally and, even more important, in your relationships. Jerry has taught CEOs and their top teams to realize their potential by using the raw material of their lives to find meaning, to build healthy interpersonal bonds, and to become more compassionate and bold leaders. What we need, sometimes, is a chance to reset our goals and to reconnect with our deepest selves and with each other. Reboot moves and empowers us to begin this journey.

QUESTIONS FOR MEDITATION:

Think of yourself in the shoes of the Other. Why do they behave in the irrational way they do? What reenactment are they playing out over and over? With a little more insight into their behavior perhaps you can have more lovingkindness toward that person even as you step away from the dysfunction?

"The most apparent thing that I noticed was how most of the people in this study derive their sense of identity and well-being from their immediate surroundings rather than from within themselves, and that's why they broke down — just couldn't stand the pressure — they had nothing within them to hold up against all of this."

WHY I LOVE THIS QUOTE:
This study revealed that the real source of resilience and strength comes from within.

WHY THIS IS A TRANSFORMATIVE BOOK:
Renowned social psychologist and creator of the "Stanford Prison Experiment," Philip Zimbardo explores the mechanisms that make good people do bad things, how moral people can be seduced into acting immorally, and what this says about the line separating good from evil. *The Lucifer Effect* explains how — and the myriad reasons why — we are all susceptible to the lure of "the dark side." Zimbardo details how situational forces and group dynamics can work in concert to make monsters out of decent men and women. Zimbardo tells the full story of the experiment the landmark study in which a group of college-student volunteers was randomly divided into "guards" and "inmates" and then placed in a mock prison environment. Within a week, the study was abandoned, as ordinary college students were transformed into either brutal, sadistic guards or emotionally broken prisoners.

He illuminates the psychological causes behind such disturbing metamorphoses, and replaces the long-held notion of the "bad apple" with that of the "bad barrel" — the idea that the social setting and the system contaminate the individual, rather than the other way around.

QUESTIONS FOR MEDITATION:

How do you find yourself absorbing and complying with your surrounding culture?

"Care of the soul is a fundamentally different way of regarding daily life and the quest for happiness."

WHY I LOVE THIS QUOTE:
Recognizing the soul within us helps us connect the spiritual with the material, the ineffable with concrete striving for the bottom line, it helps us examine our motives, and find joy in the ordinariness of our moments. Care means cultivating. Moore sees the soul as a bridge between ourselves. The care the soul needs begins deep curiosity about the ways our psyche reveals itself in ourselves in others.

WHY THIS IS A TRANSFORMATIVE BOOK:
Care of the Soul: A Guide for Cultivating Depth and Sacredness in Everyday Life by Thomas Moore is a revolutionary approach to thinking about daily life — everyday activities, events, problems and creative opportunities — and a therapeutic lifestyle is proposed that focuses on looking more deeply into emotional problems and learning how to sense sacredness in even ordinary things. Basing his writing on the ancient model of "care of the soul" — which provided a religious context for viewing the everyday events of life — Moore brings "care of the soul" into the 21st century.

QUESTIONS FOR MEDITATION:

What would it be like to live with a deeper, calmer, mindful awareness of your circumstances?

"In the morning he would sit down to work, finish his allotted task, then take the little lamp from the hook, put it on the table, get his book from the shelf, open it, and sit down to read. And the more he read, the more he understood, and the brighter and happier it grew in his heart."

WHY I LOVE THIS QUOTE:

There is a quiet simplicity in the life of the cobbler. He would perform his duties, and then he would read. There is no ostentation, no needing to share what he read, just the reading and the growing understanding or enlightening. As Joseph Campbell said, "Sit in a room and read — and read and read. And read the right books by the right people. Your mind is brought onto that level, and you have a nice, mild, slow-burning rapture all the time."

WHY THIS IS A TRANSFORMATIVE BOOK:

Where Love Is, There God Is Also by Leo Tolstoy is a short story about an impoverished cobbler who is old and without children or a wife in czarist Russia. One day, he receives a visit from a traveling priest he used to know who wishes to have his leather bound Bible repaired. As they talk, the cobbler admits that he has become estranged from God since the death of his young son. The priest promises to pray for the cobbler. That night, the cobbler has a dream in which he dreams that Jesus promises to visit him three times the very next day. Confused by the dream, he watches the window the whole day waiting for Christ's visit. He is visited by three different poor strangers, each needing the cobbler's help. He helps the three poor strangers in turn, but at the end of the day, Jesus has not come. That night, the cobbler reads the priest's Bible, and chances on the verse that says to have compassion for the least of Christ's brethren is the same as to help Christ himself. The cobbler realizes that where love is there is God also.

QUESTIONS FOR MEDITATION:

Why are words powerful to you? What books or thoughts have made an impact on your life or your thinking?

"The Enneagram is a tool that awakens our compassion for people just as they are, not the people we wish they would become so our lives would become easier."

WHY I LOVE THIS QUOTE:

Knowing my Enneagram number has deepened my self-awareness, and given me practical and specific tools for growth. It has also helped me better understand people who are wired entirely differently than me. The idea here is to also realize that for as much as we don't like it when people have agendas for us, neither should have agendas for other people. Easier said than done of course, especially when it comes to our children, with greater understanding comes greater compassion for self and others.

WHY THIS IS A TRANSFORMATIVE BOOK:

The Road Back to You: An Enneagram Journey to Self-Discovery by Ian Morgan Cron and Suzanne Stabile forges a unique approach a practical way of accessing Enneagram wisdom and exploring its connections. Cron and Stabile aren't getting into niche Enneagram topics here, like the instincts, stances, subtypes, or levels of development. For that kind of depth, check out any of the more detailed works on the topic by Riso/Hudson, Beatrice Chestnut, or Richard Rohr. This is an accessible, well-organized, witty primer on the basics.

QUESTIONS FOR MEDITATION:

Do you want to be who you are?

"Not finance. Not strategy. Not technology. It is teamwork that remains the ultimate competitive advantage, both because it is so powerful and so rare."

WHY I LOVE THIS QUOTE:

Our meditation focus is often on the self, and that is no doubt where the work begins. But a huge follow-up step is naturally how we engage and work with others. We all want to succeed and we can't do it without others. In fact, we spend so much of our time working with others to accomplish our very own goals, it's important that we are able to work well with others on teams. Most of us want to collaborate. We are ready to share our ideas and work with others, and most of us don't want conflict. This quote focuses on the power of a good team — but perhaps more importantly, that it is rare. As Henry Ford once said, "Coming together is a beginning. Keeping together is progress. Working together is success."

WHY THIS IS A TRANSFORMATIVE BOOK:

The Five Dysfunctions of a Team: A Leadership Fable by Patrick Lencioni reveals the five dysfunctions which go to the very heart of why teams, even the best ones, often struggle. He outlines a powerful model and actionable steps that can be used to overcome these common hurdles and build a cohesive, effective team. Just as with his other books, Lencioni has written a compelling fable with a powerful yet deceptively simple message for all those who strive to be exceptional team leaders.

QUESTIONS FOR MEDITATION:

Is there anyone you work with that you want to talk to them frankly about their performance?

"I don't think we did go blind, I think we are blind, Blind but seeing, Blind people who can see, but do not see."

WHY I LOVE THIS QUOTE:

The quote speaks for itself, but the book it comes from is an allegory for the breakdown of society, which is fueled in large part to our failure to "see" each other. The year 2020 has seen a global pandemic, and calls for increased attention to the issues of systemic racism. In large measure, we are called to perform radical empathy. Many refuse because it is too hard, uncomfortable, or threatening to their power. They remain blind.

WHY THIS IS A TRANSFORMATIVE BOOK:

Blindness by José Saramago is the story of a mysterious mass plague of blindness that affects nearly everyone living in an unnamed place in a never specified time and the implications this epidemic has on people's lives. It all starts inexplicably when a man in his car suddenly starts seeing — or rather stops seeing anything but a clear white brightness.

As Jeffrey Keeten writes, "There are lots of great themes in the novel, exploring the human condition and how we fail ourselves; and yet, eventually overcome the most severe circumstances. The text is a block of words with few paragraph breaks or markers to help us keep track of who is talking. This certainly adds to the difficulty of reading the novel, but I must counsel you to persevere. You will come away from the novel knowing you have experienced something, a grand vision of the disintegration of civilization and certainly you will reevaluate what is most important in your life. This is a novel that does what a great novel is supposed to do; it reveals what we keep hidden from ourselves."

QUESTIONS FOR MEDITATION:

If you wanted to change yourself for the better in one way, what would it be?

"Normally a job, fortune, or reputation has to be lost, a death has to be suffered, a house has to be flooded, or a disease has to be endured."

WHY I LOVE THIS QUOTE:
Rohr is pointing out a clear pattern that one of the primary ways we are ushered into the second half of life, of falling upward, is to experience failure or setback. It's a part of life, and it is good to be reminded that these experiences will happen. What we do with them is the real story. Another way of stating it, "Before the truth sets you free, it tends to make you miserable."

WHY THIS IS A TRANSFORMATIVE BOOK:
Falling Upward: A Spirituality for the Two Halves of Life by Richard Rohr explains why the second half of life can and should be full of spiritual richness. It offers a new view of how spiritual growth happens. This important book explores the counterintuitive message that we grow spiritually much more by doing wrong than by doing right. Most of us tend to think of the second half of life as largely about getting old, dealing with health issues, and letting go of life, but the whole thesis of this book is exactly the opposite. What looks like falling down can largely be experienced as "falling upward." In fact, it is not a loss but somehow actually a gain, as we have all seen with elders who have come to their fullness.

QUESTIONS FOR MEDITATION:

In what ways have you or are you being invited to descend or go inward and look deeply within yourself?

Is your work ever done?

"Don't just put in your time. That is not enough. You have to make great effort."

WHY I LOVE THIS QUOTE:
When the shine wears off the habits we're trying to form, when we begin to merely show up rather than put in the hard work of consistent, effortful focus, we lose hold of the very skill we're trying to develop. Trusting the process implies patience and that you're aware you're taking a long-view approach. But it also implies that you take very seriously the small micro-task in front of you. Do each step of the journey with your whole attention. While sometimes it is enough to just to "show up," it's a good reminder that on the path of personal transformation, you have to work at it.

WHY THIS IS A TRANSFORMATIVE BOOK:
Writing Down the Bones: Freeing the Writer Within by Natalie Goldberg was first published in 1986, and has stood the test of time. It remains one of my favorites on writing and life. She had already been challenging and cheering on writers with courses and workshops when she emerged on the scene with this debut book. Writing practice, as she calls it, is no different from other forms of Zen practice: "It is backed by two thousand years of studying the mind."

QUESTIONS FOR MEDITATION:

What steps can you take to bring more attention, and therefore more power, to your daily efforts?

"Progress, not perfection, is what we should be asking of ourselves."

WHY I LOVE THIS QUOTE:
For all the talk about work with purpose, and striving to be more mindful, and diligent with out habits, we need to step outside ourselves and relax too. We need grace for ourselves. Progress is going to be circuitous at times, a spiral. We're going to relapse into bad habits, or sink into holes we thought we'd climbed out of. We're not always going to be mindful. We're not always going to do our daily readings. We're not always going to exercise. We want to head in the right direction, but it's not always going to be direct. Sometimes showing up is good enough.

WHY THIS IS A TRANSFORMATIVE BOOK:
The Artist's Way by Julia Cameron is a seminal book on the subject of creativity. An international bestseller, millions of readers have found it to be an invaluable guide to living the artist's life. Still as vital today — or perhaps even more so — than it was when it was first published over two decades ago, it is a powerfully provocative and inspiring work. Somehow, Cameron is able to inspire, challenge, and actually get you to follow through with the exercises. When I went through it in the late '90s, I enjoyed the framework of it. There is the daily intensity to the practice of The Morning Pages, the weekly check-ins and work of things like the Artist's Date, and the idea that it's a 12-week program. Great content and methods for freeing up rigid thinking in general, most particularly bent toward creativity.

QUESTIONS FOR MEDITATION:

How easy or hard is it for you to make time for rest?

"Draw the art you want to see, start the business you want to run, play the music you want to hear, write the books you want to read, build the products you want to use – do the work you want to see done."

WHY I LOVE THIS QUOTE:

I love the simple pragmatism of this statement, and the optimism, and the implicit grit and courage. It's also like a statement to complainers: You don't like it, do better. And don't just do it so you'll stop complaining, do it because you must have been complaining for a good reason. Be the solution. Contribute. It's not all about you.

WHY THIS IS A TRANSFORMATIVE BOOK:

Steal Like an Artist: 10 Things Nobody Told You About Being Creative by Austin Kleon is (ironically enough) original, accessible, and even through its playful spirit, has a distilled and powerful wisdom within it. It may have few words and it does have many illustrations (he's an artist!) — but it is intended to be used more as a guide book. We celebrate a wide variety of books, and honor their unique contribution. Keeping a logbook is a great idea, especially when followed up with that incredible Nicholson Baker quote about what we remember on a given day. Lots of great takeaways from this book.

QUESTIONS FOR MEDITATION:

What would success look like in your life if nothing stood in your way?

"The more you are like others, the more secure you will feel, yet the more your heart will ache, the more dreams will be troubled and the more your soul will slip off into silences."

WHY I LOVE THIS QUOTE:
For so many, their lives are on automatic pilot because they're conditioned themselves to live in agreement with those who spout certainty. What's wrong with you? You need to get right with God — the God that is defined for you and you need to have the right attitude and spiritual practice. The only real reassurance is the others who are saying and supposedly believing in the exact same things, and supposedly that is community. Then, one day you wake up and forget that you even have a soul. Maybe that is the freedom you wanted?

WHY THIS IS A TRANSFORMATIVE BOOK:
Creating a Life: Finding Your Individual Path by James Hollis uses poetry, myths and classical allusions to add incredible insight and imagery to his ideas focused on discovering yourself, your passion, and your courage to keep discovering. Hollis encourages one to let go of the ego-attachments of youth and eagerly begin creating higher meaning and soul purpose in the second half of our ordinary lives.

QUESTIONS FOR MEDITATION:

Do you make things difficult for others to understand your own behavior?

"We've been trained to avoid creative obstacles rather than risk trying to surmount them."

WHY I LOVE THIS QUOTE:

The only way out is through, as Robert Frost once wrote. The obstacle is the way, as Ryan Holiday says. Instead of a tip-toeing around possible obstacles, let's realize that sometimes we need to push right on through.

WHY THIS IS A TRANSFORMATIVE BOOK:

Creative Calling: Establish a Daily Practice, Infuse Your World with Meaning, and Succeed in Work + Life by Chase Jarvis not only inspires readers to pursue their life's calling, it also provides valuable tactical principles for everyone who wants to create a better life. Creativity is combining things in a new way and putting these ideas out into the world. Creativity is problem solving, starting a business, social activism, building a family. Everyone is born creative, and everyone has the opportunity to exercise their creativity in their day to day lives. Our ability to choose to exercise our innate creativity is a theme woven throughout *Creative Calling*. Our agency – our ability to make decisions to help us along our creative path – is a key concept that we are encouraged to put into practice in small ways every day. It's through the use of agency in building small daily creative habits that over time, leads us to living our authentic and most creative lives.

QUESTIONS FOR MEDITATION:

How are you making things more difficult than they need to be?

"It is in playing and only in playing that the individual child or adult is able to be creative and to use the whole personality, and it is only in being creative that the individual discovers the self."

WHY I LOVE THIS QUOTE:

Two powerful thoughts wrapped up into one here. Both the child and the adult are only able to be creative and use their whole personality in play? Wow. Then, the follow up, and it is only through creativity that we discover our self? Impressive ideas. No wonder we've been emphasizing creativity as a path to growth through many of the readings during National Poetry Month.

WHY THIS IS A TRANSFORMATIVE BOOK:

Playing and Reality by D.W. Winnicott shows the reader how, through the attentive nurturing of creativity from the earliest years, every individual has the opportunity to enjoy a rich and rewarding cultural life.

As Marty Babit writes, "This is one of the most important books on the subject of psychotherapy I've read. Winnicott is a poet. He writes in images and often with a lot of jargon that is thick and hard-going. However, when he makes a discovery, and he makes quite a few, it's like he's journeyed to the center of the Earth and come back to reveal what the foundation beneath the foundation of reality is all about. As a therapist who has been practicing over twenty-five years, he is probably my greatest inspiration. His perspective turns on appreciation of the creativity and imagination that is part and parcel of psychological development. He gives therapists a way to think about authenticity and spontaneity that pushes away from preconceived notions about what is 'normal' or 'abnormal' and towards what is inventive and creative in our lives as opposed to what is deadening or deadened...This is a classic work."

QUESTIONS FOR MEDITATION:

How can I integrate more play into my life?

"If you know the enemy and know yourself, you need not fear the result of a hundred battles. If you know yourself but not the enemy, for every victory gained you will also suffer a defeat. If you know neither the enemy nor yourself, you will succumb in every battle."

WHY I LOVE THIS QUOTE:

First, start with yourself, as the readings and ideas from this book have emphasized. That is challenging enough. After you truly understand yourself, it is then just as important to understand your "enemy." Your enemy could be an obstacle, challenge, or struggle in the abstract. The better you know what you're up against, the more success you will have. It's thoughts like these that give this book such resonance.

WHY THIS IS A TRANSFORMATIVE BOOK:

Roughly 2500 years ago, Sun Tzu wrote *The Art of War.* This classic book of military strategy is based on Chinese warfare and military thought. Since that time, all levels of the military have used the teachings in warfare. Civilizations have also adapted these teachings for use in politics, business, and everyday life. It is one of the most influential strategy texts of all time. It has had a profound influence on both Eastern and Western military thinking, business tactics, legal strategy and far beyond.

QUESTIONS FOR MEDITATION:

Are there things you'd like to be able to tell your superior but are unable to for one reason or another?

What is getting in the way of the communication?

"But part of getting to know yourself is to unknow yourself — to let go of the limiting stories you've told yourself about who you are so that you aren't trapped by them, so you can live your life and not the story you've been telling yourself about your life."

WHY I LOVE THIS QUOTE:

Sometimes you almost have to reverse engineer the process. Sometimes you can't just go head on at the question: "Who do you think you are?" Sometimes you have to start with: "Who do you think you aren't?" We do often sell ourselves limiting beliefs. Sometimes it's scary how much we are capable of.

WHY THIS IS A TRANSFORMATIVE BOOK:

Maybe You Should Talk to Someone: A Therapist, Her Therapist, and Our Lives Revealed by Lori Gottlieb is an open and honest look at the therapy process that lays it out better than most depictions of therapy you're likely to come across. She starts out thinking she just needs a couple of sessions, but her conversations with Wendell make her see she could use more help than she realized. It may be tough medicine to swallow, but it also makes her a better therapist. She is even better able to understand the struggle some of her patients have in connecting the dots between their past and present, their problematic behaviors and the painful consequences, and being honest about things that don't put themselves in the best light. She makes it clear that your therapist is not there to tell you what to do, but to help you recognize how your own patterns might be causing you unnecessary pain. She is deeply committed to learning how to be better as a therapist and a patient. That is what we talk about when we talk about staying curious and having courage to keep standing up for yourself.

QUESTIONS FOR MEDITATION:

What stories do you tell yourself — big or small — that are probably holding you back in some way? It may take some time to consider because it's likely the stories are deeply embedded, and you have reasons to keep believing them.

"Pain is truth; all else is subject to doubt."

WHY I LOVE THIS QUOTE:
Pain, struggle, suffering, heartache, they get our attention. No wonder life has this perverse way of teaching us through hardship.

WHY THIS IS A TRANSFORMATIVE BOOK:
Waiting for the Barbarians is a novel by the South African-born Nobel laureate J.M. Coetzee. First published in 1980, the story is narrated in the first person by the unnamed magistrate of a small colonial town that exists as the territorial frontier of "the Empire." It is a classic in the field of postcolonial literature. The Magistrate's rather peaceful existence comes to an end with the Empire's declaration of a state of emergency and with the deployment of the Third Bureau — special forces of the Empire — due to rumors that the area's indigenous people, called "barbarians" by the colonists, might be preparing to attack the town.

Unable to stand as a mute witness to the horrendous abuse inflicted on innocent 'natives' on the false suspicion of their complicity with 'barbarians' or armed rebels who threaten the stability of the Empire, he clashes with the tyrannical administrator who represents the true face of any oppressor when divested of its sophistication. The results are as memorable as they are transformative and extreme.

QUESTIONS FOR MEDITATION:

What righteous cause are you committed to outside of yourself? Do you risk anything by making this commitment?

"Remember the small things, and the big things will work themselves out."

WHY I LOVE THIS QUOTE:

Remember the small kindnesses of strangers. Remember the ordinary love of your parents. If you keep perspective on the small things, then you turn your brain on to gratitude. Gratitude will help you face even the hardest, most unfathomable things. It begins with the small things, easily forgotten or overlooked.

WHY THIS IS A TRANSFORMATIVE BOOK:

The Tattooist of Auschwitz by Heather Morris is an unsettling, gripping novel, based on the true story of Lale, a Slovakian Jew caught up in the horrors of the Auschwitz-Birkenau concentration camp during World War 2. He speaks several languages, and soon finds himself employed in the camp as the tattooist, the man responsible for inscribing numbers on the prisoner's arms. He soon meets and falls in love with Gita, a fellow inmate, but can their love survive the horrors of life inside a concentration camp? This story shows the strength of the human spirit, and that there is always something to hope for.

QUESTIONS FOR MEDITATION:

In this time of so many unknowns in our world, what are some small things you are thankful for? What are some small things you are hopeful for?

august

"Although it's good to try new things and to keep an open mind, it's also extremely important to stay true to who you really are."

WHY I LOVE THIS QUOTE:

This point is well-taken. When we talk so much about encouraging breakthroughs, curiosity, and finding the courage to take action, there is another side to self-knowledge. We need to know when to establish healthy boundaries, both between others and within ourselves. When you do find yourself, sometimes you need to have the courage to stick with the knowledge and slowly and surely remain good at being yourself.

WHY THIS IS A TRANSFORMATIVE BOOK:

Eleanor Oliphant Is Completely Fine by Gail Honeyman is, on the one hand, a very funny novel about a socially-inept, twenty-nine year-old woman. Her attempts to become "normal" and integrate into society by having manicures and waxes are sources of hilarity. On the other hand, it is also sad. It's sad to see Eleanor's coworkers talking about her with Eleanor oblivious. She falls in love with the idea of a person, but in the end remains deeply alone. For all her quirks, she is a relatable character, even in her most extreme moments. The novel deals with serious subjects — child abuse and the growing epidemic of loneliness — without heavyhandedness, and also with insight and humor. Full of surprises, the character of Eleanor remains "who she is," and for all the sadness and issues there is loads of grace and resilience in the quirky character. Excellent storytelling, the themes of which embody the universal human experience.

QUESTIONS FOR MEDITATION:

What parts of yourself do you project onto others? What do your reactions say about you?

"Writers are really people who write books not because they are poor, but because they are dissatisfied with the books which they could buy but do not like."

WHY I LOVE THIS QUOTE:

I like how the expression is almost an outward manifestation of revealing who you are. There are the writers who write what they want to see. The idea applies to us in anything that we'd like to see in the world. "Be the change you want to see in the world," said Gandhi. But he goes on to say how cities reveal themselves through the books they offer, as well as individuals. "How many cities have revealed themselves to me in the marches I undertook in the pursuit of books!" and "You could tell a lot about a man by the books he keeps — his tastes, his interest, his habits."

WHY THIS IS A TRANSFORMATIVE TEXT:

Illuminations: Essays and Reflections by Walter Benjamin features studies on contemporary art and culture by one of the most original, critical and analytical minds of this century. The introductory essay by Hannah Arendt — who also did duty as editor of this wonderful collection — serves up her brilliant insight in categorizing Benjamin as a poetic mind who approached cultural and literary criticism in a unique manner, one that left a lasting influence upon those who followed in his wake. It is interesting how he presents the evolution of the purpose of art, how it morphed and changed from cultish function, oftentimes of a religious or social glue, to more the idea of "art for art's sake." He contends that many works of sublimity weren't in fact written for anyone. In the annals of our transformative texts, this one will indeed appeal more to our aesthetically-inclined friends.

QUESTIONS FOR MEDITATION:

What do your books say about you? If not your books, what does the content you consume say about you?

"The truth is, we only become secure in our convictions by allowing them to be challenged. Confident people don't get riled by opinions different from their own, nor do they spew bile online by way of refutation. Secure people don't decide others are irredeemably stupid or malicious without knowing who they are as individuals."

WHY I LOVE THIS QUOTE:
It does seem conclusive that when people are afraid to hear opinions other than the ones they are surrounded by they simply yell out what it is they already "know." They also tend to isolate themselves within the echo-chambers of others that think like them. The challenge is to break through the contempt opposing sides have for each other in the first place. The challenge is to find a place for dialogue over debate, and that tends to come from relationship in the first place.

WHY THIS IS A TRANSFORMATIVE TEXT:
You're Not Listening: What You're Missing and Why It Matters by Kate Murphy is an illuminating and often humorous deep dive into the difficult subject as to why we're not listening, what it's doing to us, and how we can reverse the trend. She does this through distilling the the psychology, neuroscience, and sociology behind it all.

As she writes, "People get lonely for lack of listening. Psychology and sociology researchers have begun warning of an epidemic of loneliness in the United States. Experts are calling it a public health crisis, as loneliness increases the risk of death as much as obesity, alcoholism, and heart disease combined."

QUESTIONS FOR MEDITATION:

What do you do about your need to be heard? Who listens to you? To whom do you speak?

"Everything that irritates us about others can lead us to an understanding of ourselves."

WHY I LOVE THIS QUOTE:
This simple statement can lead to numerous self insights. If you were to really ask yourself why something irritates you about another person you can learn a lot about yourself. It's not that it's necessarily negative either. Sometimes we're irritated for good reason. Sometimes not. Either way, it can be revelatory to penetrate into the sources of these irritations.

WHY THIS IS A TRANSFORMATIVE BOOK:
The Essential Jung: Selected Writings by Carl Jung is a well-organized anthology of Jung's own writings that touches on many of his most famous and important ideas, and approaches them in a mostly chronological method. Reading his own thoughts about personality types, religion, and the unconscious in his own words can be powerful, and not just how others interpret him through their own lenses. He also has a surprising amount of humor, a biting wit, and a way of bringing complex issues to light in a succinct way — at least sometimes. Anthony Storr's introductions to passages give pertinent background to set the stage for better understanding. You can really hear Jung's passion, see how he arrives at his insights, and get to know his brand of genius.

QUESTIONS FOR MEDITATION:

What would it mean to others if you were free from self-judgment? How do you think others would respond?

"I want to feel deeply, and whenever I am brokenhearted I emerge more compassionate. I think I allow myself to be brokenhearted more easily, knowing I won't be irrevocably shattered."

WHY I LOVE THIS QUOTE:
Spoken like a true master. When we build up the compassion muscle, we build up resilience as well. We can engage with the world with more courage, knowing that whatever we discover, whatever difficult truth about ourselves or others that we learn, we will integrate that with our identity and move forward as stronger and more compassionate still.

WHY THIS IS A TRANSFORMATIVE BOOK:
It's Easier Than You Think: The Buddhist Way to Happiness by Sylvia Boorstein provides readers with the benefit of her personal experience as a means to simplify Buddhist teachings. Boorstein is both a meditation teacher and a psychotherapist. She writes in a completely accessible style, using stories and anecdotes from her own life. A fellow well-known meditation instructor. She makes the point that even when we are struggling, most of us are still managing, sometimes even just somewhat gracefully. She teaches that Buddhism can help with this process, allowing us to manage life with just a bit more grace. Ideal for those brand new to Buddhist teachings and as gentle reminders for those familiar with such principles.

QUESTIONS FOR MEDITATION:

What do you long for now that you might say "yes" to if only you had the courage?

"Once you decide something put all your petty fears away. Your decision should vanquish them. I will tell you time and time again, the most effective way to live is as a warrior. Worry and think before you make any decision, but once you make it, be on your way free from worries or thoughts; there will be a million other decisions still awaiting you. That's the warrior's way."

WHY I LOVE THIS QUOTE:

If you worry over a decision, okay. That's well and good and fair enough. We probably should take our time most of the time. But if we inhabit the identity of being a warrior (as opposed to a worrier), then when we make a decision, we should move boldly. The idea that we should think of ourselves as warriors is compelling.

WHY THIS IS A TRANSFORMATIVE BOOK:

A Separate Reality is a profound book of philosophical meditations. In 1961, Carlos Castaneda, a young anthropologist, made his way to Mexico to learn more about Yaqui Indians and to do a little soul searching. What he found was a man named don Juan, a very powerful sorcerer and a force to be reckoned with. Don Juan turns Castaneda's whole world upside down through an extraordinary apprenticeship to bring back a fascinating glimpse of a Yaqui Indian's world of "non-ordinary reality" and the difficult and dangerous road a man must travel to become "a man of knowledge." Yet on the brink of that world, challenging to all that he believed, he drew back. In 1968, Castaneda returned to understand. He explains don Juan's teachings about the art of "seeing." Through the use of a hallucinogenic substance of don Juan's own creation Castaneda experiences visions that shake him to his very core.

QUESTIONS FOR MEDITATION:

What would it mean if you were to look your anxieties in the eye and tell them you are no longer willing to live with them?

"Life is an adventure to be embraced with an open mind and loving heart."

WHY I LOVE THIS QUOTE:

Whatever the struggles, this sounds like a pretty good starting point for everyone to consider as an approach to life. Life is an adventure, which means it's going to be full of mystery, wonder, doldrums, and setbacks. If we can keep our minds open and heart's loving we will experience greater empathy for one another and resilience in our own lives.

WHY THIS IS A TRANSFORMATIVE TEXT:

Girl, Woman, Other by Bernardine Evaristo is an amazing display of fictional structure and narrative intelligence, and co-winner of the 2019 Booker Prize. In the scarcity of literature portraying women of color, Evaristo's book stands out as a heartfelt contemplation of their experiences in modern times, generations after the abolishment of slavery, apartheid, and the advent of feminism.

As Tina Isaacs writes, "Evaristo's experimental style throws writing rules out the window — more 'telling than showing' and prose in stanza format. The fast-paced plot is delivered without linear chronology but never loses the reader's engagement. *Girl, Woman, Other* is definitely a case of 'know how to break the rules like a Pro'. As I delved deeper into the novel, I found myself on tether-hooks to find out how the different lives intersected. As it neared its conclusion, I was already planning a reread."

QUESTIONS FOR MEDITATION:

Which would you say is a greater strength of yours: a loving heart or an open mind?

"When the time comes to you at which you will be forced at last to utter the speech which has lain at the center of your soul for years, which you have, all that time, idiot-like, been saying over and over, you'll not talk about the joy of words. I saw well why the gods do not speak to us openly, nor let us answer. Till that word can be dug out of us, why should they hear the babble that we think we mean? How can they meet us face to face till we have faces?"

WHY I LOVE THIS QUOTE:
I remember the first time I read this as I completed the novel in the mid-90s and knew immediately how profound and eloquent it was. It has remained with me over the years as a perfect reminder of how we don't really know who we are. As a result, we don't really know how to become someone else because, again — we don't even know who we are.

WHY THIS IS A TRANSFORMATIVE BOOK:
Till We Have Faces, one of the lesser known of Lewis' fiction works, is a masterful retelling of the mythological story of Cupid and Psyche that paints a vivid picture of how selfish humanly love is, and to what extent we will go to protect it. The narrative transforms the heroine of the novel from the pitiable victim to the primary antagonist, and part of the narrative magic is that we slowly begin to realize that we are her, always pondering on our personal victimization. It's an excellent novel that speaks to how we, as humans, tend to see our own plight in life as the most dire, and perceive others as being part of our plight. It shows us how we are most likely the villains in a myriad of others' stories as much as the tragic hero of our own.

QUESTIONS FOR MEDITATION:

If there was a way for you to love every part of yourself unconditionally, could you do it?

"Part of the reason stopping seems like a death is that speed has become our core competency, our core identity. We do not know what powers we would be left with if we stopped doing what we were doing in the busy way we were doing it. Besides, there is a deeper, older human intuition at play that knows any real step forward comes through our pains and vulnerabilities, which is the reason we began to busy ourselves in the first place, so that we could stay well away from them. If we stopped, we could have to sojourn in areas that have nothing to do with getting things done but everything to do with being done to ourselves."

WHY I LOVE THIS QUOTE:
This is an unusually long quote for the reason that it keeps on giving. It takes us from the first powerful sentence of why it can be so hard to get off the merry-go-round, but it goes down the circuitous path as to insightfully explain why — or how — it happens. The truth is that the vulnerability itself — the folly — is the gateway toward self-understanding, and therefore more love and expansion.

WHY THIS IS A TRANSFORMATIVE BOOK:
Crossing the Unknown Sea: Work as a Pilgrimage of Identity by David Whyte is for anyone who wants to deepen their connection to their life's work — or find out what their life's work is — this book can help navigate the way. Whyte encourages you to take risks at work that will enhance your personal growth, and shows how burnout can actually be beneficial and used to renew professional interest.

QUESTIONS FOR MEDITATION:

At the end of my current job, how would I like to feel about myself?

"Suddenly the waters around them slowly swelled in broad circles then quickly upheaved, as if sideways sliding from a submerged berg of ice, swiftly rising to the surface. A low rumbling sound was heard; a subterrous hum; and then all held their breaths; as bedraggled with trailing ropes, and harpoons, and lances, a vast form shot length-wise, but obliquely from the sea. Shrouded in a thin drooping veil of mist, it hovered for a moment in the rainbowed air; and then fell swamping back into the deep. Crushed thirty feet upwards, the waters flashed for an instant like heaps of fountains, then brokenly sank in a shower of flakes, leaving the circling surface creamed like new milk round the marble trunk of the whale."

WHY I LOVE THIS QUOTE:

The quote shows off Melville's sensory style of observation and imagination. The sentences are dense, well-constructed, and bring you into what it describes better than even a film could replicate. Even if you're not into the aesthetics of the language, I see the whale as a profound symbol. The great whale refuses to hide. It will not be conquered, or if it is, it will take down its oppressor with it.

WHY THIS IS A TRANSFORMATIVE BOOK:

Moby-Dick or, *the Whale* by Herman Melville is the story of an eerily compelling madman pursuing an unholy war against a creature as vast and dangerous and unknowable as the sea itself. But more than just a novel of adventure, more than an encyclopedia of whaling lore and legend, the book can be seen as part of its author's lifelong meditation on America. Written with a redemptive humor, *Moby-Dick* is also a profound inquiry into character, faith, and the nature of perception.

QUESTIONS FOR MEDITATION:

What is your great whale?

"To dwell on the things that depress or anger us does not help in overcoming them. One must knock them down alone."

WHY I LOVE THIS QUOTE:

About his intellect or achievements, Einstein once said, "I have no special talent. I am only passionately curious." He also believed in the power of imagination and creativity, and this led Einstein to be unafraid when it came to upending established beliefs or questioning authority, and this probably was the key for him going the necessary step further with his theories than other scientists of his day. I love this quote because it encourages you to get unstuck if you're mired in a familiar landscape: that of being consumed by anger or depression. There is a way out but the answer begins from doing the inner work, and learning to let go.

WHY THIS IS A TRANSFORMATIVE BOOK:

Einstein: His Life and Universe by Walter Isaacson creates a vivid and engaging portrait of who Einstein was as a whole — both the brilliant and the quirky — and gives us a wonderful glimpse into how this man's amazing mind led to some of the most incredible scientific discoveries in history.

QUESTIONS FOR MEDITATION:

Am I aware of what is on my mind? Am I aware of how I'm feeling?

"What destroys us most effectively is not a malign fate but our own capacity for self-deception and for degrading our own best self."

WHY I LOVE THIS QUOTE:

This is a very similar thought to the narrator in C.S. Lewis' *Till We Have Faces* from a few days back. It's not fate or destiny or bad luck we should blame. It's our own fool self (as Huckleberry Finn might say). One doesn't want to come to the end of the road only to find one has deluded oneself all these years. Better to confront difficult truths and realities now while there is still time. We can read about what happens to people who don't through these literary representations if we'd like. And people say that fiction isn't the "truth" because it "didn't really happen." Serious literature exists because it did — and does — happen.

WHY THIS IS A TRANSFORMATIVE BOOK:

Adam Bede by George Eliot features minutely detailed empirical and psychological observations about illiterate "common folk" who, because of their greater proximity to nature than to culture, are taken as emblematic of human nature in its more pure form. So behind its humble appearance, this is a novel of great ambition, seeking to manifest a key principle of Wordsworth's aesthetic philosophy. Most say Middlemarch is Eliot's masterpiece, but the characters of her earlier Adam Bede are no less compelling.

QUESTIONS FOR MEDITATION:

In what ways have you tried to construct a life that is perfect? How has that worked out?

"My deepest belief is that to live as if we're dying can set us free. Dying people teach you to pay attention and to forgive and not to sweat the small things."

WHY I LOVE THIS QUOTE:

This quote, for some strange reason, reminds of the Coen brothers film, *A Serious Man*, which has a very Job-like feeling. Everything is going wrong for our protagonist and he keeps asking "Why?" He lectures on physics in front of a blackboard filled with bewildering equations that are mathematical proofs approaching certainty, but in his own life, what can be sure of? Very little. It's not just the small stuff, the big stuff is falling in around him from every direction. And, spoiler alert, it doesn't end well. But it's the kind of ending that leaves you a little unnerved by what it doesn't tell you. The overall point, and the connection here, is that life is short and you should live that way. If you really are tracking along in this reader, perhaps you're aware of the days passing one after the other. You're progressing, you're working on yourself, but you must be aware of how fast it passes. I certainly have in putting all these days and meditations together.

WHY THIS IS A TRANSFORMATIVE BOOK:

Bird By Bird: Some Instructions on Writing and Life by Anne Lamott is ostensibly about the art of writing, but really it too is about life and how to tackle the problems, temptations and opportunities life throws at us. It is a fun, disarming classic. The best chapter is "Shitty first drafts," which is also about mistakes in life.

QUESTIONS FOR MEDITATION:

How have you followed the script of others?

"Control the manner in which a man interprets his world, and you have gone a long way toward controlling his behavior."

WHY I LOVE THIS QUOTE:

Few other institutions as a whole probably understand this concept better than the media. All the more reason to collect our data from a wide variety of sources. The most important applicability here, however, is what this has to do with your personal transformation and fundamentally understanding with ever-growing clarity, who do you think you are?

WHY THIS IS A TRANSFORMATIVE BOOK:

Obedience to Authority by Stanley Milgram made several groundbreaking contributions to our understanding of human behavior. He was a master of particularly inventive research. Among other things, he devised the experimental method to investigate path lengths in social networks, establishing what is variously referred to as the Kevin Bacon effect or "six degrees of separation." He will always be remembered, however, as the man who conducted the "obedience studies," a controversial series of tests performed at Yale in the early 1960s. These experiments investigated the degree to which people could be persuaded to obey an authority figure who instructed them to perform cruel acts that conflicted with their personal conscience. The experiments were highly controversial, partly because of ethical questions raised by the study protocol, partly because the results were completely at variance with what psychologists had predicted (but that of course is why you conduct experiments in the first place).

QUESTIONS FOR MEDITATION:

Do you control the filters around you? Do you control others for that matter? How do you find them responding to you?

"Many people suffer from the fear of finding oneself alone, and so they don't find themselves at all."

WHY I LOVE THIS QUOTE:

It shouldn't be scary to spend time with ourselves, but for whatever the reasons, it certainly can be and often is. The readings from this book, and the design of the questions are intended to make it comfortable. We're cheering for you.

WHY THIS IS A TRANSFORMATIVE BOOK:

Man's Search for Himself: Signposts for Living and Personal Fulfillment was written in the 1950s by the great existential psychologist Rollo May, and it is still timely. May discusses the importance of becoming your own person, and how we find meaning within ourselves. He also talks about the struggle against dependency and taking responsibility for our own lives. May discusses the phenomenon of a person's inability to deal with his own condition of being alone, the anxiety that causes you to feel when being confronted with the reality of having to deal with your own exis-tence within your own context. The resulting fear, anxiety, and even panic of confronting this reality of being alone, or with people who do not want to face it when they call the state as loneliness. He draws his insights from Kierkegaard, Nietzsche and Kafka, whom he considers to have been influential on his thought with regards to the condition of humankind. He also integrated key psychodynamic concepts which are essential in the practice of therapy, case analyses, and so on.

QUESTIONS FOR MEDITATION:

Are you comfortable being alone? When you are alone how much time do you give to self-reflection, mindfulness or meditation practice?

"When we are no longer able to change a situation, we are challenged to change ourselves."

WHY I LOVE THIS QUOTE:
Frankl also expresses exasperation from people that say "What is the meaning of life?" as if someone else is supposed to answer the question for them. "You are supposed to answer the question," he says. You answer through your actions.

WHY THIS IS A TRANSFORMATIVE BOOK:
Man's Search for Meaning by Viktor Frankl has riveted generations with its descriptions of life in Nazi death camps — he survived three! — and its lessons for spiritual survival. Frankl teaches that we cannot avoid suffering but we can choose how to cope with it, find meaning in it, and move forward with renewed purpose. At the core of his theory, known as logotherapy, is a conviction that the primary human drive is not pleasure but the pursuit of what we find meaningful.

QUESTIONS FOR MEDITATION:

What actions can you control in your response to your current life situation? How do you respond to what you can't control?

"The only people for me are the mad ones, the ones who are mad to live, mad to talk, mad to be saved, desirous of everything at the same time, the ones who never yawn or say a commonplace thing, but burn, burn, burn like fabulous yellow roman candles exploding like spiders across the stars and in the middle you see the blue centerlight pop and everybody goes 'Awww!'"

WHY I LOVE THIS QUOTE:

You can certainly feel his passion for life, and curiosity to know the unknown. Comfortable people following the status quo get boring. Life has a way of dulling you when you stop questing. Keep asking questions. Keep growing. Just Kerouac also said, "Nothing behind me, everything ahead of me, as is ever so on the road."

WHY THIS IS A TRANSFORMATIVE BOOK:

Influenced by Jack London and Thomas Wolfe, Kerouac always wanted to be a writer, but his true voice only emerged when he wrote about his own experiences in On the Road. Leaving a broken marriage behind him, Sal Paradise (Kerouac) joins Dean Moriarty (Cassady), a tearaway and former reform school boy, on a series of journeys that takes them from New York to San Francisco, then south to Mexico. Hitching rides and boarding buses, they enter a world of hobos and drifters, fruit-pickers and migrant families, small towns and wide horizons. Adrift from conventional society, they experience America in the raw: a place where living is hard, but "life is holy and every moment is precious." With its smoky, jazz-filled atmosphere and its restless, yearning spirit of adventure, On the Road left its mark on the culture of the late 20th century, influencing countless books, films and songs. Kerouac's prose is remarkable both for its colloquial swing and for the pure lyricism inspired by the American landscape.

QUESTIONS FOR MEDITATION:

What important truth do very few people agree with you on?

"Learn everything. Fill your mind with knowledge — it's the only kind of power no one can take away from you."

WHY I LOVE THIS QUOTE:
In the book, Hansu never tells his son to study, but rather to learn. There is a marked difference. Learning was like playing to the boy, not work.

WHY THIS IS A TRANSFORMATIVE BOOK:
Pachinko by Min Jin Lee follows four generations of a Korean family who move to Japan amidst Japanese colonization and political warfare. The novel starts with Sunja, the beloved daughter of a poor yet well-respected family, whose unplanned pregnancy has the potential to bring great shame upon her life. After she learns that the baby's father already has a wife, she refuses to stay with him and instead marries a sickly and kind minister who moves with her to Japan. Throughout the novel we see the consequences of this choice, both through the joys of this family as they support and survive with one another, as well as the challenges and losses they experience as Korean immigrants in an unforgiving new country. Despite the persistent sexism and racism they experience, Lee shows how the perseverance of women, the strength within female friendships, and the power of individual action all can create and maintain love even under oppressive cultural conditions. Her characters adapt and strive and thrive and love one another amidst all of their hardships. In the book's acknowledgements, Lee shares that this story has been with her for almost 30 years.

QUESTIONS FOR MEDITATION:

How do you keep yourself curious? Would you call yourself a lifelong learner?

"To be aware of individuality is to realize that one has all that one needs. It also means that one needs all that one has, namely, that every psychic content and happening is meaningful."

WHY I LOVE THIS QUOTE:
I think what he is talking about here is that you are all you need to be a healthy and whole person. Of course we are social creatures, and very much in need of one another's support and community. In context, he is saying we need to be comfortable within ourselves. If we know ourselves, and are comfortable with who we are, we are also aware of what is happening in our consciousness, and understand its importance moment by moment. In order to achieve this, his premise goes, we must have a healthy integration of ego and self.

WHY THIS IS A TRANSFORMATIVE BOOK:
Ego and Archetype: Individuation and the Religious Function of the Psyche by Edward F. Edinger compares the life story of Jesus to the process of individuation and establishing a healthy ego-self axis. In the end he goes on to alchemy and this too continues what Christianity started — comparing union with God with the Philosopher's Stone. In short, the process of Christ's life on earth makes the con representative of the ego struggle. And God the father is representative of the self or soul.

QUESTIONS FOR MEDITATION:

Is it possible to be successful in the eyes of the world and achieve a healthy integration of ego and self?

"The desire is false when your personality wishes love and fulfillment, perfection and happiness, or pleasure and creative expansion without paying the price of the strictest self-confrontation."

WHY I LOVE THIS QUOTE:

This quote represents an important truth when it comes to the work of self-transformation. We often say that the work of the self begins with the self. Change your reality by changing you. Change your family systems by beginning with you. Change the way you interact with others by understanding yourself better, and also understanding the games people play (and how you choose to play them in return). But we don't often take the step back to warn against the very real possibility of self-absorption or navel-gazing. This statement says if you want these powerful realities in your life, you must be fiercely self-honest and courageous and willing to begin processes that reflect your self-understanding. It is hard work.

WHY THIS IS A TRANSFORMATIVE BOOK:

The Pathwork of Self-Transformation by Eva Pierrakos is the kind of book that really does contain the power to change your life, as well as the requirement to revisit it again and again. It's not the kind of book you just read through. You can study and meditate on the book, and assimilate the ideas into your life. Like with anything, though, timing is everything. You have to be ready. If you are, a teacher has appeared.

QUESTIONS FOR MEDITATION:

Do you ever feel an inner longing, one that even goes deeper than creative or emotional fulfillment?

"I have always believed that scientific research is another domain where a form of optimism is essential to success: I have yet to meet a successful scientist who lacks the ability to exaggerate the importance of what he or she is doing, and I believe that someone who lacks a delusional sense of significance will wilt in the face of repeated experiences of multiple small failures and rare successes, the fate of most researchers."

WHY I LOVE THIS QUOTE:

The ego is not always in the way. Sometimes, when it comes to perseverance in the face of terrible odds, we need some inflated sense of self-worth. When it comes to life-meaning and fulfillment, we need to believe in what we're doing, and sometimes what we're doing is hard. The ego can be like a machete, the blade we need to hack our way through the wilderness. Ironically enough, it's how we can sit there grinding against the hours working hard at what drives us.

WHY THIS IS A TRANSFORMATIVE BOOK:

Thinking, Fast and Slow by Daniel Kahneman is a lucid overview of research on how humans assess and navigate the world around them. Kahneman, a Nobel laureate, breaks our minds down to two parts, System 1 and System 2. System 1 is the one we use most of the time. It is intuitive, functions mainly on rules of thumb, and is essentially reactive. It applies to stereotypes, associative memories, and for anything sophisticated and counterintuitive is barely better than useless. System 2 is the part that applies analysis, considers new evidence, and wrestles with complexes. It comes into play usually when System 1 recognizes that it is in over its head, but otherwise doesn't play a major role in our cognitive lives.

QUESTIONS FOR MEDITATION:

What drives you, and why?

"To begin with clear and self-evident principles, to advance by timorous and sure steps, to review frequently our conclusions, and examine accurately all their consequences; though by these means we shall make both a slow and a short progress in our systems; are the only methods, by which we can ever hope to reach truth, and attain a proper stability and certainty in our determinations."

WHY I LOVE THIS QUOTE:

Hume argued powerfully that human reason is fundamentally similar to that of the other animals, founded on instinct rather than quasi-divine insight into things. It has served as a great corrective to any thought that lacks systematic substance. Basically the quote is saying, be sure how you start and take baby steps before you go asserting anything, but if done right, at least you'll have arrived somewhere new.

WHY THIS IS A TRANSFORMATIVE BOOK:

An Enquiry Concerning Human Understanding by David Hume is a fascinating exploration into the nature of human knowledge. Using billiard balls, candles, and other colorful examples, Hume conveys the core of his empiricism — that true knowledge can be gained only through sensory experience. No other philosopher has been at the forefront of the mind more than Hume. In physics, psychology, neuroscience, the connections to Hume are legion. Immanuel Kant confessed that this book awoke him from his "dogmatic slumber." He does appear to completely disregard a vital aspect of human consciousness: the possibility of gaining knowledge through contemplating the mind itself.

QUESTIONS FOR MEDITATION:

How do you know anything? How do you arrive at conclusions?

"By focusing on possibilities, you can see more than a potential light at the end of the tunnel. The light doesn't have to be at the end of the tunnel; it can illuminate an opportunity wherever you are."

WHY I LOVE THIS QUOTE:
I like this quote for a couple of reasons. The first is the idea of focusing on possibilities. How do you do that? How do you think about what could be? Visualize your desires. How do you want to feel? And the second part is that from this focus you don't have to be in a deep dark tunnel until you've arrived at some difficult and distant goal. The idea is that you can be present to your challenges and personal growth and remain alive to where you want to be.

WHY THIS IS A TRANSFORMATIVE BOOK:
Rewire Your Brain: Think Your Way to a Better Life by John B. Arden is a great addition to the field of neuroplasticity. It takes highly complex data and ideas, and communicates with simplicity and clarity. This is a book that you can refer to often as it has specific steps that you can keep in mind and try to put into action in order to "rewire" your brain. The brain isn't as hard-wired as once thought. It is actually "soft-wired." This book is for anyone with interest in the brain who wants to understand how to decrease anxiety or depression, improve memory, and resiliency and improve your engagement with others and in your own life.

QUESTIONS FOR MEDITATION:

Visualize your desires. How do you want to feel?

"Wherever you go, there you are."

WHY I LOVE THIS QUOTE:
I've used this phrase for decades, thinking it was a pop cultural saying or something. I had no idea its source. It's got this circuitous looping quality to it, and I've mostly used it on people who always seem to think they'll be happier at the next place. It's a great follow-up to the "grass is always greener." Another follow-up is to ask yourself where you would like to be in a few months or a year? Either way, you're going to "who you are," and you're going inhabit yourself. Would you like to have grown? Would you like to look back in wonder at how far you've come? Or would you like to remain right where you are?

WHY THIS IS A TRANSFORMATIVE BOOK:
The Imitation of Christ calls the reader to a life of intensity and discipline in following Christ. It's not comforting or particularly warm, and it makes no accommodations. What is philosophy, or science, or politics, or art, or culture for, if not to live well? Agree with all his theology or not, he was a Benedictine monk who wrote this around 1429, Thomas à Kempis illustrates that it is difficult, perhaps impossible to pick up your cross daily and truly live a life of self-denial. A rich and challenging book that in its own right could be read daily and meditated on for years.

QUESTIONS FOR MEDITATION:

Where are you, and where would you like to be?

"Only that which can change can continue."

WHY I LOVE THIS QUOTE:

Most people living well into their 80s, 90s, and 100s, tell us they continue to live with purpose. That's part of the process of self-growth and trans-formation, a constant curiosity and willingness to grow. As he also writes, "Because infinite players prepare themselves to be surprised by the future, they play in complete openness. It is not an openness as in candor, but an openness as in vulnerability. It is not a matter of exposing one's unchanging identity, the true self that has always been, but a way of exposing one's ceaseless growth, the dynamic self that has yet to be."

WHY THIS IS A TRANSFORMATIVE BOOK:

Finite and Infinite Games: A Vision of Life as Play and Possibility by James P. Carse is a brilliant thesis. The distinction between finite games and an infinite game is heuristically so powerful that once you've grasped it, it's hard to get it out of your mind. It's a lens through which you can assess almost all your actions. The nature of the game dictates that one is never at ease, always has to question oneself.

QUESTIONS FOR MEDITATION:

"A finite game is played for the purpose of winning, an infinite game for the purpose of continuing the play." What game are you playing?

"Look for people who have lots of great questions. Smart people are the ones who ask the most thoughtful questions, as opposed to thinking they have all the answers. Great questions are a much better indicator of future success than great answers."

WHY I LOVE THIS QUOTE:

This quote cuts to the heart of much of what we're exploring, teaching, meditating on throughout the course of these meditations. We're constantly trying to ask the right questions. Then, of course, comes the implementation challenge. You have to start somewhere, and questions are the answer.

WHY THIS IS A TRANSFORMATIVE BOOK:

Principles: Life and Work by Ray Dalio is a gamification of his life. He treats his failures as puzzles or missions where his goal is to reflect on the pain and get to the root of the problem. If he succeeds, he'd gain a gem in the form of a principle. He's compiled and shared his gems in this book. Harness the power of feedback, iteration, and improvement in response to failure. Simple to say. Hard to implement, and much of his efforts has gone into how to create systems, individually or for an organization, to make it more doable. For an individual, the challenge is primarily psychological — being able to reflect on your actions at a higher meta level than just doing the work itself, because you're always both the do-er and the manager.

QUESTIONS FOR MEDITATION:

What questions are you asking? What insights are you arriving at? What should you do to achieve what you want in light of what is true?

"Life will throw everything but the kitchen sink in your path, and then it will throw the kitchen sink. It's your job to avoid the obstacles. If you let them stop you or distract you, you're not doing your job, and failing to do your job will cause regrets that paralyze you more than a bad back."

WHY I LOVE THIS QUOTE:

It's hard not to be inspired by the warrior spirit of Agassi. Here he is reflecting on the crippling back pain he endured in the final years of his career.

WHY THIS IS A TRANSFORMATIVE BOOK:

Open by Andre Agassi, J.R. Moehringer is unique among sports memoirs. Why else would it be included here? Agassi brings a near-photographic memory to every pivotal match and every relationship. Never before has the inner game of tennis and the outer game of fame been so precisely limned. Alongside vivid portraits of rivals from several generations — Jimmy Connors, Pete Sampras, Roger Federer — Agassi gives unstinting accounts of his brief time with Barbra Streisand and his doomed marriage to Brooke Shields. He reveals a shattering loss of confidence. And he recounts his spectacular resurrection, a comeback climaxing with his epic run at the 1999 French Open and his march to become the oldest man ever ranked number one. In clear, taut prose, Agassi evokes his loyal brother, his wise coach, his gentle trainer, all the people who help him regain his balance and find love at last with Stefanie Graf.

As Daniel Audet writes, "The good, the bad and the ugly. It's all here. Truthfully told by a reluctant superstar with the heart of a lion and the soul of a champion. I can't recommend this book enough. You will reflect on your own life, all the way back to the beginning. The wins, the losses, the highs and the lows in life are best faced full on, with focus, and being ready - to return serve. Hit harder!"

QUESTIONS FOR MEDITATION:

If you were to achieve success what would it look like?

"Now is no time to think of what you do not have. Think of what you can do with what there is."

WHY I LOVE THIS QUOTE:
I love the pragmatic tenacity of the thought. Take this idea around with you wherever you go today.

WHY THIS IS A TRANSFORMATIVE BOOK:
The Old Man and the Sea by Ernest Hemingway is a tragic story of a Cuban fisherman in the Gulf Stream and the giant marlin he kills and loses — specifically referred to in the citation accompanying the author's Nobel Prize for literature in 1954. Two major themes are loneliness and recognition. You could say it builds upon Sartre's *The Other*, when the old man is fishing right in the middle of sea, the loneliness of human existence strikes him — a man may achieve insurmountable feats but he needs someone to share the feat. ("He looked around for the bird now because he would like him for company.") He develops a psychological association with the fish he has caught. In the end, it is a struggle for existence.

QUESTIONS FOR MEDITATION:

Today, how can you measure your worth and the value of your time?

"That of which we are not aware, owns us."

WHY I LOVE THIS QUOTE:
It's a simple distillation of some major ideas behind why we should continue to transform our lives on our own terms.

Hollis writes, "Psychological or spiritual development always requires a greater capacity in us for the toleration of anxiety and ambiguity. The capacity to accept this troubled state, abide it, and commit to life, is the moral measure of our maturity."

WHY THIS IS A TRANSFORMATIVE BOOK:
Finding Meaning in the Second Half of Life: How to Finally, Really Grow Up by James Hollis asks the question when do we finally get to say we've grown up? We assume that once we "get it together" with the right job, marry the right person, have children, and buy a home, all is settled and well. But as you know if you've done any of the readings of this reader, adulthood presents varying levels of growth, and is rarely the respite of stability we expected. He talks in depth and with perspicacity about certainty, fundamentalism, anxiety, and narcissism among many other topics critical to our age.

QUESTIONS FOR MEDITATION:

What does it really mean to be a grown up in today's world?

"But the most interesting thing that Franklin invented, and continually reinvented, was himself."

WHY I LOVE THIS QUOTE:
The idea of reinvention dovetails with many of the ideas expressed through-out this reader. It implies one is perpetually growing, that one learns from failures big and small, that one is bold and wise enough to understand one's standing among others. At one period in his life, Franklin had listed out the 13 moral virtues, and in 13-week cycles would dedicate a week to each one until he achieved "moral perfection." He found that it was best to attempt only one 13-week cycle per year, and then later every few years. The one virtue that gave him the most frustration was "order."

WHY THIS IS A TRANSFORMATIVE BOOK:
Benjamin Franklin: An American Life by Walter Isaacson makes clear, and he is quite convincing, that while Franklin had his faults, he was revered in his own time, accomplished as much or more than any other Founder, and deserves to be considered as one of America's most historically important statesmen. Franklin's personal creed was that doing good things for others was the ultimate form of religion. In life and in death (in his will he set up a trust fund for young tradesmen in Philadelphia and Boston) he practiced his religion dutifully.

QUESTIONS FOR MEDITATION:

What do you think is life's most important virtue? Are you living it out?

"The twisted paths leading to great discoveries are the rule rather than the exception."

WHY I LOVE THIS QUOTE:
This also reminds me of Steven Johnson's "adjacent principle." That leaps in progress almost never happen in giant leaps, but in sometimes vaguely connected, diagonal progressions that weren't really expected, and might only be a small step ahead. Innovation requires experimenting, which inevitably leads to failure, but it's also why we hear the need to be okay with failing so often preached. This quote says to me to keep experimenting with yourself and trying things out, you really have no idea where the next leap might happen.

WHY THIS IS A TRANSFORMATIVE BOOK:
Loonshots: How to Nurture the Crazy Ideas That Win Wars, Cure Diseases, and Transform Industries by Safi Bahcall draws on the science of phase transitions. Bahcall shows why teams, companies, or any group with a mission will suddenly change from embracing wild new ideas to rigidly rejecting them, just as flowing water will suddenly change into brittle ice. Mountains of print have been written about culture. *Loonshots* identifies the small shifts in structure that control this transition, the same way that temperature controls the change from water to ice. A fascinating shot into a range of current research.

QUESTIONS FOR MEDITATION:

Do you allow yourself freedom to know more about yourself through the time you allot yourself?

september

"To some people return to religion is the answer, not as an act of faith but in order to escape an intolerable doubt; they make this decision not out of devotion but in search of security."

WHY I LOVE THIS QUOTE:

We fear uncertainty and it is hard for us to tolerate doubt, especially about things that are effectively unknown. Therefore, many of us take Pascal's Wager — that is, we decide to join the tribe of believers and take comfort from those who seem to truly believe with the added benefit that if we are wrong there is nothing to be lost anyway. We simply die. If we are wrong about not believing when we ought to have the consequence of eternal damnation is pretty serious. People often come to religion as a kind of life insurance for the soul rather than as actually believing in faith.

WHY THIS IS A TRANSFORMATIVE BOOK:

Psychoanalysis and Religion explores the possibility of spiritual truth rather than negate it, even though Erich Fromm himself states clearly that he is not a "believer." Fromm lifts a lid off the "system" and its falsity which paves the way to a higher mysterious truth that is buried in most "mass organizations governed by a religious bureaucracy" as he puts it. It's an honest in depth look at it all rather than the usual way some people respond to religion these days which is to disregard them with superficial reasons rather than to dig deep into the psychology behind it all. When going beyond that psychology, the discovery is there must be more, but we never get it right in our human systems, which are often developed from fear and the need to control rather than faith which is an embracing of mystery that we will never fully have all the answers for.

QUESTIONS FOR MEDITATION:

Do you ever — or often — ask yourself what you really believe? Does it line up with your core values?

SEPTEMBER 2

"Leonardo had almost no schooling and could barely read Latin or do long division. His genius was of the type we can understand, even take lessons from. It was based on skills we can aspire to improve in ourselves, such as curiosity and intense observation. He had an imagination so excitable that it flirted with the edges of fantasy, which is also something we can try to preserve in ourselves and indulge in our children."

WHY I LOVE THIS QUOTE:
Our schools have been failing our kids for generations, maybe the entire history of public education in the U.S. We need to keep in mind just how far intense observation and curiosity can get you in life. Of course, da Vinci was a rebel in many respects, and incredibly gifted and driven. He's an outlier, but how can we take his inspiring story and instill parts of it into our own lives?

WHY THIS IS A TRANSFORMATIVE BOOK:
Leonardo da Vinci by Walter Isaacson loaded this volume with plates of Leonardo's artwork, but also of pages of his notebooks. Isaacson offers a thorough and highly informative piece that will educate the reader without inflating the narrative with scores of minute facts. Isaacson presents da Vinci in three distinct lights throughout this piece: the animated artist, the inquisitive inventor, and the abstract anatomist, all of which are interconnected and help to better understand the man whose name is synonymous with so many things. We have about 7,200 pages of Da Vinci's notebooks, about a quarter of what he wrote. These notebooks are filled with sketches of inventions few realized and most centuries ahead of their time, scribbles of ideas, doodles, and detailed drawings of his research into anatomy.

QUESTIONS FOR MEDITATION:

What are the things you're curious about?

"When I am attacked by gloomy thoughts, nothing helps me so much as running to my books. They quickly absorb me and banish the clouds from my mind."

WHY I LOVE THIS QUOTE:

Montaigne wrote this nearly 450 years ago, so his options were a little more limited than they are for us today, and books mean something different to us than to him. Nevertheless, we should have our sources of pleasure that come from the invested efforts of others to understand, to seek, to know our world a little better. This reader emphasizes the potential of meditation, mindfulness, and reading. These aren't the only ways to find calm and clear the mind, just two potent approaches.

WHY THIS IS A TRANSFORMATIVE BOOK:

Essays by Michel de Montaigne speak to us from across centuries in a modern voice that is never completely certain about the big questions, and that has a kind of intimacy. He's rarely concerned with seeing a thought through to its end in some systematic way. He doesn't bluster his way through his lack of knowledge, but faces it head-on with disarming cheerfulness. His arguments meander conversationally in a way that is completely unlike other writers of the time. You can enjoy these essays bit by bit, almost like talking to a good friend. In that way, Montaigne comes alive on the page. He is more interesting as a daily companion who is going to tell you about what is on his mind and the intimate details of his life, as well as his opinions and philosophies on everything from horsemanship to doctors to science to sex to his bowel movements and habits. If you approach them the right way, there is a great steady joy in Montaigne. His essays were exploratory journeys in which he works through logical steps to bring skepticism to what is being discussed.

QUESTIONS FOR MEDITATION:

Where do you turn to clear your mind, find calm, and "banish the clouds"?

"The attentions of others matter to us because we are afflicted by a congenital uncertainty as to our own value, as a result of which affliction we tend to allow others' appraisals to play a determining role in how we see ourselves. Our sense of identity is held captive by the judgements of those we live among."

WHY I LOVE THIS QUOTE:

This quote is good because it reminds us that a lot of our behavior is dictated by a vague sense (or perhaps a clear one) of what others are going to think about our actions. It is inevitable that we do this to some extent, but if it motivates too much of our behavior, or if our goals of how we set ourselves apart are directed at superficial things, we will suffer from anxiety regardless of our successes.

WHY THIS IS A TRANSFORMATIVE BOOK:

Status Anxiety by Alain de Botton reminds us that certain achievements and possessions do not give us the enduring satisfaction we believe they will. No sooner do we achieve some goal (if we are able to attain it at all), than we are met all over again with anxiety and desire. This has been proven and discussed with increasing interest and research over the past several decades as anxiety — social and otherwise — continues to rise seemingly exponentially. When we get an opportunity to do something prestigious, we're enormously flattered and pleased with ourselves, but why? Because we have a perception of being special and "above" many others. We need hierarchies. We need status places so as to know how to assess ourselves in comparison to others. Also, research shows we do not form our self assessments based on our standing in the world, but on our immediate circle, those in the same boat as ourselves. What matters is how well you did amongst the peers in your immediate group.

QUESTIONS FOR MEDITATION:

In what ways do you try to achieve status? Have you ever considered what's behind your motivation? Is it simply because you want to be known and heard? Is it because status would validate you? Is it necessarily good or bad one way or the other?

"Man will always do the thing which will bring him the MOST mental comfort — for that is THE SOLE LAW OF HIS LIFE."

WHY I LOVE THIS QUOTE:

According to Twain, we function out of selfishness one way or another. We do what makes us feel good above higher-level sensibilities like morality. There is a way to do good, however, even while only doing what makes you feel good: "Diligently train your ideals upward and still upward toward a summit where you will find your chiefest pleasure in conduct which, while contenting you, will be sure to confer benefits upon your neighbor and the community."

WHY THIS IS A TRANSFORMATIVE BOOK:

What is Man? by Mark Twain demolishes the illusion of self-sacrifice, benevolence and charity as chief motivating principles behind people's behavior. You have an inborn temperament which demands to be satisfied in its own way. If you can secure your mental comfort and self approval by doing good or even evil, you will carry out that act at any cost. According to Twain, "They follow the law of their make." Whether good or evil, that's the way they are. "It does no more and no less than the law of its make permits and compels it to do. There is nothing PERSONAL about it," he says. I've read a good bit of Twain over the years. His wit and apho-ristic style marked with his variety and seriousness makes him an author for the ages. This is a strange book in many respects, and one that Twain kept locked in his drawer for years and decided not to have published until after his death. It is added among the several hundred others in this reader as one to consider for its insights into human behavior and for its potential at stirring up opinions about what he really means. Are his opinions dated, or do they stand the test of time?

QUESTIONS FOR MEDITATION:

What motivates the work you do? Is it purely selfish, even when you do good for others?

"In other words, change is situational. Transition, on the other hand, is psychological. It is not those events, but rather the inner reorientation and self-redefinition that you have to go through in order to incorporate any of those changes into your life. Without a transition, a change is just a rearrangement of the furniture. Unless transition happens, the change won't work, because it doesn't 'take.'"

WHY I LOVE THIS QUOTE:
Whether you choose it or it is thrust upon you, change brings both opportunities and turmoil.

WHY THIS IS A TRANSFORMATIVE BOOK:
Transitions: Making Sense of Life's Changes by William Bridges takes readers step by step through the three stages of any transition: The Ending, The Neutral Zone, and, eventually, The New Beginning. Bridges explains how each stage can be understood and embraced, leading to meaningful and productive movement into a hopeful future. This book is a classic in its subject area, and has gone through an astounding 41 printings to date. It's brilliantly insightful and pragmatic at the same time. Great for individuals and business cultures.

QUESTIONS FOR MEDITATION:

Do you navigate change well? Do you embrace change? Do you resist it? If you embrace it, do you like change for its own sake, or do you seek it as a way to grow? If you resist it, how can you better prepare for the inevitability of change?

"Meditation is not about feeling a certain way. It's about feeling the way you feel."

WHY I LOVE THIS QUOTE:

Meditation is about becoming more aware of how you are actually feeling. It's about listening to your mind and body. It has enormous power for changing your perspective on reality, developing resilience, and gaining control over what would otherwise be "unconscious," reflexive-like emotional responses. Meditation, especially through the mindfulness approach that Harris favors, can also help with things like willpower. Willpower doesn't ask you to ignore the habit you want to break. Your brain will grow weary of trying to ignore it. Instead, you should look at it. You should look at the thing you want in your mind's eye as neutrally as possible. Over time it disempowers the source of anxiety, and strengthens your resolve. All of these things are related to acknowledging and accepting what is going on within.

WHY THIS IS A TRANSFORMATIVE BOOK:

10% Happier: How I Tamed the Voice in My Head, Reduced Stress Without Losing My Edge, and Found Self-Help That Actually Works by Dan Harris is a funny book about one highly successful and ambitious man's journey to grow himself up. It's a good read for those who, like Harris, are skeptical of the self-help genre claims. In truth, most of the claims are the stuff of marketers hyping their "content." Somewhere within many of these works, however, are truths. Harris traces his journey and comes to some realizations about meditation and mindfulness. He finds a form of meditation that works for him and puts it into practice. How he goes about this is often hilarious, particularly when he is so transparent about his resistance while he attempts to keep focused during a lengthy meditation retreat.

QUESTIONS FOR MEDITATION:

If you want success — and freedom from the constraints in front of you right now — what can you do about it on a daily basis?

"The purpose of learning to work with the unconscious is not just to resolve our conflicts or deal with our neuroses. We find there a deep source of renewal, growth, strength, and wisdom. We connect with the source of our evolving character; we cooperate with the process whereby we bring the total self together; we learn to tap that rich lode of energy and intelligence that waits within."

WHY I LOVE THIS QUOTE:

Perhaps one of the most succinct summaries of why there is such a thing as the "inner work" and why you stand so much to gain by paying attention to it.

WHY THIS IS A TRANSFORMATIVE BOOK:

Inner Work: Using Dreams and Active Imagination for Personal Growth by Robert A. Johnson provides a practical approach for working with dreams, and it also details the process of active imagination. This book is about as practical as a book on dreams can be. As he writes, "Once we become sensitive to dreams, we discover that every dynamic in a dream is manifesting itself in some way in our practical lives." Our egos divide the world into positive and negative, good and bad. Most aspects of our shadows, these qualities that we see as "negative," could be valuable strengths if we make them conscious. Only you will be able to say what part of you is represented by this symbol if it appears in your dream — it is your own unconscious that holds the clues. Since that inner person is part of you, its qualities are also yours. So long as you are facing your negative and immature traits squarely, you also have a duty to acknowledge the healthy qualities in yourself, and to live them consciously.

QUESTIONS FOR MEDITATION:

Have you tried to eliminate awkwardness, vulnerability, overlook ineptness, all in an attempt to make you more lovable?

"There's still time to change things."

WHY I LOVE THIS QUOTE:

Of the many powerful quotes from this collection, this one by Siri Hustvedt from *The Blazing World* stands out as a great summary. Absolutely wherever you are right now, whatever wreckage you've left behind, there is still time to change. This reader is all about the concept, and so is Out of the Wreck I Rise. It's a journey. It's a process you never finish, just like meditating and reading and guides that help you do both.

WHY THIS IS A TRANSFORMATIVE BOOK:

Out of the Wreck I Rise: A Literary Companion to Recovery edited by Neil Steinberg and Sara Bader is a collection of very short quotations from a remarkable number of literary sources which bear upon the process of getting better after active addiction. There are no books quite like this. The person in recovery looks for support wherever it may be found, and the stories of other people in recovery. This book has the potential to be a source of strength, hope, encouragement, and even humor to the recovering addict or alcoholic.

QUESTIONS FOR MEDITATION:

What is your plan to overcoming an addiction? Is it enough to remove the triggers? Do you think you need others to help you, or could you do it on your own if you decided you really wanted it?

"We're all bastards, but God loves us anyway."

WHY I LOVE THIS QUOTE:

This was Will Campbell's response to an avowed atheist who asked him to define Christianity in 10 words. Campbell distills the message into one of sweeping grace and the widespread chance for atonement for everyone. This may be more of a challenge than meets the eye because it means loving our enemies and believing in their redemption too, and in polarized times such as these it's hard to see the redemptive qualities in the opposition.

WHY THIS IS A TRANSFORMATIVE BOOK:

Brother to a Dragonfly by Will Campbell is a memoir of two brothers who grew up poor in rural Mississippi in the 1930s. They idolize each other but take different paths. Will became a Baptist minister, highly educated, and very active in the early years of the Civil Rights Movement. His older brother Joe became a pharmacist who abused and became dependent on the pills he was handing out. The brothers helped and defended each other all their lives. It's an honest story of love and family devotion. But what makes this book special is that it's also a story of the South that the author knows and loves, and the questioning of things he had always believed, including his evolving views on what he once believed, and how best to minister to people while leaving the church behind. This book is guaranteed to make you think, about family and relationships, about religion, about race, about human nature itself. And it is sure to offend almost everyone who reads it at one point or another because of it's honesty.

QUESTIONS FOR MEDITATION:

What are you, or are you not, doing that you would like to change in terms of making your beliefs line up with your actions? How do you continue to evolve with an open mind to new ideas while holding true to principles you've always believed are right?

"And this I believe: that the free, exploring mind of the individual human is the most valuable thing in the world. And this I would fight for: the freedom of the mind to take any direction it wishes, undirected. And this I must fight against: any idea, religion, or government which limits or destroys the individual. This is what I am and what I am about."

WHY I LOVE THIS QUOTE:

It is that very liberty which makes America (and any free democracy) great. The rights of the individual to choose not to explore the mind, to choose what is against the "free exploration" of the mind and liberties of others, also makes it so uneven and sometimes dangerous. They are ideals put before us, which we must aspire to live up to.

WHY THIS IS A TRANSFORMATIVE BOOK:

East of Eden is the work in which John Steinbeck created his most mesmerizing characters and explores his most enduring themes: the mystery of identity, the inexplicability of love, and the murderous consequences of love's absence. A masterpiece of Steinbeck's later years, the book is a powerful and vastly ambitious novel that is at once a family saga and some suggest a modern retelling of the Book of Genesis (I see that in certain respects). Steinbeck has to be counted as one of the top American writers of the 20th century. Like many people I had read *Of Mice and Men, The Grapes of Wrath* and, like fewer people, I loved *Tortilla Flat, Sweet Thursday, Cannery Row,* and to a lesser extent, *In Dubious Battle,* but had never gotten around to *East of Eden.* Steinbeck considered it his best work. Many critics argue that it is the pinnacle of his work. I don't disagree.

QUESTIONS FOR MEDITATION:

How are you going to keep your mind active and alert today?

"The precise person you are now is fleeting, just like all the other people you've been. That feels like the most unexpected result, but it is also the most well documented."

WHY I LOVE THIS QUOTE:

It's unlikely you'll want to do the same thing you're doing now all the rest of the days of your life. Enjoy what you're interested in now. Explore. Try new things. Fail fast. Gather information and experiences. Don't judge yourself too harshly because you didn't become a world class chess player or cyclist or tennis star. Those people aren't usually happier people anyway.

WHY THIS IS A TRANSFORMATIVE BOOK:

Range: Why Generalists Triumph in a Specialized World by David Epstein is a mythbuster against the idea that you have to know your thing at an early age, put in your 10,000 hours of deliberate practice, in order to become world class in your discipline. This book says forget all of that. Try lots of things, read broadly, and fail. Specialization is boring, and not particularly fruitful, and not the path of even most who succeed. You may need to bring your focus to bear once you do know what your "thing" is, but the truth of the matter is that most of us don't know, especially at an early age. Not only that, but hyper-focus at an early age on one thing makes you less adaptive for change as an adult. Those who tried many things and are just "pretty good" at a broader range of activities are loaded with those experiences. They're more adaptive and tend to do better as adults.

QUESTIONS FOR MEDITATION:

Who do you want to be right now? What's stopping you?

"To let go means to give up coercing, resisting, or struggling, in exchange for something more powerful and wholesome which comes out of allowing things to be as they are without getting caught up in your attraction to or rejection of them, in the intrinsic stickiness of wanting, of liking and disliking."

WHY I LOVE THIS QUOTE:

The idea behind trying to achieve calm is ultimately to become more adaptive and resilient. You're not going to be impervious to emotions, but you're going to be able to observe your emotions more readily when you feel them taking you where you don't want to go.

WHY THIS IS A TRANSFORMATIVE BOOK:

Wherever You Go, There You Are: Mindfulness Meditation in Everyday Life by Jon Kabat-Zinn provides tangible steps to improve your mindfulness, including practicing voluntary simplicity, doing non-doing, focusing on your breath, and appreciating each moment. While these actions might seem a little far-fetched or impractical if you've never tried it much before, Kabat-Zinn writes about them in thoughtful and intelligent ways. He gives practical applications alongside his more theoretical passages, and he also zones in on alternative ways to meditate based on your specific life circumstances. This is a good starter if you've only now decided that you might give this meditation thing a try. He's deep, but practical and simple.

As Dan Harris writes, "I think this guy may go down as a historical figure. He was the prime mover in turning meditation into a mainstream, secular, scientifically tested way to rewire your brain for happiness. This is a great book for beginners and the curious."

QUESTIONS FOR MEDITATION:

Are you ready for deeper life fulfillment? If not, what do you think is holding you back (that you're aware of). If so, what next step do you need to take to make fulfillment and expansion a reality?

"Read not to contradict and confute; nor to believe and take for granted; nor to find talk and discourse; but to weigh and consider. Some books are to be tasted, others to be swallowed, and some few to be chewed and digested: that is, some books are to be read only in parts, others to be read, but not curiously, and some few to be read wholly, and with diligence and attention."

WHY I LOVE THIS QUOTE:
The suggested readings from this reader probably fall into all the categories above, but most of all the latter. Take your time. Be consistent and persistent. Growth will happen.

WHY THIS IS A TRANSFORMATIVE BOOK:
In *The Essays*, Francis Bacon considers a diverse range of subjects: death and marriage, ambition and atheism, in rich and vibrant Renaissance prose. Bacon believed that rhetoric — the force of eloquence and persuasion — could lead the mind to the pure light of reason, and coupled with his great erudition, this may be some explanation as to why so many have suggested he is the real person behind Shakespeare's plays. He seems to have been a believing Christian, but he was impatient with the erudite ratiocination of the medieval Schoolmen and their idolization of Aristotle. Practical and empirical in his thinking, his ethical views show the influence of the Stoics virtue and resilience blended with some Machiavellian cunning. This book, like many of the recommendations herein, requires patience, but rewards the patient reader with mature wisdom.

QUESTIONS FOR MEDITATION:

What story would your books say about you?

Why do you read?

"Real adventure is defined best as a journey from which you may not come back alive, and certainly not as the same person."

WHY I LOVE THIS QUOTE:

This is where courage needs to be a part of the process. No one said transformation would be easy, right? If it was easy everyone would do it. It's hard. There will be something at stake. Win, lose, or draw, you will be changed from the experience. As he says, "A master in the art of living draws no sharp distinction between his work and his play; his labor and his leisure; his mind and his body; his education and his recreation. He hardly knows which is which. He simply pursues his vision of excellence through whatever he is doing, and leaves others to determine whether he is working or playing. To himself, he always appears to be doing both."

WHY THIS IS A TRANSFORMATIVE BOOK:

Let My People Go Surfing: The Education of a Reluctant Businessman by Yvon Chouinard, the legendary climber, businessman, environmentalist, and founder of Patagonia, shares the persistence and courage that have gone into being head of one of the most respected and environmentally responsible companies on earth. From his youth as the son of a French Canadian blacksmith to the thrilling, ambitious climbing expeditions that inspired his innovative designs for the sport's equipment, this book is the story of a man who brought doing good and having grand adventures into the heart of his business life. He stuck to his principles. He didn't compromise. He inculcated a culture that was authentic and distinctive. He's got quite a story.

QUESTIONS FOR MEDITATION:

Do you see work and play as a natural part of who you are and what you do? If not, is the disconnect troubling to you? How do you frame it to yourself?

"All human wisdom is contained in these two words — Wait and Hope."

WHY I LOVE THIS QUOTE:

We come across a lot of carpe diem sentiments in the books we've explored, and there's good reason for it. We need encouragement from wherever we can get it to move forward, to get unstuck, to take risks. Sometimes, however, we have to bide our time. Sometimes we have to count on the right timing and simply prepare for the next action. Meanwhile, we also need to hold onto the idea that it will get better. Things will improve. We will grow. Maybe you're doing all the right things. Maybe you're tracking good habits and taking down bad ones. Maybe you're growing, but for now you're not sure to what end. That's okay. Just keep knocking.

WHY THIS IS A TRANSFORMATIVE BOOK:

The Count of Monte Cristo by Alexandre Dumas is about Edmond Dantes, confined to the grim fortress of If for a crime he did not commit. There he learns of a great hoard of treasure hidden on the Isle of Monte Cristo, and he becomes determined not only to escape, but also to unearth the treasure and use it to plot the destruction of the three men responsible for his incarceration. Dumas' epic tale of suffering and retribution, inspired by a real-life case of wrongful imprisonment, was a huge popular success when it was first serialized in the 1840s.

It's a surprisingly compelling narrative to this day, and its themes are big, like: Why are good people so often punished by horrible tragedies when execrable people are so often able to float through life with all the rewards? Also, is it revenge or something else? Dantes spends much of his life after prison seeking the people who tossed into the oubliette. He thinks of it not as revenge, but divine retribution. He believes he has been freed from prison so he can do God's will.

QUESTIONS FOR MEDITATION:

Do you believe you are not prepared to take a leap of faith when the time is right? Do you think you'll know when the time is right?

"The greatest hazard of all, losing one's self, can occur very quietly in the world, as if it were nothing at all. No other loss can occur so quietly; any other loss — an arm, a leg, five dollars, a wife, etc. — is sure to be noticed."

WHY I LOVE THIS QUOTE:

It's so true, and so startling the way you can lose yourself, and all the while think you know perfectly well who you are and what's going on and that you are more or less doing things of your own free choice. Until, that is, something forces you to change your perspective, or occasionally, even without great disruption, you come to realize it of your own accord, perhaps through meditation and reading. Yesterday's questions were about hope and patience. Today, we bring you despair.

WHY THIS IS A TRANSFORMATIVE BOOK:

The Sickness Unto Death: A Christian Psychological Exposition for Upbuilding and Awakening by Søren Kierkegaard is a companion piece to The Concept of Anxiety. This work continues Kierkegaard's radical analysis of human nature in a spectrum of possibilities of existence. He moves beyond anxiety on the mental-emotional level to the spiritual level, where—in contact with the eternal—anxiety becomes despair. Both anxiety and despair reflect the misrelation that arises in the self when the elements of the synthesis—the infinite and the finite—do not come into proper relation to each other. Despair is a deeper expression for anxiety and is a mark of the eternal, which is intended to penetrate temporal existence. In other words, it's good to get to despair because it means you're getting somewhere.

QUESTIONS FOR MEDITATION:

How is your work or life situation causing you reason for complacency? Is it life satisfaction you're feeling, or something else?

"What we resist persists, and what we accept, we can transform."

WHY I LOVE THIS QUOTE:

If you feel the beginnings of a panic attack, respond to those initial waves of anxiety with a "so what, whatever." You're safe. Your body can handle it. As the waves increase, accept and allow all the uncomfortable anxious thoughts and sensations to just be. Don't resist them. Bob up and down with them. Repeat to yourself, "I accept and allow this anxious feeling." If a wave of anxiety peaks into a panic attack, run toward it. Tell yourself that you feel excited and then call fear's bluff by demanding more. Ride up and over the wave of adrenaline. Once the initial flood of adrenaline has passed, understand that there may be a few more minor waves of adrenaline.

WHY THIS IS A TRANSFORMATIVE BOOK:

Dare: The New Way to End Anxiety and Stop Panic Attacks Fast by Barry McDonagh uses empathy and insights from his own experiences into his encouraging style for a relatively quick and easy to read, at least in comparison to many of our selections. He explains the DARE Response in simple steps and explains how, where, and when to utilize them. McDonagh teaches you to have confidence and love for yourself which are both essential to recover from anxiety.

QUESTIONS FOR MEDITATION:

What do you resist? Do you accept the possibility that you can transform your response?

"In the wild struggle for existence, we want to have something that endures, and so we fill our minds with rubbish and facts, in the silly hope of keeping our place."

WHY I LOVE THIS QUOTE:
It says something about our own view of existence, and our naivete, as transient as it is, that we want "something that endures." It's true enough, and hasn't changed in the 130+ years since this novel was published. We live in shallow and anxious times still. We hold on to that which is passing and trivial as if it were to ground us in something important here and now, but it is all going to be replaced by tomorrow's cute cat YouTube video, or the latest hot topic on the 24-hour newscycle.

WHY THIS IS A TRANSFORMATIVE BOOK:
The Picture of Dorian Gray by Oscar Wilde is the story of a fashionable young man who sells his soul for eternal youth and beauty. The tale of Dorian Gray's moral disintegration caused a scandal when it first appeared in 1890, but though Wilde was attacked for the novel's corrupting influence, he responded that there is, in fact, "a terrible moral in Dorian Gray." Just a few years later, the book and the aesthetic-moral dilemma it presented became issues in the trials occasioned by Wilde's homosexual liaisons, which resulted in his imprisonment. Dorian Gray was a character who was vapid internally. He begins so young and full of potential, but invests all his sense of worth in his external beauty, and does nothing to grow the inner man. His mentor Lord Henry teaches him that experience has no value, yet he is strangely curious as to how they will affect his soul. He's tragic in a sense, but it's hard to feel sorry for his choices, and his lack of taking responsibility for himself. A fascinating piece of late Victorian literature and also notable for Wilde's prose style.

QUESTIONS FOR MEDITATION:

How do you spend your time on things you do think will endure? What can you do today that will pay dividends tomorrow?

"For me, running is both exercise and a metaphor. Running day after day, piling up the races, bit by bit I raise the bar, and by clearing each level I elevate myself. At least that's why I've put in the effort day after day: to raise my own level. I'm no great runner, by any means. I'm at an ordinary — or perhaps more like mediocre — level. But that's not the point. The point is whether or not I improved over yesterday. In long-distance running the only opponent you have to beat is yourself, the way you used to be."

WHY I LOVE THIS QUOTE:

Murakami's dedication to running every day, just like his dedication to writing, comes from his belief that maintaining consistency in anything you do will lead to accomplishing the goals you are seeking. This is not to say that there won't be fears to be faced, injuries, delays, or frustrations, but that's part of the experience.

WHY THIS IS A TRANSFORMATIVE BOOK:

What I Talk About When I Talk About Running by Haruki Murakami is equal parts training log, travelogue, and reminiscence. In 1982, having sold his jazz bar to devote himself to writing, Murakami began running to keep fit. A year later, he'd completed a solo course from Athens to Marathon, and now, after dozens of such races, not to mention triathlons and a dozen critically acclaimed books, he reflects upon the influence the sport has had on his life and — even more important — on his writing. Through this lens of sport and dedication emerges a panorama of memories and insights: the eureka moment when he decided to become a writer, his triumphs and disappointments, his passion for vintage LPs, and the experience, after fifty, of seeing his race times improve and then fall back. Murakami does not make any claims about how running has completely transformed his life. He is simply sharing his thoughts on running, and the profound impact it can have on a person without even realizing it.

QUESTIONS FOR MEDITATION:

What do you work at step by small step, brick by brick, that you stick with? What are you most consistent at?

"I don't like work — no man does — but I like what is in the work — the chance to find yourself. Your own reality — for yourself not for others — what no other man can ever know. They can only see the mere show, and never can tell what it really means."

WHY I LOVE THIS QUOTE:

It's true, we don't "like" sitting down and working hard at something for hours on end when we could be riding a bike, walking along a coast, reading a good book, watching a movie, talking idly with our friends, and so forth. But what we like is the "indirect" fruits of our labor, the identity that emerges step by step, hour by hour, as a result of our concentrated effort.

WHY THIS IS A TRANSFORMATIVE BOOK:

Heart of Darkness by Joseph Conrad is a slim volume with massive implications. The "immense darkness" is simultaneously the real unknown of the jungle, as well as the symbolic "darkness" that hides within the human heart. But then it is also something that pervades society — so the narrator has been made aware that London, just upstream, really should be understood to be as frightening as the Congo. For all the difficulties with the racism issues within the text, one thing is undeniable: Conrad does provide a harsh critique for colonialism. That cannot be ignored. Firstly, it is detrimental to the colonized. The Westerners exploit the tribes for their ivory and ship it back home. They take the wealth of the tribe folk, rouse their wrath and cause war between neighboring villages. All in all, they shape the culture of the colonized by destroying it. It provides an image of a society totally obsessed with monetary wealth, and how much they can gain through the evils of Imperialism.

QUESTIONS FOR MEDITATION

What have you learned about yourself through work that you didn't think you'd like at first?

"In the murky water of the aquarium, furtive shadows pass — an undulation whose vague existence dissolves of its own accord...and afterward it is questionable whether there had been anything to begin with. But the dark patch reappears and makes two or three circles in broad daylight, soon coming back to melt, behind a curtain of algae, deep in the protoplasmic depths. A last eddy, quickly dying away, makes the mass tremble for a second. Again everything is calm...Until, suddenly, a new form emerges and presses its dream face against the glass."

WHY I LOVE THIS QUOTE:

That is our consciousness and this is our world. We are sure that we know everything about the world we live in but we're just wandering the labyrinths of our own misconceptions.

WHY THIS IS A TRANSFORMATIVE BOOK:

The Erasers by Alain Robbe-Grillet was the author's first novel. The combination of detailed visual description and vagueness in most other respects is a hallmark of the nouveau roman, which he virtually invented. That staircase will come back in the book again and again, in different contexts, often mutually contradictory. The entire novel is a web of simple acts and shape-shifting repetitions. Robbe-Grillet takes the conventions of the policier or French detective novel and turns them on their head. You might think that the genre is a model of logical deduction, a chain of clues leading to the inevitable denouement. But Robbe-Grillet goes his own way. The narrative spans a 24-hour period following a series of eight murders in eight days, presumably the work of a terrorist group. After the ninth murder, the investigation is turned over to a police agent, who may in fact be the assassin. Thematically, it could be said to be an erasing of values.

QUESTIONS FOR MEDITATION:

What are you curious about? Have you ever pursued your curiosities? When was the last time you did? Did it get you into trouble? Were there unexpected surprises?

"Those who are in ideology believe themselves by definition outside ideology: one of the effects of ideology is the practical denegation of the ideological character of ideology by ideology: ideology never says, 'I am ideological'. It is necessary to be outside ideology, i.e. in scientific knowledge, to be able to say: I am in ideology (a quite exceptional case) or (the general case): I was in ideology. As is well known, the accusation of being in ideology only applies to others, never to oneself (unless one is really a Spinozist or a Marxist, which, in this matter, is to be exactly the same thing). Which amounts to saying that ideology has no outside (for itself), but at the same time that it is nothing but outside (for science and reality)."

WHY I LOVE THIS QUOTE:
So, how do you get outside your ideological framework? It's good to keep asking questions, and possibly reading those who have given their life and thought to the task.

WHY THIS IS A TRANSFORMATIVE BOOK:
On Ideology by Louis Althusser is a classic. It provides an excellent analysis and a very insightful contribution, while remaining approachable and highly readable. Is a book of theory always pure pleasure to read? Not exactly. It can be tedious. It's not necessarily the joy you get from reading experience, but from the challenge. Entertaining new and complex ideas in order to better examine your perceived reality turns your mind on. Althusser's examination of ideology is a mental workout. It tires you out at first, only to have made you stronger. That's the pep talk for today, but if you've stuck with this reader for any length of time and possibly have picked up on a book here and there along the practical lines of writing, I'd like to encourage you to try some theory too.

QUESTIONS FOR MEDITATION:

Who do you want to be? Why? What are you doing to be that person?

"Perhaps the ultimate test of a leader is not what you are able to do in the here and now — but instead what continues to grow long after you're gone."

WHY I LOVE THIS QUOTE:

This quote asks us to consider the use of our strengths — the application of our talents — toward a purpose or cause larger than ourselves. When we're already thinking about what continues to grow from what we've left behind, we're getting out of the ego and into the larger pool of others whom we might actually be serving (or providing usefulness). It's not that everything we do is going to grow after we're gone, but if one in a leadership position is looking toward that horizon, it's likely that a lot of other things have taken place. Healthy leadership has dropped the pretense of being the best at everything, and instead has shown authority by what and how they have shared responsibility, delegated wisely.

WHY THIS IS A TRANSFORMATIVE BOOK:

Strengths Based Leadership: Great Leaders, Teams, and Why People Follow: A Landmark Study of Great Leaders, Teams, and the Reasons Why We Follow by Tom Rath advocates a different approach to strengths. Lean into them rather than try to compensate for your weaknesses. Great leaders have the acute awareness of their strengths as well as their weaknesses. But they don't struggle to fix their weaknesses, instead they find the complements. This way, they build strong, well-rounded teams.

QUESTIONS FOR MEDITATION:

How do you maximize your strengths, and delegate the tasks you're not as good at? Are you aware of what you're not as good at? Do you spread yourself too thin trying to be good at everything?

"Morality binds and blinds. It binds us into ideological teams that fight each other as though the fate of the world depended on our side winning each battle. It blinds us to the fact that each team is composed of good people who have something important to say."

WHY I LOVE THIS QUOTE:

It's a good reminder that the very things that make us comfortable, and that we often think are sources of strength and possibly even wholesome, can also be weaponized. We can use our teams to be echo-chambers, validating what we already believe (or "know") to be true. We can use the strength of our tribe to keep ourselves protected, and to keep others out. While there is plenty of privilege and strength to be had in these fortressed places of our lives, we are blind to so much else. Many are fine with that and want to remain safe and blind, but not you. That's why you're here.

WHY THIS IS A TRANSFORMATIVE BOOK:

The Righteous Mind: Why Good People Are Divided by Politics and Religion by Jonathan Haidt covers far more territory than the subtitle of the book implies. Not only is he attempting to explain why people are morally tribal, but also the way morality works in the human brain, the evolutionary origins of moral feelings, the role of moral psychology in the history of civilization, the origin and function of religion, and how we can apply all this information to the modern political situation — among much else along the way.

QUESTIONS FOR MEDITATION:

How do you thrive within the culture of your tribe? How could you make it more welcoming to others?

"All truth passes through three stages. First, it is ridiculed. Second, it is violently opposed. Third, it is accepted as being self-evident."

WHY I LOVE THIS QUOTE:
Just remember that next time you have a big idea.

WHY THIS IS A TRANSFORMATIVE BOOK:
The World as Will and Representation, Vol. 1 by Arthur Schopenhauer attempts to form a coherent unified expression of how he saw human experience. Well, maybe you could say that all philosophers are trying to do just that. Schopenhauer, however, is important for many reasons, and this book, which he published when he was 30, argued for and developed all the rest of his further writings around. Schopenhauer is perhaps most famous for his extreme pessimism. Seeing the world as something horrific and bleak, he urged that we turn against it. As a follower of Kant, he took space, time, and causality to be, not things-in-themselves, but categories of the mind through which we interpret and make sense of things. He was the only major Western philosopher to draw serious and interesting parallels between Western and Eastern thought, as well as being the first major philosopher to openly identify as an atheist. He had a significant influence on many great thinkers and artists, including Nietzsche, Freud, Wittgenstein, and Wagner. The arts were particularly important for Schopenhauer not only because he thought they give us a glimpse into the underlying reality, but because they help us to escape our individuality and thus the inherent suffering and meaningless absurdity of existence. Because he was also a brilliant writer, he is often quoted from, but to truly understand him, you really should read his work in its entirety because his thinking is best understood within a system.

QUESTIONS FOR MEDITATION:

What is being violently opposed in our culture now that was once ridiculed that you think will soon (or eventually) be self evident?

"Whatever the times, suffering eventually touches every life. How we live with it, and help others to, is one of the great creative and ethical opportunities"

WHY I LOVE THIS QUOTE:
Do you have a keen imagination and vivid dreams? Is time alone each day essential to you? Are you considered shy? Do noise and confusion tend to overwhelm you?

WHY THIS IS A TRANSFORMATIVE BOOK:
The Highly Sensitive Person: How to Thrive When the World Overwhelms You by Elaine N. Aron contributes to our understanding of sensitive people by shedding light on our relationships, our work lives, and how we can thrive in the world around us. Aron frames sensitivity as a trait that carries both strengths and weaknesses, as any facet of an individual does. She provides helpful tools to highly sensitive people on how to maximize the assets of sensitivity as well as strategies to cope with it. If you aren't sure whether or not you're highly sensitive, Aron shows you how to identify this trait in yourself and make the most of it in everyday situations. Drawing on her many years of research and hundreds of interviews, she shows how you can better understand yourself and your traits to create a fuller, richer life.

QUESTIONS FOR MEDITATION:

What three words would others use to describe you? Would their descriptions line up with yours?

"The shadow is the image of ourselves that slides along behind us as we walk toward the light. The persona, its opposite, is named after the Roman term for an actor's mask. It is the face we wear to meet the social world around us."

WHY I LOVE THIS QUOTE:

This is an excellent way of illustrating the difference between the shadow and the persona. It's especially interesting visually to consider what it means about the shadow, but each sentence provides you with a clear image to remember the concept. If you're like most of us, you've given a lot more thought to your persona than your shadow. You probably think about how others perceive you and the face you present to the world at work and at school and everywhere else far more than you've thought about your shadow. That's the nature of the shadow. A part literally pushed into the shade. Ignored, suppressed, but still there.

WHY THIS IS A TRANSFORMATIVE BOOK:

Jung's Map of the Soul: An Introduction by Murray Stein is an excellent book summarizing the theories of Carl Jung. Stein puts Jung into context while starting with the fundamental constructions of Jung's thought. It's better than most of the scores, if not hundreds, of other Jungian distillations and summary-interpretations. Yes, we all need to read every primary source, and grabbing a copy of Jung's collections is never a bad idea, but Jung is difficult in part simply because he is so discursive. Here, Stein makes it easy, starting with the Ego, then to its Shadow, followed by the Persona and Animus. Only then is the Self brought in, the concept most in need of clear definitions. From there he turns to the realm of the outer world through synchronicity and extra sensory perception. We conclude with a clear view of the collective unconscious that reaches from inside our psyche (or the self) and into participation with the whole universe. When can we get started?

QUESTIONS FOR MEDITATION:

How do you get to know your shadow? Do you think it would be uncomfortable, or would you just be curious to understand more about yourself?

"The real universe of ordinary language is that of the struggle for existence. It is indeed an ambiguous, vague, obscure universe, and is certainly in need of clarification. Moreover, such clarification may well fulfill a therapeutic function, and if philosophy would become therapeutic, it would really come into its own."

WHY I LOVE THIS QUOTE:

But perhaps philosophy is becoming therapeutic before our very eyes. Perhaps that is a part of the construct of this reader, asking you of your own creative free will and subjective biases and interpretations and experiences to construct a self that is "you." It is also asking you to consider ways that you make meaning.

WHY THIS IS A TRANSFORMATIVE BOOK:

One-Dimensional Man: Studies in the Ideology of Advanced Industrial Society by the German-American philosopher Herbert Marcuse, offers a wide-ranging critique of both contemporary capitalism and the Communist Soviet Union, documenting the parallel rise of new forms of social repression in both these societies, as well as the decline of revolutionary potential in the West. His argument is that the system's much lauded economic, political, and social freedoms, formerly a source of social progress, lose their progressive function and become subtle instruments of domination which serve to keep people in bondage to the system that they strengthen and perpetuate. An enlightening and disturbing read at the same time.

QUESTIONS FOR MEDITATION:

What is lost when we only consider the world as it is, rather than as it should be?

"When the situation is hopeless, there's nothing to worry about."

WHY I LOVE THIS QUOTE:

While this may be an absurd outlook on the one hand — you can almost hear Dr. Pangloss from *Candide* say it — it also has the ring of a powerful truth. The things that are out of our control cannot be controlled. We can only control our response. We must still persevere in what we've set out to accomplish.

WHY THIS IS A TRANSFORMATIVE BOOK:

The Monkey Wrench Gang by Edward Abbey is about a group of four passionate environmental activists comprising an eco-feminist, a wealthy medical doctor, a Vietnam vet, and a wilderness guide who commit mayhem and liberate parts of Utah and Arizona from evil developers. They wage war on billboards, construction machinery, roads and dams. There are plenty of rollicking exploits, and nail biting dramatic episodes, but the characters also provide a vehicle for Abbey to voice his concerns on environmental preservation and the essential relationship between a healthy planet and healthy human beings. You are left with a heightened awareness of the serious moral questions concerning the nature of our relationship with wilderness and our personal responsibility and culpability.

QUESTIONS FOR MEDITATION:

What task sits in front of you that seems impossible right now?

october

"Knowledge about life is one thing; effective occupation of a place in life, with its dynamic currents passing through your being, is another."

WHY I LOVE THIS QUOTE:

The difference between being a distanced observer and a fully engaged participant, and it a person of any class or social status can be one or the other. Similarly, there is a huge gulf between knowledge and self-knowledge. You can possess vast knowledge and still function, at least in many respects, utterly like a child under the right (or wrong) conditions if you lack self-knowledge. For how vital it is for personal and spiritual growth it's stunning how little we've done to educate ourselves and our children in self-knowledge. Perhaps it explains a lot. They say understanding history is a way to keep from repeating the past. Understanding yourself may be more important. It's where empathy comes from, which is where tolerance can be built.

WHY THIS IS A TRANSFORMATIVE BOOK:

The Varieties of Religious Experience by William James is a project that, upon completion, stands as one of the most important texts on psychology ever written. At the same time it is also a vitally serious contemplation of spirituality, and for many critics one of the best works of nonfiction written in the 20th century. Applying his analytic clarity to religious accounts from a variety of sources, James elaborates a pluralistic framework in which "the divine can mean no single quality, it must mean a group of qualities, by being champions of which in alternation, different men may all find worthy missions." It's an intellectual call for serious religious tolerance, understanding, and respect, the vitality of which has only grown through the subsequent decades.

QUESTIONS FOR MEDITATION:

What is the most important moral lesson you've ever learned, and on a scale of 1-10 to what degree would you say you've built it into your daily life?

"The position is, then, that at any given moment each individual in a social aggregation will exhibit a Parental, Adult or Child ego state, and that individuals can shift with varying degrees of readiness from one ego state to another."

WHY I LOVE THIS QUOTE:

This rather simple construct was a major contribution to social interactions in the late '60s. At first, I would think about it just between myself and other family members, but once I started applying the concept within work situations, it became even more fascinating. We are constantly fluctuating between different communication styles, and not nearly as often are communicating Adult to Adult as we think (and what is more healthy and ideal).

WHY THIS IS A TRANSFORMATIVE BOOK:

Games People Play revolutionized our understanding of what really goes on during our most basic social interactions. Eric Berne's classic is astonishing and revealing. We play games all the time — sexual games, marital games, power games with our bosses, and competitive games with our friends. Detailing status contests like "Martini" (I know a better way), to lethal couples combat like "If It Weren't For You" and "Uproar," to flirtation favorites like "The Stocking Game" and "Let's You and Him Fight," Berne exposes the secret ploys and unconscious maneuvers that rule our intimate lives. Explosive when it first appeared, it is now widely recognized as one of the more original and influential popular psychology books.

QUESTIONS FOR MEDITATION:

What games do you find yourself playing with others? What happens when you try to break the rules of the game?

"Whatever happens around you, don't take it personally...
Nothing other people do is because of you. It is because of
themselves."

WHY I LOVE THIS QUOTE:
Easier said than done, but when you put the other parts of Ruiz's "agreements" together, it can be a powerful way of operating in the world. So
long as it really isn't about you (that's the tricky part), it does help to realize that many of people's actions are about them. It can at least helped
to not get "hooked."

WHY THIS IS A TRANSFORMATIVE BOOK:
The Four Agreements: A Practical Guide to Personal Freedom by Miguel
Ruiz reveals the source of self-limiting beliefs that rob us of joy and create
needless suffering. Based on ancient Toltec wisdom, the Four Agree-
ments offer a powerful code of conduct that can rapidly transform our
lives to a new experience of freedom, true happiness, and love. The Four
Agreements are: Be Impeccable With Your Word, Don't Take Anything
Personally, Don't Make Assumptions, Always Do Your Best.

As Jim Mitchell writes, "I am not reading with a hope that I will attain
some mystical state, but I read because I find the author's explanation
of how our mind, our society, and importantly, our relationships work to
be insightful, even though it is based on a paradigm that is completely
outside my heritage of growing up in a small New England town...Read-
ing this book, I have started to formulate a good answer to a question
that originally began in childhood. 'What is the meaning of life?' is not a
good question to be unanswered when one has piled up decades in this
mortal realm. Ruiz has helped me drop many of my limited belief structures and has opened up insights into living that are valuable to young
and old souls alike."

QUESTIONS FOR MEDITATION:

Do you feel you have to be liked as a way of doing business?

"I've been thinking about five intersecting problems: first, how the internet is built to distend our sense of identity; second, how it encourages us to overvalue our opinions; third, how it maximizes our sense of opposition; fourth, how it cheapens our understanding of solidarity; and, finally, how it destroys our sense of scale."

WHY I LOVE THIS QUOTE:
She also observes that "writing is either a way to shed my self-delusions or a way to develop them." We need to develop our thinking without the need for need and tidy bows and perfectly developed conclusions.

WHY THIS IS A TRANSFORMATIVE BOOK:
Trick Mirror: Reflections on Self-Delusion by Jia Tolentino is an enlightening trip through the river of self-delusion that surges just beneath the surface of our lives. This is a book about the incentives that shape us, and about how hard it is to see ourselves clearly in a culture that revolves around the self. As Roxane Gay writes, "This is an outstanding, rigorously researched and written collection of cultural criticism. I really admired the depth of thought here. I felt like each essay was a master class on how to write cultural criticism. I was definitely taking notes. Some of the essays ran too long and could use some tightening but that is a subjective opinion. I was particularly interested in the essay about the UVA rape case and the one about uncritical feminism and how it can flatten discourse in really troubling ways. This is well worth a read. I read it slowly so I could really think through each piece. It is a rare book that encourages me to do that."

QUESTIONS FOR MEDITATION:

How do you get off the internet and seek sources of clarity and perspective?

"The next thing I want to do is to make a prophecy to you, the ones who voted against me; I'm now at that moment when human beings are most prone to turn prophet, when they're about to die. I tell you, you Athenians who have become my killers, that just as soon as I'm dead you'll meet with a punishment that – Zeus knows – will be much harsher than the one you've meted out to me by putting me to death...If you think killing people will stop anyone reproaching you for not living correctly, you're not thinking straight."

WHY I LOVE THIS QUOTE:
After he's been sentenced to death, Socrates becomes introspective with his friends, and his inspiring advice and requests serve as indicators of his real personality (as opposed to his philosopher persona). He loved his family and neighbors so much that he was willing to risk his life to make them good people.

WHY THIS IS A TRANSFORMATIVE BOOK:
The Trial and Death of Socrates (Euthyphro, Apology, Crito, Phaedo) by Plato traces the trial, conviction, and death sentence at 399 B.C.E. of Socrates who was already seventy years old. He had lived through the imperialistic spread of Athenian democracy and culture under Pericles, twenty-five years of first cold and then heated war with Sparta, the defeat of Athens in 404 B.C.E., the short-lived oligarchy imposed on that city by the Spartans, and finally the reestablishment of democracy in his homeland. During all of that time, the former bricklayer was known for practicing philosophy in the public spaces of Athens questioning those in authority who feigned virtue and wisdom while in reality lacking it. This technique gradually garnered him powerful enemies.

QUESTIONS FOR MEDITATION:

What regular work do you put in to keep yourself sharp even in areas where you're already strong?

"Fortunately, you don't need to change who you are as a person to make change last. You just need to understand the science behind lasting change and how to create a process that fits who you are."

WHY I LOVE THIS QUOTE:
Know the science. Create a customized process. Boom. Everything else is just details.

WHY THIS IS A TRANSFORMATIVE BOOK:
Stick with It: The Science of Lasting Changes by Sean Young is for anyone who wants to improve and live a better, more satisfying and productive life. Who doesn't, right? The book is by a medical school professor who has had repeated successes practicing these very techniques. He tells you how to change your behavior (spoiler: change your process). He describes seven psychological forces that undergird lasting behavior changes. You need to know the why behind motivation, start with small steps, learn the power of the community, understand what is important and use it, discover how to make things easy, change actions not thoughts, grasp how to convince yourself to keep doing what is right, and use the power of efficiency. Lots of practical, useful information based on science and practice. See how we balance these readings with theory and philosophy?

QUESTIONS FOR MEDITATION:

What habit do you want to include in your life consistently that you never find yourself sticking with?

"I want people, when they realize they have been wrong about the world, to feel not embarrassment, but that child-like sense of wonder, inspiration, and curiosity that I remember from the circus, and that I still get every time I discover I have been wrong: 'Wow, how is that even possible?'"

WHY I LOVE THIS QUOTE:

And as we have seen from other readings in this book, we have an inclination to do just the opposite. When confronted with empirical, factual evidence that we are wrong about something we held to be true, we double down. We explain away, justify, rationalize, or do all kinds of mental gymnastics to continue the untruth. How hard, then, do you think it might be to change that within you for which there is no "empirical" data showing you the error of your ways? That's where relationships and emotions step in and do the work where facts won't.

WHY THIS IS A TRANSFORMATIVE BOOK:

Factfulness: Ten Reasons We're Wrong About the World – and Why Things Are Better Than You Think by Hans Rosling (and his two long-time contributors Ana and Ola) is devoted to ten instincts that keep us from seeing the world factfully. These range from the fear instinct (we pay more attention to scary things) to the size instinct (standalone numbers often look more impressive than they really are) to the gap instinct (most people fall between two extremes). With each one, he offers practical advice about how to overcome our innate biases. Hans argues that these instincts make it difficult to put events in perspective. He also wants you to have facts behind your opinions. Wishful thinking?

QUESTIONS FOR MEDITATION:

It's a fact that we change. What are five facts about yourself that used to be true that are no longer true? What are five facts about yourself that you expect to no longer be true in five years?

"While our first instinct is usually attempting to push harder, it's more valuable to figure out where to push."

WHY I LOVE THIS QUOTE:

And part of knowing where to push is knowing what's going on, and part of knowing what's going on is engaging, and part of engaging at the core comes with being adaptive. Adaptive to what? Everything and anything. It's not just for a young person to be inclined toward adaptation. We all do better for ourselves and in our relationships when we are fluid with mind's like water. The idea here isn't just to be adaptive, but to proactively do so.

WHY THIS IS A TRANSFORMATIVE BOOK:

The End of Jobs: Money, Meaning and Freedom Without the 9-to-5 by Taylor Pearson is all about the need to adapt. If you are in college, starting a career, or really at any point in your career, it is becoming clear that traditional jobs are a less secure social script than ever before, whereas the entrepreneurship opportunities have never been better. Pearson's Stair-Step method and Apprenticeships provide compelling social scripts for that very thing. College is increasing in cost but decreasing in value. There are more graduates each year than relevant job openings. There are equally-skilled knowledge workers overseas that are much more affordable to hire on a full-time, part-time, or contract basis. Capital is abundant, time is scarce. This book is brave, bold, and specific and gives some clear process ideas and advantages.

QUESTIONS FOR MEDITATION:

Why do people follow others? What ideas or values do you possess that others would be willing to follow?

"Sometimes, people who hate on your dream aren't really mad about your dream. They're mad because you're making them jealous."

WHY I LOVE THIS QUOTE:
In the idea of self-examining, one thing should be noted that rarely is, and that is the power that you have to re-create yourself. And you know one of the early stage setbacks we all feel when we take even just the first few tentative steps in what should feel like a bold decision? We feel the resistance from others. Well, let's have grace for the others. We've all been the others at one time or another, but let's not let them make us feel inhibited to re-make ourselves. It's inauthentic to re-create yourself. It doesn't even mean you "failed" at something, and even if you did fail, so what? Isn't that what we're supposed to do from time to time? Aren't we supposed to experiment?

WHY THIS IS A TRANSFORMATIVE BOOK:
Do Over: Rescue Monday, Reinvent Your Work, and Never Get Stuck by Jon Acuff is all about boldly re-creating yourself. The thesis embodies Robert Greene's "Law of Power #25," Re-Create Yourself, which goes: "Do not accept the roles that society foists upon you. Re-create yourself by forging a new identity, one that commands attention and never bores the audience. Be the master of your own image rather than letting others define it for you. Incorporate dramatic devices into your public gestures and actions — your power will be enhanced and your character will seem larger than life." Acuff makes fun and creative. Don't apologize for "starting over."

QUESTIONS FOR MEDITATION:

Take a few moments now to think of yourself as an actor. Think of yourself as taking complete control of your behavior and actions, your appearance, even your emotions. Now, who are you going to be?

"New information muddies the picture. Once we finally reach a decision, we are relieved to have the uncertainty of decision making behind us. And now somebody turns up and tells us things that call the wisdom of that decision into question again. So we prefer not to listen."

WHY I LOVE THIS QUOTE:
We have seen how people like to double down in the face of factual or empirical data that muddies the picture they have of something they already decided on. They don't like it. It doesn't seem rational the way they hem and haw and make excuses and refuse to believe the facts. Facts are stubborn things, but people have a lot of tricks up their sleeves for pushing back against reality. This idea gives us a clear reason why, which isn't necessarily irrational.

WHY THIS IS A TRANSFORMATIVE BOOK:
The Logic of Failure: Recognizing and Avoiding Error in Complex Situations by Dietrich Döerner shows that our habits as problem solvers are typically counterproductive. One huge reason why is that we oversimplify problems. Dörner offers a long list of self-defeating behaviors, but common to all of them is our reluctance to see any given problem is part of a whole system of interacting factors. Full of real world case studies and experiments showing how bad planning results in inadequate understanding of the interrelationships between complex systems, inability to visualize non-linear causation chains and, more importantly, the inadequate self-testing of the relationships between our mental models of reality and reality itself. He looks at how better planning helps in major ways, and he challenges you to ask the right questions in the first place, and keep on asking after. Never stop asking. What?

QUESTIONS FOR MEDITATION:

What's being said to you that you're not hearing?

"The key to good decision making is not knowledge. It is understanding. We are swimming in the former. We are desperately lacking in the latter."

WHY I LOVE THIS QUOTE:

The new trend is that the best leaders are the best listeners, and maybe it's even more than a trend. Maybe it's a new level of collective self-understanding. We live in the information age, so it's really pretty rare these days to seriously lack knowledge. It's far more the experiential, and the interpretive, listening stance that is what is needed. So much talking. So much zealous over-confidence.

WHY THIS IS A TRANSFORMATIVE BOOK:

Blink: The Power of Thinking Without Thinking is Malcolm Gladwell's effort to make you more aware of your gut instincts and to urge you to consider trusting it more frequently than you do. People tend to make decisions that are supported by a huge number of rationalizations and explanations, but do we always really have reasons for why we do or think what we do. Gladwell argues that we don't, and that sometimes it takes the unconscious mind to make those decisions for us. On the flip side, he also argues that sometimes we unconsciously make negative decisions based on that same quick judgment and our predetermined stereotypes, such as with people of other sexes or other races than ourselves.

QUESTIONS FOR MEDITATION:

Do you imagine yourself as a good decision-maker?

"Your ability to generate power is directly proportional to your ability to relax."

WHY I LOVE THIS QUOTE:

The Internet Age constantly pushes us to do more. Even if it's an article preaching the benefits of mindfulness, it seems everyone is always out to make us better and get us to do more. The incredible benefit to this age of information — for all its clutter and speed — is that something that for most of history that was scarce now flows freely. The information we need is out there. But now we have new problems. Things come in so rapidly, we have to figure out methods of processing and systemizing and prioritizing the super small to the super big things we have to get done. The idea here of the principle of power being an inverse relationship from relaxing being proportional to generating power is essential. However hard you plan on working at your task, you must know yourself well enough to know how much recharge time you need, and you must recharge by relaxing.

WHY THIS IS A TRANSFORMATIVE BOOK:

Getting Things Done: The Art of Stress-Free Productivity by David Allen takes a practical approach to digging yourself out of your mountain of commitments, and how to stay on top of your mountain once you get there. In short, the GTD method (as it is popularly known) focuses on getting stuff — commitments, to do items, reminders to gather information, requests for information or actions — out of your short-term memory and into a physical, organized system that reminds you of the right stuff at the right time. Dumping everything out of your short-term memory allows you to do something critical to productivity: focus on one thing at a time. Have a mind like water, friends. Get stuff done because you have the right containers to put stuff in, and because you can readily assess what is worth your time and what isn't, and all while relaxing more. It's a complex system, but definitely with principles that work when put into action.

QUESTIONS FOR MEDITATION:

Where do you find your deepest moments of relaxation? When you're getting lots of stuff done and being highly organized are you more or less able to relax?

"To increase your self-affirmation, get in the habit of remembering your successes, your good qualities and characteristics, and forgetting your failures."

WHY I LOVE THIS QUOTE:

This is the kind of habit development that can readily become a part of your natural mental process. It's important for our efforts toward trans-formation as a process, and our ability to synthesize failures and make them into something better than we ever could have imagined.

WHY THIS IS A TRANSFORMATIVE BOOK:

Thinkertoys: a handbook of creative-thinking techniques by Michael Michako is a gem, a treasure-trove of specific and clearly-rendered techniques and processes to ideate and funnel ideas of literally all kinds. Creativity, as is everything, depends on your perception: of your-self, of things happening and of the world. If you believe and act like you're creative and use the tools with a faith in the process then you'll be creative. This is the kind of book that can be used again and again in powerful recombinant ways.

QUESTIONS FOR MEDITATION:

Record all the things you like about yourself — your positive qualities, characteristics, and traits. Include the successes you have had in every area of your life: work, home, school, and so on. Keep adding to this list as you think of more things and as you accomplish more. Acknowledging yourself, your abilities, and your own unique qualities will encourage you to get moving.

"Failure is only the opportunity to begin again more intelligently."

WHY I LOVE THIS QUOTE:

Seelig gives specific, practical techniques to expand everyone's creativity. She begins with the reframing because that's part of the roadblock for most people. Everyone can be more creative, sometimes much more. Sometimes you have to start from right where you are.

WHY THIS IS A TRANSFORMATIVE BOOK:

inGenius: A Crash Course on Creativity by Tina Seelig has a lot to do with reframing the way we think about creativity. Ideas aren't cheap. Also they don't — as commonly believed — just because we lacked the capacity to "execute" the vision. Our biggest failures usually have to do with lack of imagination. A Stanford Professor for over 14 years now, Seelig has seen the theory behind her ideas in full-fledged practical application. She's tried them out on her students, and in a variety of corporate settings. A cut above your typical creativity book, Seelig's ideas are infectious and widely applicable. She has a way of making you feel like anything is possible. It really is an exciting time to be alive when so much collaboration of cross-disciplinary ideas are bearing fruit. You can be in the arts and humanities, the tech industry, religion, science, or any field and discover new ways of knowing.

QUESTIONS FOR MEDITATION:

Be an artist of yourself. You're allowed right here, right now in this moment to remake yourself. Who else is in control of who defines you? Who else is allowed to mold you? Will your biggest failure be a lack of imagination about how you define yourself?

"Recognize the call as a prime fact of human existence; align life with it; find the common sense to realize that accidents, including the heartache and the natural shocks the flesh is heir to, belong to the pattern of the image, are necessary to it, and help fulfill it. A calling may be postponed, avoided, intermittently missed. It may also possess you completely. Whatever; eventually it will out. It makes its claim. The daimon does not go away."

WHY I LOVE THIS QUOTE:
Hillman hypothesizes that each individual is born into the world with a daimon or destiny, a guardian angel that seeks to order our lives with a destiny. Similar to Plato's Myth of Er, Hillman proposes that we each choose this path before birth and that we choose our parents and the station in life that will best suit this innate potential. It's wired into the code of our soul.

WHY THIS IS A TRANSFORMATIVE BOOK:
The Soul's Code: In Search of Character and Calling by James Hillman offers observations on the human experience and the nature of the mind that stands outside of the mainstream of American psychology, refreshingly so, with its current emphasis upon reducing all our experience to biological processes, whether it be sociobiology, neuropsychology, cognitive-behavioral, or applied behavior analysis. Material reality isn't the only reality. There are other ways to study outcomes and predict behaviors. Hillman aligns himself with the anthropomorphic cosmological orientation of the ancient Greeks, and really most of our so-called indigenous peoples, that to fully understand the nature of our human experience, we have to return to the concept of soul. To unquestioningly accept the idea that we exist only on a "horizontal" dimension of material extension and eventual personal finality, is to live utterly blind to what gives our lives meaning, the "vertical" dimension of the soul.

QUESTIONS FOR MEDITATION:

What is your soul's mandate?

"Closings, conclusions, and culminations reveal something essential about the human condition: In the end, we seek meaning."

WHY I LOVE THIS QUOTE:
Research has proven that people prefer happy endings over sad endings. People prefer conclusions, time-captured narratives, not just open-endedness. We prefer not only happy endings that elevate, we want something richer, a rush of unexpected insight, a fleeting moment of transcendence, the possibility that by discarding what we wanted we've gotten what we need.

WHY THIS IS A TRANSFORMATIVE BOOK:
When: The Scientific Secrets of Perfect Timing by Daniel Pink should be compulsory reading for bosses, educators, schedulers, policymakers, company executives, and performers...I could go on. There is plenty in this fascinating book that the average person will find applicable to their lives. He distills everything from the latest research about our natural biorhythms — our low and high points throughout the day — to our sleeping schedules, to when judges and doctors do their best work, to how complex delivery services and human organizations can sync together in such precise ways. The information leads to easy takeaways for how you can adapt and arrange your days, when you choose to do certain tasks (and why), as well as longer term habit-building strategies.

QUESTIONS FOR MEDITATION:

Why do you think they say: Timing is everything?

"The place God calls you to is the place where your deep gladness and the world's deep hunger meet."

WHY I LOVE THIS QUOTE:

This famous quote is about as good as it gets when it comes to trying in an epigrammatic way to parse out the complexity of vocation, or labor that is meaningful and that you can get paid for. He unwraps his formula a little more clearly in the book, saying essentially that it's somewhere in the middle between the easy and the hard. It's also hard to see clearly the difference between what could be God's voice or society's or the superego or just plain old self-interest.

WHY THIS IS A TRANSFORMATIVE BOOK:

Wishful Thinking: A Theological ABC by Frederick Buechner takes common terms, theological and otherwise, and turns them into unexpected moments of humorous delight and punches to the gut. While much of the book is lighthearted, he never shies away from cutting his reader to the quick.

On Grace: "The grace of God means something like: Here is your life. You might never have been, but you are because the party wouldn't have been complete without you. Here is the world. Beautiful and terrible things will happen. Don't be afraid. I am with you. Nothing can ever separate us. It's for you I created the universe. I love you."

On Anger: "Of the Seven Deadly Sins, anger is possibly the most fun. To lick your wounds, to smack your lips over grievances long past, to roll over your tongue the prospect of bitter confrontations still to come, to savor to the last toothsome morsel both the pain you are given and the pain you are giving back — in many ways it is a feast fit for a king. The chief drawback is that what you are wolfing down is yourself. The skeleton at the feast is you."

QUESTIONS FOR MEDITATION:

What do you think Buechner means by your "deep gladness," and do you think you've met the criteria for finding your "thing" vocationally?

"Modern man is drinking and drugging himself out of awareness, or he spends his time shopping, which is the same thing."

WHY I LOVE THIS QUOTE:

If you can look past the dated gender construction (the book was originally published in 1973), this quote epitomizes so much of what this masterpiece of a book stands for: we are painfully self-aware. We are higher order beings flooded with too much truth. Perhaps it is true that one way or another we're going to live under some form of illusion, but this quote reminds us that there are oblivious and unhealthy ways to avoid reality — and there are healthy ones.

WHY THIS IS A TRANSFORMATIVE BOOK:

The Denial of Death by Ernest Becker is his brilliant and impassioned answer to the "why" of human existence. In bold contrast to the predominant Freudian school of thought, Becker tackles the problem of the vital lie — humankind's refusal to acknowledge mortality. The primary repression is not sexuality, as Freud said, but our awareness of death. Becker relies extensively on Otto Rank, a psychoanalyst with a religious bent who was one of the most trusted and intellectually potent members of Freud's inner circle until he broke away, and Danish theologian Søren Kierkegaard. Becker's solution for ridding humankind of this vital lie is what he calls "a fusion of psychology and religion." The only way is to give yourself to something outside the physical.

QUESTIONS FOR MEDITATION:

What does death or the fact that your life is finite have to do with your current joy, or lack thereof, right now? Does it energize you, depress you, or have you packed it far away?

"People learn from their failures. Seldom do they learn anything from success."

WHY I LOVE THIS QUOTE:

We especially learn (or are more likely to) from the big failures, the painful ones, the ones that find us saying, "I'll never do that again." Failures can also mean certain resistances we hit as we try to advance, which makes us rethink, recalculate, reassess. If all we're met with is success we naturally feel like whatever we're doing is right. The disruptive moments are there for a reason, you may even be unconsciously asking for the disruptions, you self-sabotage, and behave in a way that is not healthy or sustainable. Sometimes only when you hit rock bottom you become truly capable of achieving what you truly desire.

WHY THIS IS A TRANSFORMATIVE BOOK:

Ego Is the Enemy by Ryan Holiday is similar in quality in our estimation to the earlier *The Obstacle is the Way*, and the later *Stillness is the Key*. They each take a single, powerful, clear concept and reinforce it through a three-part sequence of historical examples. The examples range from any time period, but Holiday's brand is to funnel everything through a stoical lens. Some critics skewer his books as saying nothing new, but I find that his clarity, historic choices, and the distillation of his message combine into an inspiring and practical message. Through the other readings in this reader, it is probably clear that we believe in a healthy, integrated ego, not "no ego at all." But as a question of semantics, when ego means narcissism, hubris, over-confidence so that all you do is talk and never listen, and unwillingness to adapt even when faced with all kinds of evidence to do just that, then, yes, we agree, that definition of ego is destructive.

QUESTIONS FOR MEDITATION:

What healthy ways are you tapping into your own awareness?

"Would you have a great empire? Rule over yourself."

WHY I LOVE THIS QUOTE:

It's another way — an ancient and epigrammatic way — of saying what we have revealed and thought about through many of the readings herein. Before you seek to change someone else, before you seek to change your team, your family, your organization, start with yourself.

BONUS QUOTES:

"Rivers are easiest to cross at their source."

"Divide the fire and you will sooner put it out."

WHY THIS IS A TRANSFORMATIVE BOOK:

The Moral Sayings of Publius Syrus were written by a Syrian slave in the first century BCE. Publius Syrus is a fountain of quick, helpful wisdom that you cannot help but recall and apply to your life.

QUESTIONS FOR MEDITATION:

Are you willing to examine a blind spot — obviously you have to be aware of it to be willing to bring it into the light of your attention — but is there something that is just on the edge of your self-awareness, perhaps something that others have point out, that you really don't like to think about or acknowledge?

"It is quite remarkable how firmly belief and conviction stand in the way of reasoning."

WHY I LOVE THIS QUOTE:

Even though this is about the scientific research of "internal time" based on different biological chronotypes, the quote applies to the human condition in general.

WHY THIS IS A TRANSFORMATIVE BOOK:

Internal Time: Chronotypes, Social Jet Lag, and Why You're So Tired by Till Ronnenberg pulls together some of the best research now being conducted on the science of "when," as in time, timing, sleep patterns, and other body clock research. The style of his writing combines story-telling with reasonably accessible science tutorials to explain how our internal clocks work. Many of the factors that make us early or late "chro-notypes" are beyond our control, but that doesn't make us powerless. While we have control over when we want to wake and sleep, at our core there is a mechanism that has a preset when we should wake and sleep. Not only does this impact on how we feel, but also how we digest, think and function. This sleep preset is, however, not fixed, rather it follows a natural pattern over the course of our lives — varying with age. There is also a divergence between male and female sleeping patterns. If there is a limitation to this book's overall transformative impact, it's because it gives you the science, but perhaps not so much what to do about it. That's where our previous look at Daniel Pink's When steps in.

QUESTIONS FOR MEDITATION:

List five things about sleeping you hold to be true, then look at the latest research and see if you learn anything that can change your habits and improve your life.

"People say that what we're all seeking is a meaning for life. I don't think that's what we're really seeking. I think that what we're seeking is an experience of being alive, so that our life experiences on the purely physical plane will have resonances with our own innermost being and reality, so that we actually feel the rapture of being alive."

WHY I LOVE THIS QUOTE:
This is a memorable and distinctive observation of what so many seek.

WHY THIS IS A TRANSFORMATIVE BOOK:
The Power of Myth by Joseph Campbell is a pretty major contribution to the 20th century. The "collective hero" journey is still realizing itself today. Now the question becomes how enduring Campbell will be to other generations. Like C.S. Lewis, Campbell thought humans were disconnected from themselves in ways crucial to their (loss of) humanity. And also like Lewis, he made it "okay" to have an intellectual conversation on the topic of God and beliefs without being written off as small-minded — or of a limited worldview (or "meta" narrative). His audience shared a larger segment of the population too. He's more Jungian than Freudian, but he has assimilated his Freud into the equation too. Freud brought the "ego" into discussion after all. Campbell's lasting genius is probably most what he did through his application of such a cross-section of world myths.

QUESTIONS FOR MEDITATION:

How do you tap into your "innermost being" and experience reality outside of the physical plane of existence?

"Competition doesn't kill creativity: it facilitates creative output by supplying motivational drive. Competition also teaches people to be comfortable with conflict and opposition, which is a necessary building block for developing the creative psyche."

WHY I LOVE THIS QUOTE:

Becoming a better competitor is about controlling your psychological state, which in turn alters your underlying physiology. Simply put, if you can control your fear, then you can control your biology, too. It can lead to a growth mindset over a fixed one.

WHY THIS IS A TRANSFORMATIVE BOOK:

Top Dog: The Science of Winning and Losing by Po Bronson and Ashley Merryman set out on a quest to find out what it is that makes competitors tick. How people respond to challenges, rise to the occasion or flop. How they work individually and as teams. In a time of decreased concentration on competitiveness and more collaboration on the field — or the ever present "everyone gets a trophy" mantra — social scientists want to know if people benefit from competition and if we're hard wired for it. The short answer is yes and yes. And, competition often facilitates improvement.

QUESTIONS FOR MEDITATION:

In your experience, how does competition give you an edge and keep you refined and strong, and how does competition inhibit your energies or decrease your creativity? Is it one or the other?

"Without realizing that the past is constantly determining their present actions, they avoid learning anything about their history. They continue to live in their repressed childhood situation, ignoring the fact that it no longer exists, continuing to fear and avoid dangers that, although once real, have not been real for a long time."

WHY I LOVE THIS QUOTE:
It can be overwhelming and discouraging to realize you've lived out of a false self most or all of your life, and that has a great deal to do with personal resistance.

WHY THIS IS A TRANSFORMATIVE BOOK:
The Drama of the Gifted Child: The Search for the True Self by Alice Miller is an excellent book for learning more about yourself, how you became the way you are, and also as a possible source of help regarding the causes and cure of any emotional difficulties you may have. It will also help you better understand the people around you and how they came to be the way they are. "Gifted" does not refer necessarily to academic or artistic gifts (though these are common in the patient group Miller describes), rather a kind of emotional sensitivity. Miller describes narcissism as an internalization of the great expectations of one's parents, the consequent lasting feelings of inadequacy and drive to greater and greater successes. After all, Narcissus did not fall in love with himself, but with a false reflection of himself. The twin manifestations of narcissism are grandiosity and depression. Each is a defense against the other. Grandiosity arises as you feel your achievements render you superior to everyone else. Depression strikes when you realize you will never achieve as much as "necessary" to support your ego, or that all achievements are empty. Both manifestations can be traced back to a failure to express your true self and an idealization of a false-self.

QUESTIONS FOR MEDITATION:

Who is most responsible for molding you into the person you are? Who is most responsible for adapting and evolving now? Who challenges you the most?

"It is solely by risking life that freedom is obtained...the individual who has not staked his or her life may, no doubt, be recognized as a Person; but he or she has not attained the truth of this recognition as an independent self-consciousness."

WHY I LOVE THIS QUOTE:
It's a powerful distillation of why growth and personal freedom is hard. It takes real risk.

WHY THIS IS A TRANSFORMATIVE BOOK:
Hegel's Phenomenology of Spirit by Georg Wilhelm Friedrich Hegel, is perhaps one of the most revolutionary works of philosophy ever presented. The work as a whole is a remarkable study of the mind's growth from its direct awareness to scientific philosophy, proving to be a difficult yet highly influential and enduring work. As Roy Lotz writes, "Many have described the dialectic process as consisting of thesis, antithesis, and synthesis. The problem with this characterization is that Hegel never used those terms; and as we've seen he disliked logical formulas. Nevertheless, the description does manage to give a taste of Hegel's procedure. Mind, he thought, evolved through stages, which he calls 'moments'. At each of these moments, mind takes a specific form, in which it attempts to grapple with its reality. However, when mind has an erroneous conception of itself or its reality (which is just mind itself in another guise), it reaches an impasse, where it seems to encounter a contradiction. This contradiction is overcome via a synthesis, where the old conception and its contradiction are accommodated in a wider conception, which will in turn reach its own impasse, and so on until the final stage is reached."

QUESTIONS FOR MEDITATION:

Do you ever feel lost even while struggling to move forward?

"Everything about her spoke of alternatives and possibilities that if considered too deeply would wreak havoc with the neat plan I had laid out for my life."

WHY I LOVE THIS QUOTE:
It's easy to feel threatened by new ideas, even in the form of a burgeoning friendship. We've taken a long time to arrive at our plans. We've held onto them for a long time, and they intersect with our identity, of who we think we are.

WHY THIS IS A TRANSFORMATIVE TEXT:
Nervous Conditions by Tsitsi Dangarembga is a modern classic in the African literary canon and voted in the Top Ten Africa's 100 Best Books of the 20th Century. This novel brings to the politics of decolonization theory the energy of women's rights. This book is a work of vision. Through its deft negotiation of race, class, gender, and cultural change, it dramatizes the "nervousness" of the postcolonial conditions that are with us still. These are the questions Tambu has to ask herself. She's a young black girl living in a small, rural, improvised village in postcolonial Rhodesia. She initially believes that her ticket to self-improvement is through education. However, the only education available is the white man's education. She learns to speak English, and eventually she looks back on her origins with an air of indifference and woe. Not as much as her brother did, but to a degree that considers them under-developed and primitive. She has opportunities afforded to few, but is this a good thing if she comes to scorn her origins?

QUESTIONS FOR MEDITATION:

If you are forced to accept another culture's ways and customs, who is the "you" that is left?

"When I look at a sunset as I did the other evening, I don't find myself saying, 'Soften the orange a little on the right hand corner, and put a bit more purple along the base, and use a little more pink in the cloud color'. I don't do that. I don't try to control a sunset. I watch it with awe as it unfolds. I like myself best when I can appreciate my staff member, my son, my daughter, my grandchildren, in this same way. I believe this is a somewhat Oriental attitude; for me it is a most satisfying one."

WHY I LOVE THIS QUOTE:

Toward the end of his life, especially, Rogers assimilated other world views into his methods. I love the illustration as a way of unconditionally observing and appreciating the others in our lives. It reminds me of Parker Palmer's instructions in *A Hidden Wholeness*. When we listen to the struggles of others, don't try to fix or offer advice. Simply listen. Nothing more or less. Our presence with each other is enough. We need community and acceptance first and foremost. For all the ways in which you are encouraged through the readings and meditations in this book to have the courage to change, you should also occasionally take a step back and have grace for yourself, and gratitude for where you are and the others in your life.

WHY THIS IS A TRANSFORMATIVE BOOK:

A Way of Being by Carl Rogers shows us what is possible out of pre-constructed roles. He shows us a way to empathy, a fascinating journey into the experience of the other. This book is a classic for a reason. It serves as a guidepost towards phenomenology in the abstract and humanity in the concrete.

QUESTIONS FOR MEDITATION:

What are you grateful for today? Who are the others in your life that you can love exactly for who they are right now?

"Knowing that what you are doing is the most important thing for you to be doing at that moment is surprisingly powerful."

WHY I LOVE THIS QUOTE:
This idea applies to being present in the moment, as well as doing your one job well. While inner growth and life itself is a process, it's all about the sum total of our present moments. The quote is also helpful because it implies that you have made conscious and/or strategic decisions ahead of time in order to be focused and present in the task at hand.

WHY THIS IS A TRANSFORMATIVE BOOK:
The Organized Mind: Thinking Straight in the Age of Information Overload by Daniel J. Levitin doesn't have much good to say about multitasking. It increases the production of the stress hormone cortisol and the fight-or-flight hormone adrenaline. These chemicals overstimulate the brain and cause scrambled thinking. Multitasking puts the brain into a feedback loop that rewards it for losing focus, and causes one to constantly search for external stimulation. There are many practical takeaways from the book, although it is much more about the latest research than specific things you should do to be more organized. One thing he stresses is to make use of 3x5 cards and make To Do lists frequently. The cards can be reordered and re-prioritized whenever desired. By writing things down, you give your mind permission to focus on other things. Some chapters are more directly applicable to transformation than others, but overall it is packed with well-assimilated and groundbreaking research.

QUESTIONS FOR MEDITATION:

How can you be wholly present and attentive to your tasks today? Track your consciousness. When does it want to tune out? When does it engage?

"The road to enlightenment is long and difficult, and you should try not to forget snacks and magazines."

WHY I LOVE THIS QUOTE:
Lamott also writes, "I do not at all understand the mystery of grace — only that it meets us where we are but does not leave us where it found us." Between these two quotes we should continue to remember that the road you are traveling is uneven. Growth will happen. Change will come with greater compassion for yourself and others, which is the best form of grace we can give ourselves.

WHY THIS IS A TRANSFORMATIVE BOOK:
Traveling Mercies: Some Thoughts on Faith by Anne Lamott demonstrates her ability to look at the ugly and petty, along with the sublime of her life. She inspires without resorting to preaching mainly because you really feel she has been there with you. Her irreverence and humor don't hurt either. Lamott's faith isn't about easy answers, which is part of what endears her to believers as well as nonbelievers. Against all odds, she came to believe in God, and then, in herself. As she puts it, "My coming to faith did not start with a leap but rather a series of staggers."

QUESTIONS FOR MEDITATION:

Can a rational, free-thinking, independent person have religious faith?

"Two things fill the mind with renewed and increasing awe and reverence the more often and the more steadily that they are meditated on: the starry skies above me and the moral law inside me. I have not to search for them and conjecture them as though they were veiled in darkness or were in the transcendent region beyond my horizon; I see them before me and connect them directly with the consciousness of my existence."

WHY I LOVE THIS QUOTE:
As you can see throughout the course of these readings there is a steady drumbeat of philosophers over the course of the past several hundred years up to the current moment that stress the congruence of the inner and outer reality we experience. It would seem that for as critical as science is to our understanding of reality, that the inner reality comes under a kind of stress test.

WHY THIS IS A TRANSFORMATIVE BOOK:
Critique of Pure Reason by Immanuel Kant is a brilliant and incalculably important book which, it could be argued, created modern thought. Kant's critical turn shows that the problem of self-knowledge, not metaphysics, is the true subject matter for philosophy. It argues that it is not metaphysics that should serve as a meta-science, or as the discipline that can critique science in order to discern its underlying logical systematic discourse, but rather the theory of self-knowledge that can perform that function. Kant shows that it is the theory of self-knowledge alone that can identify the logical principles by which we can conceive the unity of knowledge. Knowledge is one because experience is one, and all knowledge is based on principles that are ultimately drawn from the structure of experience. Kant introduces a new starting point for thought itself.

QUESTIONS FOR MEDITATION:

How can we value and define that which isn't measurable or verifiable in a scientific or financial sense?

"Searcher, there is no road. We make the road by walking."

WHY I LOVE THIS QUOTE:

Not all who wander are lost because we are making the very road as we go. Of course we don't have to reinvent the wheel. There are plenty of others who have done a great deal of thinking and struggling ahead of us, and we would do well to consider their arguments and experiences. But in the end we do walk our journey in our own particular way. We have to find what works for us.

WHY THIS IS A TRANSFORMATIVE BOOK:

Brian Christian's *The Most Human Human: What Talking with Computers Teaches Us About What It Means to Be Alive* is a profound exploration of the ways in which computers are reshaping our ideas of what it means to be human. Did you know that the term "computers" was originally a job description for people who could perform calculations for a living? Not until the 20th century did the word begin to refer to a device. Far from being a mere rhetorical exercise, reading this book asks us serious questions about how we live our life, questions literary writers, such as David Foster Wallace, have asked, and that spiritual pioneers such as Alan Watts anticipated. Christian points out that throughout history we have largely defined ourselves as separate and distinct from other species and as a "soul" through our rational ability.

QUESTIONS FOR MEDITATION:

What does it mean to "act human"?

november

"What you think you are is a belief to be undone."

WHY I LOVE THIS QUOTE:

The persona we project to the world — our best, most affable self — is the part of us under the spotlight. The shadow, by contrast, has long been trained to "hide" from the light. Our defense mechanisms keep our shadows repressed and out of view for reasons we may not be aware of, which makes it all the harder to "out" the shadow. Of all the paths to self-knowledge, the shadow is one of the most important (if not the most important) and is also the least understood. Remaining unconscious of the shadow hurts our relationships with our spouses, family, and friends, and it will impact our professional relationships, as well as our leadership abilities. Those are the kind of self-beliefs that should be undone and reworked into our emerging and ever-expanding compassionate identities.

WHY THIS IS A TRANSFORMATIVE BOOK:

A Course in Miracles by Helen Schucman is a profound, direct, non-dualistic pathway to spiritual renewal and awakening. The wisdom and clear instructions support a total transformation of consciousness, from identification with the voice and thought patterns of the ego (fear-based thinking) to identification with Spirit (Love) and the still, small voice within. Many find it a life study.

QUESTIONS FOR MEDITATION:

How can you completely and wholeheartedly accept who you are if there are sides of yourself that you're too afraid to explore?

"The idea that leading in a 'fast world' always requires 'fast decisions' and 'fast action' — and that we should embrace an overall ethos of 'Fast! Fast! Fast!' — is a good way to get killed. 10x leaders figure out when to go fast, and when not to."

WHY I LOVE THIS QUOTE:

It speaks to me. When I get excited about something I race toward its execution with my hair on fire in search of a pond. There is so much to be said for deliberation, analysis and study first. Ready, aim, fire, not the other way around. There is a Latin phrase, *Gradatim Ferociter*, which translates to *step by step, ferociously*.

WHY THIS IS A TRANSFORMATIVE BOOK:

Great by Choice: Uncertainty, Chaos, and Luck — Why Some Thrive Despite Them All by Jim Collins and Morten Hansen is another case of Collins' exhaustive research (reviewing 20,400 companies with 7,000 historical documents) and synthesizing them down to 11 fixed criterions. Collins, along with Hansen, a faculty member at Harvard Business School, spare no effort in coming up with bold new theories and thought provoking concepts. The foundation is based on the following premise: uncertainty is permanent; the worst will always be round the corner; chaotic times are normal; sudden great fortune is always dangerous; change is accelerating; and instability will characterize the rest of our lives.

QUESTIONS FOR MEDITATION:

Why do some thrive in the face of immense uncertainty, and others do not?

"The world will tell you how to live, if you let it. Don't let it. Take up your space. Raise your voice. Sing your song. This is your chance to make or remake a life that thrills you."

WHY I LOVE THIS QUOTE:
Nobody can live it for you, although a lot of people would probably offer to do just that. It's amazing how many people live under others' oppressive rules, agendas, expectations (tactic and otherwise). This is your one life. If anyone is taking notes on your every move, then they need to get their own life. Meanwhile, follow your desires and find yours.

WHY THIS IS A TRANSFORMATIVE BOOK:
Present Over Perfect: Leaving Behind Frantic for a Simpler, More Soulful Way of Living by Shauna Niequist is an invitation to this journey that changed my life. I'll walk this path with you, a path away from frantic pushing and proving, and toward your essential self, the one you were created to be before you began proving and earning for your worth. Written in Niequist's warm and vulnerable style, this collection of essays focuses on the most important transformation in her life, and maybe yours too: leaving behind busyness and frantic living and rediscovering the person you were made to be. Shauna offers an honest account of what led her to begin this journey, and a compelling vision for an entirely new way to live: soaked in grace, rest, silence, simplicity, prayer, and connection with the people that matter most to us.

QUESTIONS FOR MEDITATION:

When it comes to your decision-making processes, do you find yourself resistant to asking yourself hard questions? Do you substitute your answers with smaller, easier ones?

"There is only one thing that makes a dream impossible to achieve: the fear of failure."

WHY I LOVE THIS QUOTE:
There are so many great quotes from this jewel of a book. This one says something that strikes me as elemental — the weird stuff that the fear does to us. Structurally, the sentence is also interesting in that the subject (the dream) is curtailed by the antecedent, the fear (of failure).

WHY THIS IS A TRANSFORMATIVE BOOK:
The Alchemist by Paulo Coelho, is a tiny masterpiece that tells the mystical story of Santiago, an Andalusian shepherd boy who yearns to travel in search of a worldly treasure. His quest will lead him to riches far different, and far more satisfying, listening to our hearts, of recognizing opportunity and learning to read the omens strewn along life's path, and, most importantly, to follow our dreams.

QUESTIONS FOR MEDITATION:

It might require listening, watching, suffering, gathering whatever self-knowledge you can, but if you can then can you take the next step toward making choices based on your knowledge, no matter how hard?

"There is the risk you cannot afford to take, and there is the risk you cannot afford not to take."

WHY I LOVE THIS QUOTE:
This speaks for itself, but the tricky part is knowing the difference between the two. It's a different choice when it comes to a business decision and a personal life choice. The way to be best prepared for making tough choices and taking the right risk is to thoroughly know who you are, what you value, and what will bring the most joy to you and those closest to you. Hopefully, you do this in advance of the opportunity. Having a mentor, or at least following a leader you admire, can also be of immense help.

WHY THIS IS A TRANSFORMATIVE BOOK:
Leadership Lessons from Peter Drucker covers everything from politics and economics of the environment to knowledge workers and the Knowledge Society to computer and information literacy to managing nonprofit organizations and the increasing demands of working in a globalization economy. During his life, Drucker well understood that over the last 150 years the world had become a society of large institutions — and that they would only become larger and more powerful. He contended that unless these institutions were effectively managed and ethically led, the good health of society as a whole would be in peril. His prediction is unfolding before our eyes.

QUESTIONS FOR MEDITATION:

What leader has had the most positive influence in your daily life? What three words best describe what this person contributes to your life?

"This process of being mature in an anxious organization has been likened to learning to sail against the wind; and as any sailor will tell you, this requires concentration and tolerating some tension as the wind pressures the vessel to let it take over the controls. Good skippers know how to tolerate sufficient tension to keep a steady course...There's only one path to growing this ability: through patient, thoughtful perseverance in the midst of experience...no shortcuts to be found."

WHY I LOVE THIS QUOTE:
It's a nice metaphor for working on yourself as it relates to others, and of course the recognition that it takes hard, patient, and persistent work.

WHY THIS IS A TRANSFORMATIVE BOOK:
Growing Yourself Up: How to Bring Your Best to All of Life's Relationships by Jenny Brown is a guide to growing up based on a lifelong inner process from the inner child to the inner adult. Based on the Bowen Theory of family systems, you are introduced to the concept that human relations are not based on individuals, but on a vast network of reactions starting from your families of origin over generations. In light of all the complex inter-relations within the family dynamics, however, in the end you are responsible for your own reactions, not the other member's behavior. Nowhere is it more clear that you must begin with yourself in order to expect change within a family, and even then it is no guarantee that the system will change because each individual has to take personal ownership for their own growth. Whether it's a parent or a child or a significant other you expect change from, first begin with yourself.

QUESTIONS FOR MEDITATION:

Have you seen your inner growth influence the behavior of others in your tribe?

"Authentic happiness derives from raising the bar for your-self, not rating yourself against others."

WHY I LOVE THIS QUOTE:

Another reminder that transformation comes from the work you do on yourself through another turn of the multifaceted diamond of the self. It should be noted, too, that "raising the bar" for yourself doesn't necessarily mean doing more, more, more. It may mean the opposite. Or it may mean doing what you do with greater clarity and mindful purpose.

WHY THIS IS A TRANSFORMATIVE BOOK:

Authentic Happiness: Using the New Positive Psychology to Realize Your Potential for Lasting Fulfillment by Martin Seligman effectively launched the revolutionary new science of Positive Psychology — and sparked a coast-to-coast debate on the nature of real happiness. According to Seligman, happiness comes from focusing on one's personal strengths rather than weaknesses — and working with them to improve all aspects of one's life. Using practical exercises, brief tests, and a dynamic website program, he shows readers how to identify their highest virtues and use them in ways they haven't yet considered.

QUESTIONS FOR MEDITATION:

How can you raise the bar for yourself and do less? What would that mean? How would it look?

"When asked about what they regret most in the last six months, people tend to identify actions that didn't meet expectations. But when asked about what they regret most when they look back on their lives as a whole, people tend to identify failures to act."

WHY I LOVE THIS QUOTE:

Trevor Noah, Elisabeth Kubler-Ross, and several others in our readings throughout the year have pointed to this very idea. These are the kinds of choices you think are in unlimited supply when they're presented to you, but only in retrospect do you realize they never come again. It's part of why, after our Peter Drucker reading from a few days back, we consider how to be prepared to take the right risks when they come.

WHY THIS IS A TRANSFORMATIVE BOOK:

The Paradox of Choice: Why More Is Less by Barry Schwartz is one of those books that, once you've read it, permanently shifts your perspective. It makes you think altogether differently about the diminishing value of having more choices. As the author argues, your sense of well-being increases when you go from having no choices to having a few choices. But as you go from having a few choices to having many choices, your happiness typically goes down. It's time-consuming and stressful to choose between all those alternatives. You become fearful of making a mistake, of not making the absolute best choice. And often the more time you spend making that perfect choice, the more unhappy you are second-guessing yourself after the fact.

QUESTIONS FOR MEDITATION:

What choices do you make by simply not choosing? How can you create the conditions for better options in your short-to-medium term future without compromising on doing what gives you joy?

"A second chance is not a repeat of the first chance. A second chance is a moving forward to something new."

WHY I LOVE THIS QUOTE:

This quote speaks to me as I sometimes struggle with projects that I spent great time and energy on, but that were abandoned along the road for one reason or another. The reasons might have been good or realistic, but some projects were left behind due to life circumstances more than the project really needing to be abandoned. This thought inspires the idea of renewal or recovering from that which has been left behind.

WHY THIS IS A TRANSFORMATIVE BOOK:

Never Go Back by Henry Cloud teaches what we might call common sense principles to a certain extent: never trust something that seems too perfect, always do due diligence, never turn from short-term pain that brings long-term success. At the same time, it's amazing how many people don't practice them, and the lessons from the book are inspiring about finding inner clarity and resources to find the right direction. Cloud relates his ten principles to scripture without didacticism. He is a person of faith who can talk about matters of psychology and culture without exclusivity.

QUESTIONS FOR MEDITATION:

Is there a profession or perhaps even a creative project that you could return to without "going back"? Could you re-envision yourself from who you are now with a new opportunity? On the other hand, are there professions or projects that you refuse to return to no matter how good the opportunity?

"Most enjoyable activities are not natural; they demand an effort that initially one is reluctant to make. But once the interaction starts to provide feedback to the person's skills, it usually begins to be intrinsically rewarding."

WHY I LOVE THIS QUOTE:

This is the kind of activity we want you to have more of in your life.

WHY THIS IS A TRANSFORMATIVE BOOK:

Flow: The Psychology of Optimal Experience is the landmark text of psychologist Mihaly Csikszentmihalyi's investigations of "optimal experience." The discoveries of his 1990 classic revealed that what makes an experience genuinely satisfying is a state of consciousness called flow. During flow, people typically experience deep enjoyment, creativity, and a total involvement with life. Csikszentmihalyi demonstrates the ways this positive state can be controlled, not just left to chance. The book teaches how, by ordering the information that enters our consciousness, we can discover true happiness, unlock our potential, and greatly improve the quality of our lives. It is highly applicable across all industries, and was groundbreaking to generate ideas and practices in clinical psychotherapy, the rehabilitation of juvenile delinquents, the organization of activities in old people's homes, the design of museum exhibits, and occupational therapy with the handicapped. Flow examines the fundamental process of achieving happiness through control over your inner life.

QUESTIONS FOR MEDITATION:

How is consciousness controlled? How is it ordered so as to make experience enjoyable? How is complexity achieved? How can meaning be created?

"If I take death into my life, acknowledge it, and face it squarely, I will free myself from the anxiety of death and the pettiness of life — and only then will I be free to become myself."

WHY I LOVE THIS QUOTE:

Recent brain studies confirm that when it comes to dealing with an anxiety, the best approach is not to resist it by acting like you aren't aware of the thought, trying to repress it, or ignore it. Let your mind look at the anxiety as a neutral observer. This has been shown again and again to take the power of the anxiety away, especially over time and with calm resolve. Death is the ultimate anxiety, and Heidegger is showing us a way to freedom by acknowledging its presence rather than ignoring it.

WHY THIS IS A TRANSFORMATIVE BOOK:

On Being and Time by Martin Heidegger opened awareness to the complexities of Dasein, a German word, referring to the experience of being peculiar to human beings. It is a form of being that is self-aware, and must confront such issues as personhood, mortality, and the dilemma or paradox of living in relationship with other humans while being ultimately alone with oneself. Cultural studies, sociology, psychology, philosophy, history, and creative disciplines alike have been affected by this and other ideas in this book. *Being and Time* stands with few other books in terms of their influence on subsequent Continental Philosophic thinking. His ontological and epistemological investigations have profoundly influenced his successors.

QUESTIONS FOR MEDITATION:

Be present to your emotions as you consider how short life is. Try to climb out of your head and acknowledge it on a feeling level. How do you want to be remembered?

"'Had you not seen [the world] from birth and thereby bled it of its strangeness it would appear to you for what it is, a hat trick in a medicine show, a fevered dream, a trance bepopulate with chimeras having neither analogue nor precedent, an itinerant carnival, a migratory tentshow whose ultimate destination after many a pitch in many a mudded field is unspeakable and calamitous beyond reckoning.'"

WHY I LOVE THIS QUOTE:
This is one of the judge's unyielding diatriabes, and what's interesting are the incantatory-like speech. He sounds somewhat like God explaining to Job his answer to Why?: "Where were you when I laid the foundations of the earth?" Similarly, we are forced to puzzle out for ourselves just what to make of the judge. Another interesting thought from a theological angle at least is: What should we expect from God? Should we only expect comfort and grace, even when we know part of the very design of existence is that growth comes through struggle. Maya Angelou called it "the perverse truth."

WHY THIS IS A TRANSFORMATIVE BOOK:
Blood Meridian, or the Evening Redness in the West by Cormac McCarthy is an epic novel of the violence and depravity that attended America's westward expansion, brilliantly subverting the conventions of the Western novel and the mythology of the Wild West. Based on historical events that took place on the Texas-Mexico border in the 1850s, it traces the fortunes of the Kid, a fourteen-year-old Tennesseean who stumbles into a nightmarish world where Indians are being murdered and the market for their scalps is thriving.

QUESTIONS FOR MEDITATION:

What can we learn about ourselves even through terrible suffering that we did not deserve?

"I find I am more effective when I can listen acceptantly to myself, and can be myself. I have learned to become more adequate in listening to myself; so that I know...what I am feeling at any given moment. One way of putting this is that I feel I have become more adequate in letting myself be what I am....The curious paradox is that when I accept myself as I am, then I change."

WHY I LOVE THIS QUOTE:

The true self can be complex to define in some ways, in another it can be distilled quite simply. The true selves are the selves that profoundly see into all parts of their character, and love them with compassion. When we can stand before our self, and see through the wilderness of good and bad, of where we're proud and ashamed, where we present the persona, and hide the shadow, with acceptance, then when we turn outward, our actions toward others have changed as well. It's two things: great inner self-knowledge, and a deeply compassionate self. That speaks to Jung's shadow, and this "curious paradox."

WHY THIS IS A TRANSFORMATIVE BOOK:

On Becoming a Person: A Therapist's View of Psychotherapy by Carl Rogers is his landmark book. His influence has spanned decades, but that influence has become so much a part of mainstream psychology that the ingenious nature of his work has almost been forgotten. Rogers' "client-centered therapy" remains timely and important.

QUESTIONS FOR MEDITATION:

What characteristics do you most judge in others? What characteristics were not tolerated or seen as unacceptable in your family growing up? Therein lies your shadow.

"If you are unsure of a course of action, do not attempt it. Your doubts and hesitations will infect your execution. Timidity is dangerous: Better to enter with boldness. Any mistakes you commit through audacity are easily corrected with more audacity. Everyone admires the bold; no one honors the timid."

WHY I LOVE THIS QUOTE:

"Most of us are timid," Green writes. "We want to avoid tension and conflict and we want to be liked by all. We may contemplate a bold action but we rarely bring it to life. We are terrified by the consequences, of what others might think of us, of the hostility we will stir up if we dare go beyond our usual place. Although we may disguise our timidity as a concern for others, a desire not to hurt or offend them, in fact it is the opposite — we are really self-absorbed, worried about ourselves and how others perceive us. Boldness, on the other hand, is outer-directed, and often makes people more at ease, since it is less self-conscious and less repressed."

WHY THIS IS A TRANSFORMATIVE BOOK:

The 48 Laws of Power by Robert Green is a one-of-a-kind book. We can talk all day about being open and flexible, having a mind like water, and forgiving others their trespasses upon us. But life is also about creating and maintaining good boundaries. And while it's great to be gentle as a lamb, it's also a bottom line to realize the way human beings and their relationship with power works. Power is a force we are always bumping up against. People have power over us, we seek power to accomplish our goals. We must understand power, how it works and how to get it. This book synthesizes the philosophies of Machiavelli, Sun Tzu, and Carl Von Clausewitz with the historical legacies of statesmen, warriors, seducers, and con men throughout the ages. With fascinating, in-depth historical detail followed by scrupulous and creative analysis and application, Green has created a masterpiece.

QUESTIONS FOR MEDITATION:

What actions are you behaving timidly in that you dream of being bold and just doing?

"'That is very well put', said Candide, 'but we must cultivate our garden.'"

WHY I LOVE THIS QUOTE:

In the end, Candide concludes, all we can do is tend to our own garden. *Il faut cultiver nos jardins.* Some may find this cynical, but I find it a good beginning point. Family systems Bowen theory, for instance, says that for you to create the change in the system's dynamics do one thing first: work on yourself. Of course, you should turn your attention to others as you grow. Don't just sit there in your garden for the rest of your life.

WHY THIS IS A TRANSFORMATIVE BOOK:

Candide by Voltaire is a classic from the Enlightenment that I loved from the first time I had to read it in Western Civ. I worked it into my own curriculum whenever I had the chance in World Literature classes. Despite the fact that the book is about suffering, torture, the ignorance and corruption of the powerful, it is also a light-hearted satire that pokes fun at optimism, philosophy, politics, and power. I also identify with Candide's naive, exploratory open-mindedness. I too have fallen under the spells of people's false philosophies, creeds, and ways of viewing the world, like Candide experiences against the "expert" Pangloss and the foolishness of his blind optimism.

QUESTIONS FOR MEDITATION:

How long do you tend your garden before you help others tend their own?

"I am convinced that something positive begins to happen within me when I do look death, my death, straight in the eye. When I say 'Yes' to it, however haltingly, something new and fresh stirs in my soul."

WHY I LOVE THIS QUOTE:

This is an inverse way of seeing the opportunity of beauty within our finitude. I love the extra spin he puts on it as he unpacks the idea. Death puts our whole existence into question without providing an answer. When we look death in the eye we are surrendering. The surrender can lead in various directions, such as despair, or just to the unknown. It can also be an act of faith that a "radical rescue is at hand."

WHY THIS IS A TRANSFORMATIVE BOOK:

Soul Making: The Desert Way of Spirituality by Alan Jones distills the elements that made the orthodox way of inner transformation from early Christian monks in the Egyptian desert a unique and important part of the early church. Filled with rich insights, *Soul Making* draws together the spirituality of modern literature with elements of psychology. Jones admits to finding it increasingly difficult to feel at home with fellow Christians while becoming more comfortable with non-Christians. The two characteristics he admires most in both kinds of people are honesty and reverence. The two marks of the Christian, he says, are joy and penitence.

QUESTIONS FOR MEDITATION:

How will you know when your work is done?

"Even when you have an organization brimming with talent, victory is not always under your control. There is no guarantee, no ultimate formula for success. It all comes down to intelligently and relentlessly seeking solutions that will increase your chance of prevailing. When you do that, the score will take care of itself."

WHY I LOVE THIS QUOTE:
The mainstay of your happiness will come from living in alignment with your values. If part of your values is to succeed, all you can do is create the conditions. Control what you can control, and be observant of your motivations. Living an integrated life can tolerate a wide variety of outward successes and maintain fulfillment. With all that said, the main focus of the idea is maximize your chances for success and truly create successful conditions.

WHY THIS IS A TRANSFORMATIVE BOOK:
The Score Takes Care of Itself: My Philosophy of Leadership by Bill Walsh has a lot of powerful gems. It's about structure, culture, discipline, habits, and finding your inner purpose. Great results come from small improvements made on a regular basis over a long period of time. Walsh's story is also a cautionary tale. His career was one of the most successful in NFL history, but shows us that success alone is not enough. Despite, or perhaps because of, his incredible accomplishments, Walsh felt extreme stress to always succeed. The relentless striving and perfectionism finally broke him down. The book preaches to focus on improvement over success. Tie your identity to how you go about getting results rather than the results themselves. Walsh wasn't able to do this himself, and it cost him dearly.

QUESTIONS FOR MEDITATION:

How do you create the conditions for success in your own life?

"Not every story has a happy ending...but the discoveries of science, the teachings of the heart, and the revelations of the soul all assure us that no human being is ever beyond redemption. The possibility of renewal exists so long as life exists. How to support that possibility in others and in ourselves is the ultimate question."

WHY I LOVE THIS QUOTE:

"Addictions arise from thwarted love, from our thwarted ability to love children the way they need to be loved, from our thwarted ability to love ourselves and one another in the ways we all need," writes Maté. This is why through some of our readings we hit on the power of needing to have self-compassion even while examining all the parts of ourselves.

WHY THIS IS A TRANSFORMATIVE BOOK:

In the Realm of Hungry Ghosts: Close Encounters with Addiction by Gabor Maté theorizes that addiction is an issue of society at large. Addiction is neither a choice nor a disease. It is a rational adaptation to that society by members who have been traumatized by circumstances. Addiction to sex, consumption, popularity, religion, politics, computer games, and power are much more common, and could easily involve most of the human population of industrialized countries. Each has their own form of damage. All these addictions have the same ultimate source, and the same prognosis. You will not overcome your addiction without inner transformation, and removing the triggers.

QUESTIONS FOR MEDITATION:

How do you support the possibility of renewal in your own life?

"Your life is yours to create. Be grateful for the opportunity. Seize it with passion and boldness. Whatever you decide to do, commit to it with all your strength...and begin it now."

WHY I LOVE THIS QUOTE:

It's easy enough to still see Buffett's inherent privilege, but in some ways, as the son of a billionaire, you could also see how there was even more at stake for him to prove himself. More than an average amount of pressure. His idea lines up with our recent quote from Robert Green's Law 28, Enter Action with Boldness.

WHY THIS IS A TRANSFORMATIVE BOOK:

Life Is What You Make It: Find Your Own Path to Fulfillment by Peter Buffett is a book about personal and fundamental values. The son of one of the world's richest billionaires, Peter Buffett received from his dad what many would call a questionable inheritance: a $90,000 check at age 19. That was it. Peter was raised to expect nothing unearned. He understood from early on that his father's substantial fortune would never trickle down his way, because he needed to find his own path, prove himself, make his own living, and discover his self-worth, self-respect, and the meaning of his life all on his own. His true inheritance was less tangible: uncompromising moral and ethical values, true love of knowledge and learning, and a strong work ethic that was based not on acquiring wealth but on committing to his passion. Eventually Peter carved out his own successful career as a music composer and author, and later also created a way to give back to society by starting a foundation that helps girls and women find equality and opportunities.

QUESTIONS FOR MEDITATION:

If you are taking Peter Buffett's advice to heart, what are you waiting for?

"Enjoy making decisions. You must know that in any moment a decision you make can change the course of your life forever: the very next person you stand behind in line or sit next to on an airplane, the very next phone call you make or receive, the very next movie you see or book you read or page you turn could be the one single thing that causes the floodgates to open, and all of the things that you've been waiting for to fall into place. If you really want your life to be passionate, you need to live with this attitude of expectancy."

WHY I LOVE THIS QUOTE:

Rather than just say, "Be bold," this is an incisive way to open the floodgates of optimism. Enjoy making decisions because you're cranking on the gears one way or another. You're progressing even if sometimes the decisions aren't good ones. You learn from failing. At least by making decisions you are moving the needle.

WHY THIS IS A TRANSFORMATIVE BOOK:

Awaken the Giant Within: How to Take Immediate Control of Your Mental, Emotional, Physical and Financial Destiny! by Tony Robbins teaches about the power of the mindset to impact everything from your persistence to your self-confidence. The book introduces you to Neuro Linguistic Programming which proves effective with practice. Robbins offers plenty of personal anecdotes and some of the struggles he faced growing up. While some may be resistant to his slick marketing and excessive use of exclamation points, it's actually a very well thought-out book. This first book of Robbins' is a practical, strategic guide and not a book of mere superficial hope.

QUESTIONS FOR MEDITATION:

What are examples of good decisions you've made and how did you make them? What are examples of poor decisions you've made and how did you make them?

"All of humanity's problems stem from man's inability to sit quietly in a room alone."

WHY I LOVE THIS QUOTE:

Well, that's partially the thesis upon which we constructed this book. Maybe with a bit more optimism. We're saying, "It can be done, but you do actually have to find the right books and do the work." This is a quintessential Pascal quote: it's funny and sad, true in a certain sense, but not meant to be taken too terribly literally.

WHY THIS IS A TRANSFORMATIVE BOOK:

Pensées by Blaise Pascal were never intended to be read, much like Marcus Aurelius' *Meditations*. As such, they honestly reveal the private thoughts of great philosophers on the human condition, and they speak of how miserable people are. Both were lonely men made so by their great intellect and great character. While Marcus continues to strive with Ragnarokian futility to fulfill all his duties in a life of perfect virtue, Pascal is a bit more pessimistic, yet in the end more hopeful when he looks to Christ for ultimate purpose. Even those who don't believe in God will extract much wisdom from Pascal. His one-liners are some of the most devastating observations of human psychology. Even a cursory exercise in quote-mining will yield many seeds for extended thought. This book should be read carefully and digested fragment by fragment, line by line.

QUESTIONS FOR MEDITATION:

When did reading make a huge difference in your enrichment and understanding?

"Some men give up their designs when they have almost reached the goal, while others, on the contrary, obtain a victory by exerting, at the last moment, more vigorous efforts than ever before."

WHY I LOVE THIS QUOTE:

I've seen men and women get right up to the thing they wanted the very most, that they had driven for and dreamed of, and then walk away. I've seen a whole lot of the latter, especially when it comes to any of us trying to beat a deadline. The point seems to be to drive all the way to the very end. Finish strong.

WHY THIS IS A TRANSFORMATIVE BOOK:

The Histories by Herodotus converted legend-writing into the science of history in the fifth century BCE. The prime subject of The Histories is the twenty years (499-479 B.C.E) of war between Greece and Persia for domination of the Greek world. Herodotus is a consummate storyteller who had a fine eye for the fantastical, although to his credit, he always qualified his more improbable assertions by stating that they are based on hearsay or other sources that he could not wholly verify. Much of the pleasure of reading his book is found in the lush descriptions of long lost nations and their exotic customs. He doesn't focus solely with history in the modern sense. It is also a book of travelogue, ethnography, zoology, geography, and botany. He is an excellent raconteur, almost always entertaining, except when he drones about speculative geography. Literary-wise we could say he is a precursor to Tristram Shandy — progress through digression. One of the masterpieces of classical literature.

QUESTIONS FOR MEDITATION:

Have you ever given up on a goal even when it was within view? Do you stick with your goals in general, or do you frequently stop after given just some effort?

"It is not for me to judge another man's life. I must judge, I must choose, I must spurn, purely for myself. For myself, alone."

WHY I LOVE THIS QUOTE:

It may sound a little harsh, but he's seeking truth for himself. There is one person he must concern himself with, and one person only forever and ever, and that is himself. That is the foundation of Bowen Family Systems, and connects to insights and readings throughout this reader. "Want to rule an empire? First, rule yourself."

WHY THIS IS A TRANSFORMATIVE BOOK:

Siddhartha by Hermann Hesse is a classic novel that has delighted, inspired, and influenced generations of readers, writers, and thinkers. A wealthy Indian Brahmin casts off a life of privilege to seek spiritual fulfillment. Hesse synthesizes disparate philosophies — Eastern religions, Jungian archetypes, Western individualism — into a unique vision of life as expressed through one man's search for true meaning.

In order to attain enlightenment, he must first realize the true state of emptiness. And to understand emptiness one must first experience temporary fullness. He walks into the world of the everyday man. He indulges in their pleasure, gains possessions, and takes a lover. He forms attachments and begets a household of servants and wealth. Through experiencing such things, he learns that they are shallow and transitory. They will never create the feeling of lasting happiness within his soul, so he walks out once more with the full realization that peace can only come from one place: himself.

QUESTIONS FOR MEDITATION:

Do you think it's possible in your day-to-day interactions to judge no one but yourself? Is that even reasonable to assume of anyone?

"Optimism is, in the first instance, a way of explaining failure, not prophesying success. It says that there is no fundamental barrier, no law of nature or supernatural decree, preventing progress."

WHY I LOVE THIS QUOTE:
It's a pretty engaging idea about the inevitability of progress. We're going to stay curious. We're going to keep testing, and we're going to keep failing, but by the very nature of curiosity, testing, and a willingness to fail, we are going to progress at some point. May we apply the same optimism to our own lives.

WHY THIS IS A TRANSFORMATIVE BOOK:
The Beginning of Infinity: Explanations That Transform the World by David Deutsch is about rational optimism. The West owes science and logical thinking an awful lot. Deustch's main idea is that science is defined by seeking explanations for the universal laws that govern reality — and the places we're bound to go know no bounds. Nothing is sacred to Deutsch — least of all religion — only human ingenuity. We're thinkers and doers. We read and write and pass on critical knowledge from generation to generation. Our intelligence has "reach," and eventually even, we're going to be immigrants to other worlds. Get your Passport ready. The Enlightenment for everyone. Mind-bending and wholly surprising from chapter to chapter. A one-of-a-kind book, wherever it may land.

QUESTIONS FOR MEDITATION:

You'll see books from time to time that suggest "try things out," and "don't be afraid to fail." We've seen many quotes and ideas along these very lines. While you may agree in theory, does it ever make you willing and ready to try something new out? What personal growth or life challenges are you experimenting with right now?

"All the world's stupidest people are either zealots or atheists. If you want to truly deduce how intelligent someone is, just ask this person how they feel about any issue that doesn't have an answer; the more certainty they express, the less sense they have. This is because certainty only comes from dogma."

WHY I LOVE THIS QUOTE:

This is a parallel to Voltaire's famous quote, "Doubt is not a pleasant condition, but certainty is absurd." In my own life, I have learned to keep clear of people with their "certainty," whatever system that may be. They tend to be certain of all their opinions, which means they aren't listening, and that they're only ready to convert you into their ideological vortex. They may be good for information-gathering and research on the folly of what it means to be human, but generally speaking they are not healthy for those pursuing wisdom and personal growth.

WHY THIS IS A TRANSFORMATIVE BOOK:

Chuck Klosterman IV: A Decade of Curious People and Dangerous Ideas may rank lower on the transformational potential of the hundreds named and briefly discussed in this book, but we bring it in because it's funny. It's pop-cultural, and therefore relevant to our time through a different lens. A book with some general levity and upside-down thinking seems in order — especially if you're going through this book in order. In which case, you deserve a pat on the back.

QUESTIONS FOR MEDITATION:

Would you say you are rigid or flexible in your beliefs and opinions? Can you be both?

"The mind commands the body and is instantly obeyed. The mind commands itself and meets resistance."

WHY I LOVE THIS QUOTE:

He also says, "And men go abroad to admire the heights of mountains, the mighty waves of the sea, the broad tides of rivers, the compass of the ocean, and the circuits of the stars, yet pass over the mystery of themselves without a thought." The inner journey is so hard for some just to try. Oddly, some of the very ones who need to take the inner journey the very most are the ones who will never know it.

WHY THIS IS A TRANSFORMATIVE BOOK:

Confessions by Augustine of Hippo is one of the most influential and most innovative works of Latin literature. Written in the author's early forties in the last years of the fourth century A.D. and during his first years as a bishop, they reflect on his life and on the activity of remembering and interpreting a life. Books 1-4 are concerned with infancy and learning to talk, schooldays, sexual desire and adolescent rebellion, intense friendships and intellectual exploration. Augustine evolves and analyzes his past with all the resources of the reading which shaped his mind: Virgil and Cicero, Neoplatonism and the Bible. Socrates may have insisted, "Know thyself," but no one took up the task with so much earnestness and persistence as Augustine some 800 years later. Here, we find the first great instance of a condition we now understand to be uniquely modern, infinite self-contradiction, as well as the associated activity, infinite self-analysis.

QUESTIONS FOR MEDITATION:

What is the hardest part for you about developing self-knowledge?

"In fact, of course, there is no secret knowledge; no one knows anything that can't be found on a shelf in the public library."

WHY I LOVE THIS QUOTE:
This embodies one of the premises of this very meditation book: that it is our civic duty to read. Reading challenges us. Reading awakens us. Reading enlivens us. There are no shortcuts to wisdom and growth. It is a timeless — and democratic — process. And like Mark Twain says, "A person who won't read has no advantage over one who can't read."

WHY THIS IS A TRANSFORMATIVE BOOK:
Ishmael: An Adventure of the Mind and Spirit by Daniel Quinn changed the way I saw the world when I first read this novel in college. Then, in 2002, when I first began teaching college composition, I assigned it. Those students had the same experience I did. And without fail, teaching Ishmael off and on for 10 years, students continue to marvel at their reading experience, saying to the effect: I don't like to read, but I love this book. Ishmael is a bit of a miracle in that way. It's philosophical, spiritual, and countercultural. It's just challenging enough and entertains at the same time. Many of our readings, whether fiction or nonfiction, have been challenging. This has challenging ideas, but doesn't rank as high on the reading challenge level, which is nice for a break when you're taking on Heidegger or Kant.

QUESTIONS FOR MEDITATION:

What books have you picked up along the way over the course of the year? These books are for you and your personal growth? What could be more important? Treat yourself to a good read and some mindful meditation today.

"So, this is my life. And I want you to know that I am both happy and sad and I'm still trying to figure out how that could be."

WHY I LOVE THIS QUOTE:

As adults, we get used to containing polarities. We're often in a state of both happiness and sadness. Sometimes one runs through us stronger than the other, and often without us being particularly aware. Sometimes when things are good we aren't as grateful because, hey, it's always supposed to be good, right? And sometimes when things aren't so good we get inured to the same slow sad state and before we know it we're depressed or burnt out. While his emotions are simple, they're strong, and through his writing it down and reflecting about it, he's bringing awareness to them.

WHY THIS IS A TRANSFORMATIVE BOOK:

The Perks of Being a Wallflower by Stephen Chbosky is a spectacular coming-of-age story starring Charlie as the wallflower. The story is told in a series of letters that chronicles his experiences during his freshman year in high school that he writes to an unnamed friend. At the novel's opening, Charlie is very much alone and unpopular. His unique way of thinking draws special attention from his English teacher and a few older students who teach Charlie about the ways of the world. Chbosky's lush high school setting paints vivid pictures of adolescents who — as a result of their environments and own unique perspectives on the world — grow up fast. The book makes you feel nostalgic with longing and a desire to dive back into the dreams of our teenager. In some ways at least. As a bildungsroman, the novel provides a window through which to view a world unadulterated by expectations and regret.

QUESTIONS FOR MEDITATION:

How often are you aware of feeling contradictory emotions at the same time? How often are you aware of your emotions at all?

"This strategy is classic digital minimalism. By removing your ability to access social media at any moment, you reduce its ability to become a crutch deployed to distract you from bigger voids in your life. At the same time, you're not necessarily abandoning these services. By allowing yourself access (albeit less convenient) through a web browser, you preserve your ability to use specific features that you identify as important to your life — but on your own terms."

WHY I LOVE THIS QUOTE:

Cal Newport is encouraging us to make the habit of constantly being on social networks a little less convenient. Put the phone away. Make rules for yourself, not only to get the unhealthy habits out — or to make them a little harder to do — and pull some healthy ones in. If you're reading this book, you probably already sense the need for a little more clarity and stillness.

WHY THIS IS A TRANSFORMATIVE BOOK:

Digital Minimalism: Choosing a Focused Life in a Noisy World by Cal Newport is summed up best by his own definition: "Digital minimalists see new technologies as tools to be used to support things they deeply value — not as sources of value themselves. They don't accept the idea that offering some small benefit is justification for allowing an attention-gobbling service into their lives, and are instead interested in applying new technology in highly selective and intentional ways that yield big wins. Just as important: they're comfortable missing out on everything else."

QUESTIONS FOR MEDITATION:

Is technology aiding you in being a more fully realized human being, or is distracting you from yourself?

"I see in myself, Lucilius, not just an improvement but a transformation, although I would not venture as yet to assure you, or even to hope, that there is nothing left in me needing to be changed."

WHY I LOVE THIS QUOTE:

The difference between transformation and improvement is vast. I think of transformation as the result of a process made up of thousands of micro-improvements. It may come from a single determining moment, but it is a process. Transformation is always a process. I also like the modesty in Seneca's statement, that for all his change, he would not be so bold as to say he is a finished product. Therein may be a key toward ever-deepening growth: that we are never a finished product.

WHY THIS IS A TRANSFORMATIVE BOOK:

Letters from a Stoic by Seneca is rich and beautiful writing and sometimes surprising that it was written as long ago as it was, which clearly indicates my "chronological snobbery." Seneca was the outstanding figure of his age. The Stoic philosophy which he professed in his writings, later supported by Marcus Aurelius, provided Rome with a passable bridge to Christianity. Seneca's major contribution to Stoicism was to spiritualize and humanize a system which could appear cold and unrealistic. These letters illustrate the upright ideals admired by the Stoics and extol the good way of life from their standpoint. They also reveal how far in advance of his time were many of Seneca's ideas — his disgust at the shows in the arena or his criticism of the harsh treatment of slaves. Philosophical in tone and written in the "pointed" style of the Latin Silver Age these "essays in disguise" were clearly aimed by Seneca at posterity.

QUESTIONS FOR MEDITATION:

What processes — what micro-choices — are you inculcating your life with on a daily basis for transformation? Why do you want to be transformed and not merely improved? What is the difference to you?

december

"Once there was a tree, and she loved a little boy."

WHY I LOVE THIS QUOTE:

"... and she loved a boy very, very much — even more than she loved herself." The follow up quote to the quote suggests a different story under the story. I've known a lot of parents who give up their identities in raising their children. It's not healthy for either party to have your happiness so attached to another's that you aren't happy as a separate and whole person unto yourself.

WHY THIS IS A TRANSFORMATIVE BOOK:

The Giving Tree by Shel Silverstein was read to me as a child. What I remember most about this early introduction to the story was that it made me sad, even at an age when most things are forgotten. Often we present children with "feel-good," happy characters whose sole purpose is to entertain, presented in such a sanitized manner that no real message or lasting impression is made on the reader or listener. I have since gone on to read it to my children. It is not a perfectly clear message by any means, but this strangeness adds to its appeal. On one hand, this story can be taken as an open, honest exhortation toward selfless, unconditional love. Love which asks nothing. Love which gives everything. On the other hand, this story can be read as a horrifying condemnation of dysfunctional unrequited codependency.

QUESTIONS FOR MEDITATION:

What steps can you undertake to separate yourself from a relationship where you're a little too close, maybe too invested? Even if you're "just trying to help," how can you start with yourself?

"But misfortunes do not last forever (this they have in common with joys) but pass away or are at least diminished and become lost in oblivion. Life on the kapia always renews itself despite everything and the bridge does not change with the years or with the centuries or with the most painful turns in human affairs. All these pass over it, even as the unquiet waters pass beneath its smooth and perfect arches."

WHY I LOVE THIS QUOTE:
There are a lot of ways to extrapolate the meaning of the perfect and seemingly timeless bridge with the turbulent waters passing beneath and the generations coming and going. Certainly one thing to consider is perspective, the transience of the good times and the bad.

WHY THIS IS A TRANSFORMATIVE BOOK:
The Bridge on the Drina by Ivo Andric is a stunning depiction of the suffering experienced by the people of Bosnia from the late sixteenth century to the beginning of World War I. The novel earned the author the Nobel Prize for Literature in 1961. A great stone bridge built three centuries ago in the heart of the Balkans by a Grand Vizier of the Ottoman Empire dominates the setting. Spanning generations, nationalities, and creeds, the bridge stands witness to the countless lives played out upon it. Radisav, the workman, who tries to hinder its construction and is impaled on its highest point. The lovely Fata throws herself from its parapet to escape a loveless marriage. Milan, the gambler, risks everything in one last game on the bridge with the devil his opponent. Fedun, the young soldier, pays for a moment of spring forgetfulness with his life. War finally destroys the span, and with it the last descendant of that family to which the Grand Vizier confided the care of his pious bequest — the bridge. An unforgettable novel with one of the most powerful metaphors you'll ever encounter.

QUESTIONS FOR MEDITATION:

What are some of the most shocking or memorable incidents you can recollect since the last ten years? How do they or don't they have an impact on your life now?

"The family is the cradle of the world's misinformation. There must be something in family life that generates factual error. Over-closeness, the noise and heat of being. Perhaps even something deeper like the need to survive. Murray says we are fragile creatures surrounded by a world of hostile facts. Facts threaten our happiness and security. The deeper we delve into things, the looser our structure may seem to become. The family process works towards sealing off the world. Small errors grow heads, fictions proliferate."

WHY I LOVE THIS QUOTE:
It's a fascinating point. On the one hand, we often use family as the ultimate excuse for resigning from a job, or a kind of getting back to basics and the nobler call to what's really important. "I've got to do what's best for my family," we say. Murray is saying the family can become tribal and sealed off from the world. And this was written in 1985, way before the social media echo chambers emerged. An unsettling idea.

WHY THIS IS A TRANSFORMATIVE BOOK:
White Noise by Don DeLillo is a visionary satire on the chemical and electronic hum that surrounds us all, clouds our reasoning, and distracts us from what should be important in our lives...but doesn't distract us enough to ameliorate our base fears. Sometimes downright hilarious and often very touching, this is a memorable book with resonant themes.

QUESTIONS FOR MEDITATION:

How does technology impact your relationship with your children? How has it changed social interactions? On the whole, would you say technology improves our lives or not?

"Dogmatic, apocalyptic predictions about the collapse of liberal culture or the disappearance of high culture may be right or wrong; but one thing about them seems certain: they are more likely to instill self-pity and despair than the will to resist or the confidence to make the most of one's creative energies. It is possible, of course, that under modern conditions the avenues of choice are being closed, and that the culture of the future will be dominated by single-minded men of one persuasion or another. It is possible; but in so far as the weight of one's will is thrown onto the scales of history, one lives in the belief that it is not to be so."

WHY I LOVE THIS QUOTE:

Hofstadter is concluding with some reason for hope that liberal culture will endure despite various anti-intellectual viruses attacking it.

WHY THIS IS A TRANSFORMATIVE BOOK:

Anti-Intellectualism in American Life by Richard Hofstadter was awarded the 1964 Pulitzer Prize in Nonfiction. It is a book which throws light on many features of the American character. Its concern is not merely to portray the scorners of intellect in American life, but to say something about what the intellectual is, and can be, as a force in a democratic society. He sets out to trace the social movements that altered the role of intellect in American society from a virtue to a vice. In so doing, he explores questions regarding the purpose of education and whether the democratization of education altered that purpose and reshaped its form. A serious and helpful book in getting a sense of the puzzle that is America.

QUESTIONS FOR MEDITATION:

How does what you know set you apart? How is education dangerous? What do you know that you would rather not have learned?

"Change is hard because people wear themselves out. And that's the second surprise about change: What looks like laziness is often exhaustion."

WHY I LOVE THIS QUOTE:
Sometimes in a very real sense, less is more. Sometimes it's what you choose not to do that is the best decision in the process of growth and transformation.

WHY THIS IS A TRANSFORMATIVE BOOK:
Switch: How to Change Things When Change Is Hard by Chip Heath, Dan Heath is their follow-up book to the critically acclaimed international bestseller Made to Stick, Chip and Dan Heath talk about how difficult change is in our companies, our careers, and our lives, why change is so hard, and how we can overcome our resistance and make change happen. The Heaths liken the human mind to two distinct entities — the animal mind, or what psychologist Jonathan Haidt calls the elephant, and the logical brain, which Haidt describes as the rider. The elephant is instinctive; it acts on emotion. It likes gorging on Oreos and sleeping in. And it loves routines — doing things the same old way, every day.

QUESTIONS FOR MEDITATION:

Why is change so difficult and frightening? How do you create change when you have few resources and no title or authority to back you up?

"Our task in life consists precisely in a form of letting go of fear and expectations, an attempt to purely give oneself to the impact of the present."

WHY I LOVE THIS QUOTE:

We live with so much anxiety. It becomes a part of the cultural stew we swim in. Part of why mindfulness, yoga practices, health and wellness, and meditations practices have sprung up in such intensity over the past few decades in the West can be directly associated with our stress levels. There is emerging science showing how certain drug-induced escapes can actually lead to deeper and ongoing wellbeing.

WHY THIS IS A TRANSFORMATIVE BOOK:

How to Change Your Mind: What the New Science of Psychedelics Teaches Us About Consciousness, Dying, Addiction, Depression, and Transcendence by Michael Pollan opens your mind to the history and treatment of psychedelics, as well as his own personal history, and where we stand with research today. Truly a fascinating experience. "Psilocybes gave our hominid ancestors access to realms of supernatural power...catalyzed the emergence of human self-reflection...and brought us out of the animal mind and into the world of articulated speech and imagination," he writes. This hypothesis about the invention of language turns on the concept of synesthesia, the conflation of the senses that psychedelics are known to induce: under the influence of psilocybin, numbers can take on colors, colors attach to sounds, and so on. Language, Pollan contends, represents a special case of synesthesia, in which otherwise meaningless sounds become linked to concepts. Hence, the stoned ape: by giving us the gifts of language and self-reflection psilocybin mushrooms made us who we are, transforming our primate ancestors into Homo sapiens. It's a far-out theory, but could just be weird enough to have a spark of truth to it.

QUESTIONS FOR MEDITATION:

Could psychedelic drugs change our worldview?

"Solitude allows us to get comfortable being with ourselves, which makes it easier to be ourselves in interactions with others. That authenticity helps build strong connections."

WHY I LOVE THIS QUOTE:
Therefore, solitude is actually a defense against loneliness. Solitude is different than merely being alone. In solitude you are attending to yourself. You are present to yourself, asking yourself questions, reflecting on your emotions, desires, needs, and hopefully, if you've been doing any of the readings from this reader, doing so with self-compassion aimed toward realization and growth. This is often scary and challenging for any number of reasons, and people tend to fend these unconscious fears off through addictions, which increases loneliness.

WHY THIS IS A TRANSFORMATIVE BOOK:
Together: Why Social Connection Holds the Key to Better Health, Higher Performance, and Greater Happiness by Vivek H. Murthy is for anyone interested in the science behind social connectivity. Vivek does an amazing job connecting together concepts like shame, social infrastructure, natural disasters, medical problems, and cultural differences to form a cohesive story about loneliness. The personal stories collected and explored by Murthy will resonate with anyone who has experienced loneliness, which is surprisingly and increasingly common in this digital age. Reading about loneliness can itself feel like a human connection. You are not alone in this.

QUESTIONS FOR MEDITATION:

How can you attend to yourself when you're both alone and with others?

"There's a wonderful Chinese proverb that says: 'When the winds of change rage, some build shelters while others build windmills'."

WHY I LOVE THIS QUOTE:

Like a lot of proverbs the saying hinges on being an observation of human behavior without advising one way or the other. The implicit challenge asks the listener: What kind of person are you?

WHY THIS IS A TRANSFORMATIVE BOOK:

Insight: Why We're Not as Self-Aware as We Think, and How Seeing Ourselves Clearly Helps Us Succeed at Work and in Life by Tasha Eurich is superbly positioned as a classic on self awareness. While Daniel Goleman gets all the credit for popularizing Emotional Intelligence, self-awareness didn't get the much-needed spotlight it deserves amongst all other components of emotional intelligence. This book serves the purpose of putting the spotlight back on self-awareness. Fortunately, self-awareness is a surprisingly learnable skill. Eurich helps readers uncover the areas they are weakest in and discover the areas of their life they'd be better off focusing on.

QUESTIONS FOR MEDITATION:

Do you ever wonder how other people really see you? And do you think the person they see is an accurate representation of who you really are?

"It is a fact of life that certain people are corrosive to others' self esteem simply as a function of who and what they are."

WHY I LOVE THIS QUOTE:
You know who these people are in your life. You rarely, if ever, feel good about yourself after spending any length of time with them. Either they're in power over you and are like the never-can-be-pleased-quite-enough parent, or they're a peer who constantly wants to give advice, or persuade you to do something (with the underlying message that you aren't quite good enough).

WHY THIS IS A TRANSFORMATIVE BOOK:
Oblivion by David Foster Wallace is challenging and transportive and for me, held a perfect tension between inventive, exhaustive detail and moving the storyline forward. I could not suffer through Infinite Jest, especially on an e-reader, it felt literally infinite. Here, you find the postmodern playfulness reigned in somewhat. Also, unlike the layered interviews and broken portraits of *Brief Interviews with Hideous Men*, these are more clearly stories (or even novellas, as two are quite lengthy), winding yet carefully plotted, and fully invested in the narrative. Characteristic of his style, the prose creates a vicarious experience of anguish and identification with the character. Wallace's slyly subversive humor is apparent throughout. The title piece, "Oblivion" had the most immersive effect, putting you in the consciousness of someone who's thinking is completely obliterated by the marketing and jargon-like language of the corporate, marketing world.

QUESTIONS FOR MEDITATION:

How can we develop and maintain a strengthened sense of self when we are forced to interact with unhealthy people or to perform in unhealthy environments?

"This is what I know — Sam is dead. My brother is dead. My mother is dead. My father is dead. My husband is dead. My cat is dead. My dog, who was dead in 1957, is still dead. Yet still I keep thinking that something wonderful is about to happen. Maybe tomorrow."

WHY I LOVE THIS QUOTE:

The quote reminds me a little of the beginning of the quote from *The Perks of Being a Wallflower:* "So this is life..." and he goes on to say how he's happy and sad and trying to reconcile that feeling. Here, with decades of life experience under her belt beyond that adolescent observation, we see that even a huge accumulation of loss doesn't have to be the final statement on your outlook. You stay alive by living in expectation.

WHY THIS IS A TRANSFORMATIVE BOOK:

Year of the Monkey by Patti Smith melds the western landscape with her own dreamscape. Taking us from California to the Arizona desert; to a Kentucky farm as the amanuensis of a friend in crisis; to the hospital room of a valued mentor; and by turns to remembered and imagined places, this haunting memoir blends fact and fiction with poetic mastery. The unexpected happens. Grief and disillusionment set in. But as Smith heads toward a new decade in her own life, she offers her wisdom, wit, and determined optimism in the face of all the hardship and suffering.

As David W. Berner writes, "Marvelous. Already re-reading passages. Patti Smith is a true artist; she is the closest we have to what may be left of the Beat movement. The writing is close to the bone and insanely, keenly observant. It's about self, but yet universal. Loved *Just Kids*, and especially *M Train*. *Devotion* is a sleeper favorite for me."

QUESTIONS FOR MEDITATION:

What's next in your decision-making tree? What answers are you receiving? How are you living in expectation?

"Someone once said anyone can be great under rosy circumstances, but the true test of character is measured by how well a person makes decisions during difficult times."

WHY I LOVE THIS QUOTE:
Well, it's not just someone, many people have said this very thing, but it is wisdom, and one important source is our good friend, Seneca. From him, Marcus Aurelius also considers the virtue of how to deal with rugged and difficult times with grace and resilience.

WHY THIS IS A TRANSFORMATIVE BOOK:
Hole in My Life by Jack Gantos is his autobiographical account of how, lost and adrift after high school, basically homeless, poor, and envious of great authors like Kerouac and Hemmingway, longing for adventures, he agrees to help pilot a boat from the Virgin Islands to New York, smuggling drugs. Gantos' account is unabashed, unsentimental, unapologetic, unsympathetic for his own self, which is refreshing for the genre and the young adult audience. He makes no excuses (except foolishness) for his behavior, the consequences of which are disturbing and disquieting. Many contributing factors led to Gantos' agreeing to help sail that boat and smuggle in drugs. Mostly he wanted money to pay for college so he could become a writer. An enthralling book about Gantos' time in prison. He has since gone on to become an award-winning author and a charismatic writing teacher.

QUESTIONS FOR MEDITATION:

When things are out of control what can you control?

"When someone is telling you their story over and over, they are trying to figure something out."

WHY I LOVE THIS QUOTE:
They also may not feel heard. Carl Rogers innovated the mirroring technique in couples counseling that when people repeat themselves or begin to raise their voices it's because they are literally not feeling heard. The technique to help each other feel heard (or actually be heard) is to mirror back what is being said from the other. Similarly, that may help when someone is repeating a part of their story over and over. It may help them to feel heard to repeat back to them what they are saying at the appropriate time.

WHY THIS IS A TRANSFORMATIVE BOOK:
On Grief and Grieving: Finding the Meaning of Grief Through the Five Stages of Loss by Elisabeth Kübler-Ross is another classic in the field of Death and Dying, and applies the theories first introduced by Kübler-Ross in the '70s.

As Gautham Vasan writes, "I believe this is one of the most important books ever written. The landscape of grief is dark and dreary. When you lose a loved one, all you experience is excruciating pain, emptiness and numbness. One moment you are laughing at a shared memory of a loved one, the next moment you are curled up in your bed, wading through a deep well of sadness in isolation. Interactions with regular, functioning people made me feel somehow deeply, irreparably broken. This book helped me validate all the emotions I've experienced over my mourning period so far. I think a lot of people, even ones who have lost loved ones themselves earlier in life haven't really processed their grief in a healthy fashion. There's a lot of incorrect advice floating out there based on ridiculous and inhumane societal expectations. Every grief is unique and it is a deeply personal experience."

QUESTIONS FOR MEDITATION:

How do you channel grief? Have you experienced much in your life?

"It's the trying that heals you. That's all you have to do. Just try."

WHY I LOVE THIS QUOTE:

This is a novel about learning to roll with the punches, good and bad, as well as about taking stock in loved ones. It's also about life lessons. This is a grace-filled thought. Sometimes when we struggle to grow, even when our first steps feel hopeless and maybe even pathetic and weak, there is still a mindset play.

WHY THIS IS A TRANSFORMATIVE BOOK:

How to Walk Away by Katherine Center has written a compelling story about how in a split second life can change in dramatically different ways. What was supposed to be a romantic flight where they become engaged, turns into a nightmare. During landing they crash, and her fiance Chip walks away without any injuries while Margret is not so lucky. In the hospital, she learns the extent of her injuries. Yet at the very moment when all she wants to do is wallow, she has to deal with those around her as well. Chip is drowning in self-pity and wants Margaret to forgive him and give him the easy way out. Her mother has taken on this challenge as she's taken on every other obstacle in life — full steam ahead — and will stop at nothing to make her daughter fight to get every ounce of her life back. Margaret's sister Kit returns after a three-year absence and tries to help her with her quirky sense of humor and her unflagging sense of enthusiasm.

QUESTIONS FOR MEDITATION:

What have you ever lost by trying?

"The greatest fear in the world is of the opinions of others. And the moment you are unafraid of the crowd you are no longer a sheep, you become a lion. A great roar arises in your heart, the roar of freedom."

WHY I LOVE THIS QUOTE:

He also writes: "Commit as many mistakes as possible, remembering only one thing: don't commit the same mistake again. And you will be growing." Today we revisit two themes we've been turning over from time to time: living unafraid of other's judgments and of failing. From others we need to remind ourselves that for the most part they simply want to keep you down because they aren't striving for much themselves, and/or your change is threatening to their sense of self. That fear probably plays the most into our fear of failure.

WHY THIS IS A TRANSFORMATIVE BOOK:

Courage: The Joy of Living Dangerously by Osho provides a bird's-eye view of the whole terrain of fears — where they originate, how to understand them, and how to find the courage to face them. In the process, Osho proposes that whenever you are faced with uncertainty and change in your life, it should actually be a cause for celebration. Instead of trying to hang on to the familiar and the known, you can learn to enjoy these situations as opportunities for adventure and for deepening our understanding of yourself and the world around you. It begins with an in-depth exploration of the meaning of courage, and how it is expressed in your everyday life. Unlike books that focus on heroic acts of courage in exceptional circumstances, the focus here is on developing the inner courage that enables you to lead an authentic and fulfilling life on a day-to-day basis.

QUESTIONS FOR MEDITATION:

How does freeing yourself up from the judgments of others help you feel freer to fail (or at least be willing to try things that might fail)?

"We have been led to imagine all sorts of things infinitely more marvelous than the imagining of poets and dreamers of the past. It shows that the imagination of nature is far, far greater than the imagination of man. For instance, how much more remarkable it is for us all to be stuck — half of us upside down — by a mysterious attraction, to a spinning ball that has been swinging in space for billions of years, than to be carried on the back of an elephant supported on a tortoise swimming in a bottomless sea."

WHY I LOVE THIS QUOTE:

We get so tied to the same old ways of doing things along the lines of social expectations we really do lose a sense of mystery and wonder about the amazing reality of our existence and the incredible imagination of the natural world. Often the world's leading innovators and designers take their inspiration and ideas from nature.

WHY THIS IS A TRANSFORMATIVE BOOK:

What Do You Care What Other People Think? by Richard P. Feynman is his last literary legacy, prepared with his friend and fellow drummer, Ralph Leighton. There is something quasi-religious about Feynman's combination of naïveté, simplicity, and keen wonder at the natural world; there is something indeed mystical about his way of cutting through everything distracting and irrelevant, of putting aside all unhelpful conventions, and getting to the core of the issue.

QUESTIONS FOR MEDITATION:

When was the last time you were inspired by nature? How can nature transport you outside of yourself and lead you to important, potentially transformative, insights?

"We are all in the depths of a cave, chained by our ignorance, by our prejudices, and our weak senses reveal to us only shadows. If we try to see further, we are confused; we are unaccustomed. But we try. This is science."

WHY I LOVE THIS QUOTE:
Sometimes we are like reluctant churchgoers, sitting in the pew because we feel like we're supposed to (or maybe we feel we have to), and we're open to hearing a good message, maybe vaguely curious that something good within ourselves might come of it. People don't get "saved" every time they go to church, but for those seeking transformation, they meet the need within themselves with expectancy and even urgency. There is a spiritually-minded belief behind the potential for our own transformation, even if we view the possibilities through the lens of scientific hypothesis and curiosity.

WHY THIS IS A TRANSFORMATIVE BOOK:
Reality is Not What it Seems: The Journey to Quantum Gravity by Carlo Rovelli asks questions like: What are time and space made of? Where does matter come from? And what exactly is reality? Rovelli has spent his whole life exploring these questions and pushing the boundaries of what we know. Here he explains how our image of the world has changed throughout centuries. Tracking a range of brilliant minds and compelling personalities, he takes us on a journey to show us that beyond our ever-changing idea of reality is a whole new world that has yet to be discovered.

QUESTIONS FOR MEDITATION:

Right now, are you doing your daily tasks taking you anywhere? Do you feel a sense of purpose? Are you doing too much?

"The central riddle I've set out to solve concerns the self's continuity in change: how can we remain the same people over time, even as we change, sometimes considerably?"

WHY I LOVE THIS QUOTE:
It's a fascinating thought to explore and makes the subject for a compelling book, whether or not you agree with his conclusions or not. In fact, research does show that we change considerably more than we predict we will.

WHY THIS IS A TRANSFORMATIVE BOOK:
The Ego Trick: In Search Of The Self by Julian Baggini argues that "I" is a verb masquerading as a noun. "I" is not a "thing" but what my brain and my body "does." The self, is a function of what a certain collection of stuff does. It's the fact that I can use my memories and experiences to develop a sense of continuity in my life without actually having a central command center. It's a fascinating quest that draws on the history of philosophy, and also anthropology, sociology, psychology, and neurology. Baggini talks to theologians, priests, possibly reincarnated Lamas, and delves into real-life cases of lost memory, personality disorders and personal transformation. He discusses his own experiences candidly, and he searches with earnestness.

QUESTIONS FOR MEDITATION:

What and who is the real you? Does it remain constant over time and place, or is it something much more fragmented and fluid? Is it known to you, or are you as much a mystery to yourself as others are to you?

"If there is one lesson I've learned from failure and success, it's this. I am not the outcome. I am never the result. I am only the effort."

WHY I LOVE THIS QUOTE:

I love this one. But to be honest I feel like there were so many things to quote from this book, just one doesn't manage to crystallize the whole essence of it. I found it relaxingly liberating. Being present, forgiving yourself and loving yourself, those are things that take time mastering and require practice. It's all worth the effort. And I like the overall optimism this book showed. This takes honesty, vulnerability, and lots of grace for yourself.

WHY THIS IS A TRANSFORMATIVE BOOK:

Live Your Truth by Kamal Ravikant shows that you don't just stumble accidentally into an amazing life. It takes a conscious commitment to figuring out what you stand for — finding your truth. It begins by looking inside yourself, because when it rises from within, you then have no choice but to express it, to live it. That is when the magic happens: fulfillment, happiness, relationships, and success. This book gives you continued encouragement to be bold, to lead a life of thoughtful integration of your values and your lived reality.

QUESTIONS FOR MEDITATION:

Have you been rejecting yourself? How could you affirm yourself more and increase your freedom and confidence?

"My perfectionism arose as an attempt to gain safety and support in my dangerous family. Perfection is a self-persecutory myth. I do not have to be perfect to be safe or loved in the present. I am letting go of relationships that require perfection. I have a right to make mistakes."

WHY I LOVE THIS QUOTE:

Have you noticed a theme this month? As we conclude our readings and meditations in anticipation of the year's end, we continue to chip away at the idea of freeing yourself to take calculated risks, to try things out in your life, and to free yourself from the judgments of others who might hold you back and make you afraid to fail. You simply have to accept that you will fail at some point along your growth path.

WHY THIS IS A TRANSFORMATIVE BOOK:

Complex PTSD: From Surviving to Thriving by Pete Walker is an excellent resource for anyone who had an abusive or neglectful childhood, whether you have a formal diagnosis of Complex PTSD or not. This is practical advice on learning to be free from toxic shame and the inner critic. This book also contains an overview of the tasks of recovering and a great many practical tools and techniques for recovering from childhood trauma. Key concepts include managing emotional flashbacks, understanding the four different types of trauma survivors, differentiating the outer critic from the inner critic, healing the abandonment depression that come from emotional abandonment and self-abandonment, self-reparenting and reparenting by committee, and deconstructing the hierarchy of self-injuring responses that childhood trauma forces survivors to adopt. It's powerful content designed from a practitioner.

QUESTIONS FOR MEDITATION:

You might fail even if you don't take risks. Isn't it more empowering to imagine doing so with a purpose in mind?

"Knowledge is a function of being. When there is a change in the being of the knower, there is a corresponding change in the nature and amount of knowing."

WHY I LOVE THIS QUOTE:

This is a fantastic quote on the subject of the difference between knowledge and self-knowledge. The key is "change in the being" part. Huxley inversely connects knowledge to being, so "being" changes as a result of knowledge. You could spend a lot of energy defining "different kinds of knowledge" compared to specifically "self" knowledge, but it seems clear that Huxley means knowledge which results in behavior (or you could say action). He also compares it on macro terms. How does a nation's behavior reflect on its majority religion? Is it fair to do that?

WHY THIS IS A TRANSFORMATIVE BOOK:

The Perennial Philosophy by Aldous Huxley is defined by its author as, "The metaphysic that recognizes a divine Reality substantial to the world of things and lives and minds." With a combination of wit and penetrating insight, Aldous Huxley examines the spiritual beliefs of various religious traditions and explains them as experiences of reality without the mediation of time-oriented, results-driven thought. Awareness is a way out of the self, a way out of what David Foster Wallace famously called our default setting, in which I am and you are and everyone is at the center of their own little universes, in which one's self is what processes all incoming information. Huxley says, "There has to be a conversion, sudden or otherwise, not merely of the heart, but also of the senses and of the perceiving mind... metanoia, as the Greeks called it, this total and radical 'change of mind'." This change of mind is about, in large part, "the elimination of self-will, self-interest, self-centered thinking, wishing and imagining."

QUESTIONS FOR MEDITATION:

Is it fair to say that you will change your behavior based upon the amount of self-knowledge you acquire? What is the kind of knowledge you value more highly than self-knowledge?

"Words save our lives, sometimes."

WHY I LOVE THIS QUOTE:

Maybe they save us if we take the time to read them in the first place, as Mark Twain alludes to when he says, "A person who won't read has no advantage over one who can't read." Maybe words save us when they teach us to think about who we are, and how we belong to the world.

WHY THIS IS A TRANSFORMATIVE BOOK:

The Ocean at the End of the Lane by Neil Gaiman is a fantasy, and like all good fantasy, it offers insights into human existence — the complexity and nuances and plain old relations that make us unique. There's an almost dreamlike quality to the story and there are many reasons it's hard to know what's real and what is not. It's a beautiful story, which I also enjoyed from its style, which is not often mentioned. It reads with a lucid dreaming kind of rhythm. I felt a sense of dreaming even while following exactly what my mind imagined through the clarity of each sentence. Every now and then a novella pulls this off somehow more profoundly than a short story, but with more immediacy than you could expect from a novel. *Train Dreams* by Denis Johnson is a more recent example of this aesthetic experience. Rick Bass achieves similar lyrical effect in *The Sky, The Stars, The Wilderness.*

QUESTIONS FOR MEDITATION:

How real is the magic and monsters of our childhood?

"One cannot change, that is to say become a different person, while continuing to acquiesce to the feelings of the person one has ceased to be."

WHY I LOVE THIS QUOTE:

I appreciate the finer point Proust is making about returning to the emotional state of the person you once were. In other words, it's implied that what makes you a different person is having achieved a whole different set of consistent — and mature — feelings. Feelings are the guide to transformative change. We almost certainly won't change unless something is urging us on a passionate level.

WHY THIS IS A TRANSFORMATIVE BOOK:

Swann's Way by Marcel Proust engages the senses with immersive synesthesia. Really like no other. Consider this sentence on asparagus: "At the hour when I usually went downstairs to find out what there was for dinner...I would stop by the table, where the kitchen-maid had shelled them, to inspect the platoons of peas, drawn up in ranks and numbered, like little green marbles, ready for a game; but what most enraptured me were the asparagus, tinged with ultramarine and pink which shaded their heads, finely stippled in mauve and azure, through a series of imperceptible gradations to their white feet — still stained a little by the soil of their garden-bed — with an iridescence that was not of this world, I felt that these celestial hues indicated the presence of exquisite creatures who had been pleased to assume vegetable form and who, through the disguise of their firm, comestible flesh, allowed me to discern in this radiance of earliest dawn, these hinted rainbows, these blue evening shades, that precious quality which I should recognize again when, all night long after a dinner at which I had partaken of them, they played (lyrical and coarse in their jesting like one of Shakespeare's fairies) at transforming my chamber pot into a vase of aromatic perfume."

QUESTIONS FOR MEDITATION:

How do we feel our way to the change we want to make?

"We don't really learn anything properly until there is a problem, until we are in pain, until something fails to go as we had hoped...We suffer, therefore we think."

WHY I LOVE THIS QUOTE:

Proust also writes, "Reality will take shape in the memory alone," which is an interesting followup thought. What is also well-established about memory is that it isn't always reliable, isn't always verifiable, and is also often laced with nostalgia, filtered through the context of our current emotional state. But as Botton reminds us too, "When Proust urges us to evaluate the world properly, he repeatedly reminds us of the value of modest scenes." While it is a cliche to say "find the extraordinary in the ordinary," Proust actually demonstrates that very thing through his majestic prose while describing something that could be considered completely banal.

WHY THIS IS A TRANSFORMATIVE BOOK:

How Proust Can Change Your Life by Alain de Botton is a wonderful and rather unusual book — a combination of literary biography, life reflection and self-help manual. It's a wonderful, witty, philosophical, and reflective read. Botton masters the task of connecting our modern world and Proust's thoughts and considerations of life and time. Did you know reading Proust nearly silenced Virginia Woolf? She loved his novel almost too much. There wasn't enough wrong with it — a crushing recognition when one considers Walter Benjamin's assessment of why people become writers: because they are unable to find a book already written that they are completely happy with.

QUESTIONS FOR MEDITATION:

How does the past combine with the present to make you who you are right now? What would you say plays the biggest role in your knowledge: What you learned a long time ago, or what you learned over the last few years?

"Freedom of choice regarding occupation is a relatively novel social phenomenon. Those of us who are faced with such a choice are, historically speaking, a very small minority indeed."

WHY I LOVE THIS QUOTE:
All the more reason for us to deeply know the history that brought us here, the rare good fortune, and the collective hard work. It should inform our generation as to the work ahead of us now. It should ask us what role we will play as individuals and how we participate in the collective in meaningful ways.

WHY THIS IS A TRANSFORMATIVE BOOK:
Leading Lives That Matter: What We Should Do and Who We Should Be, edited by Mark R. Schwehn and Dorothy Bass, draws together a wide range of texts — including fiction, autobiography, and philosophy — offering challenge and insight to those who are thinking about what to do with their lives. Instead of giving prescriptive advice, the editors approach the subject of vocation as an ongoing conversation. They include some of the western tradition's best writings on human life — its meaning, purpose, and significance — ranging from ancient Greek poetry to contemporary fiction. While you may not want to read all the readings in the anthology, it certainly asks some very compelling questions and offers a range of interesting styles of writing to answer them. Fun for the whole family!

QUESTIONS FOR MEDITATION:

What is your purpose? Is it more to discover or to invent?

"Explorers depend on the North Star when there are no other landmarks in sight. The same relationship exists between you and your right life, the ultimate realization of your potential for happiness. I believe that a knowledge of that perfect life sits inside you just as the North Star sits in its unaltering spot."

WHY I LOVE THIS QUOTE:

I like the inner and outer reality that she posits here. I also like the idea that within you is an "unaltering spot" within that will guide you if only you choose to journey.

WHY THIS IS A TRANSFORMATIVE BOOK:

Finding Your Own North Star: Claiming the Life You Were Meant to Live by Martha N. Beck is a step-by-step program that will help you take the exhilarating and frightening journey to your own ideal life. The book, which is somewhat of a course, will teach you how to read your internal compasses, articulate your core desires, identify and repair the unconscious beliefs that may be blocking your progress, nurture your intuition, and cultivate your dreams from the first flicker of an idea through the planning and implementation of a more satisfying life. Beck offers thoroughly tested case studies, questionnaires, exercises, and her own trademark style to guide you. It can motivate and guide you to figure out what you need to do.

She writes, "People who don't honor their losses don't grieve. They may lose all joy in living, but they don't actively mourn, and this means that they don't heal."

QUESTIONS FOR MEDITATION:

Where do you need to look for guidance and inspiration? How far can you take yourself? Do you believe aid will come on its own, or do you need to seek it out?

"In awakening, our whole sense of identity shifts. We let go our small sense of self and enter the unbounded consciousness out of which we come. What becomes known with absolute certainty is that we are not and never have been separate from the world... When our identity expands to include everything, we find peace with the dance of the world. The ocean of life rises and falls within us — birth and death, joy and pain, it is all ours, and our heart is full and empty, large enough to embrace it all."

WHY I LOVE THIS QUOTE:

Those who research on the subject of habits emphasize the need to shift your identity as a way of embracing either what you — or don't — want to do. I am a non-smoker, not just someone who is trying to quit smoking. I am an athlete, not just someone who is trying to work out. Similarly, you will know you have achieved a level of awakening when your very identity shifts. The shift in identity makes the changes you want to make seamless, an integrated living out of who you have now become.

WHY THIS IS A TRANSFORMATIVE BOOK:

After the Ecstasy, the Laundry: How the Heart Grows Wise on the Spiritual Path by Jack Kornfield draws on the experiences and insights of leaders and practitioners within the Buddhist, Christian, Jewish, Hindu, and Sufi traditions. The book offers a uniquely intimate and honest understanding of how the modern spiritual journey unfolds — and how we can prepare our hearts for awakening. After the ecstasy we are faced with the day-to-day task of translating that feeling of freedom into our imperfect lives. We are faced with the laundry. The journey is consistent for all (though not exactly the same) no matter what your tradition is.

QUESTIONS FOR MEDITATION:

If this day in the lifetime of a hundred years is lost, will you ever touch it with your hands again?

"Do you feel bad enough now to make some changes or would you rather wait until you feel even worse?"

WHY I LOVE THIS QUOTE:
It's a fair question you might consider when it comes to change. On the one hand we realize that transformation might only come when our emotions get strong enough to get our attention, but maybe your emotions already are speaking. Maybe there's a part of you that refuses to acknowledge just how bad you feel right now.

WHY THIS IS A TRANSFORMATIVE BOOK:
Words That Change Minds: The 14 Patterns for Mastering the Language of Influence by Shelle Rose Charvet is a relatively simple system for pulling out complex data points in communicating. It applies to how you communicate in your personal life, but also to businesses and teams. Nothing is more frustrating than finding yourself misunderstood. Research has shown how people respond to words, and how they process what they hear. Charvet has taken that research and shown how words impact those who listen to us. By understanding how people receive communications, we can change the way we say things so that the receiver better understands what it is we are trying to communicate. And the key that Charvet opens is that by asking some basic questions, people will actually tell us how they prefer to communicate and under what conditions. This book identifies the traits, then shows you which questions to ask to get the best outcome at each point.

QUESTIONS FOR MEDITATION:

Do you feel bad enough to bring yourself to some change and identity shifts right now? Are you hopeful that things will somehow become better without having to do any specific work?

"Happiness is not a destination: Being happy takes constant weeding, a tending of emotions and circumstances as they arise. There's no happily ever after, or any one person or place that can bring happiness. It takes work to be calm in the midst of turmoil. But releasing the need to control it — well, that's a start."

WHY I LOVE THIS QUOTE:
All you can be is you. Let your self shine through in a calm, compassionate way and let the chips fall where they may.

WHY THIS IS A TRANSFORMATIVE BOOK:
Life From Scratch: A Memoir of Food, Family, and Forgiveness by Sasha Martin is compelling. Martin lays bare her entire life for the reader to see: the eclectic chaos of her childhood, particularly her mother. Martin's love for her shines through, even while her free-spirited mother makes a series of disastrous choices. You can feel the grace in her writing, which could only have come through a lot of inner work. Her descriptions of people's behaviors throughout her life are unflinching, yet charitable. The instrument of Martin's redemption and her tools for forgiveness come in the form of her food blog, and her family. She weaves a variety of recipes into the book, which gives the transformational value an added seasoning. A wonderful book of love, forgiveness and great food. What's not to love?

QUESTIONS FOR MEDITATION:

How do you pursue happiness even though you know parts of your reality are out of your control? How do you deal with what you can and can't control? Do you often step back and consider the difference between the two?

"The vicious cycle starts: if you fail at something, you think it is your fault. Therefore you think you can't do that task. As a result, next time you have to do the task, you believe you can't, so you don't even try. The result is that you can't, just as you thought."

WHY I LOVE THIS QUOTE:

As a followup, Norman writes, "The idea that a person is at fault when something goes wrong is deeply entrenched in society. That's why we blame others and ourselves. Unfortunately, the idea that a person is at fault is also embedded in the legal system. When major accidents occur, official courts of inquiry are set up to assess the blame. The person involved can be fined, punished, or fired. Maybe training procedures are revised. The law rests comfortably. But in my experience, human error usually is a result of poor design: it should be called system error. Humans err continually; it is an intrinsic part of our nature. System design should take this into account."

WHY THIS IS A TRANSFORMATIVE BOOK:

The Design of Everyday Things by Donald A. Norman will make you never look at any human-made object the same. You will question everything from doors to tea kettles to the most sophisticated computer program. The next time you fumble with an answering machine, web page, or light switch you will think back to the lessons from this book.

QUESTIONS FOR MEDITATION:

Pinning the blame on the person within your ecosystem may be a comfortable way to proceed, but why was the system designed so that a single act by a single person could cause the chaos in the first place? Maybe you should think about your personal systems? How can you create the conditions for greater success?

"I believe that most of us have false beliefs about our own nature, and our identity over time, and that, when we see the truth, we ought to change some of our beliefs about what we have reason to do."

WHY I LOVE THIS QUOTE:
Parfit also writes, "Until this century, most of mankind lived in small communities. What each did could affect only a few others. But conditions have now changed. Each of us can now, in countless ways, affect countless other people. We can have real though small effects on thousands or millions of people. When these effects are widely dispersed, they may be either trivial, or imperceptible." It seems reasonable to consider whether we really collectively understand how interwoven our lives now are. It may take another decade of social media and internet technology to evolve to get a better idea of where we're headed. So many leaps have only just occurred.

WHY THIS IS A TRANSFORMATIVE BOOK:
Reasons and Persons by Derek Parfit is a challenging, but also incredibly rigorous and important philosophical book from the 20th century. Unless you're schooled in ethics it will be hard to fully follow all of his arguments (as it was for me), and he doesn't purport to solve all the problems he raises, but even reading and understanding what you can is enough to pull forth plenty of transformative potential.

QUESTIONS FOR MEDITATION:

To what extent are you "the same person" you were 10 years ago? What is your connection to that person? Parfit shows that most of our conventional answers to why we are "the same person" are woefully deficient.

"And though all these things are difficult, almost inconceivable, and quite contrary to the opinion of the multitude, nevertheless in what follows we will with God's help make them clearer than day — at least for those who are not ignorant of the art of mathematics."

WHY I LOVE THIS QUOTE:

And one of these mathematical principles is that the wheel goes round and round. It feels right to end these 365 meditations with Copernicus because this book should be used cyclically, like a sphere of possibilities any one of which could lead you to your shadow or to your light.

WHY THIS IS A TRANSFORMATIVE BOOK:

On the Revolutions of Heavenly Spheres by Nicolaus Copernicus was published on his deathbed, because he feared the fallout from his truth proofs. And lo, it was a voice out of Poland, saying that this earth, this footstool of God, and home of his redeeming pilgrimage, was a minor satellite of a minor sun. It seemed so simple a thing to say. We cannot be moved to fear or wonder by it now, only by those who still want to argue that the earth is flat. People will choose to believe whatever they want. We take it for granted that the soil on which we stand is a passing thing, transiently compact of elements that will one day disintegrate. Even if one has trouble following his proofs (like me), there is something undoubtedly sublime about reading his book. To watch as a 1200-year-old geocentric planetary system is dismantled is amazing enough.

QUESTIONS FOR MEDITATION:

What supposed truths about yourself are you ready to break down as you head into a whole planetary system of catalogued days?

index

A

Acceptance — Jan. 16, Mar. 2, 5, June 25, July 2, 13, Oct. 27, Nov. 13

Achievement — Jan. 29, Mar. 22, Apr. 16, Aug. 11, Sept. 4, Oct. 24

Action — Jan. 8, 11, 18, 23-24, Feb. 6, 14, 18, Mar. 4, 11, 14, Apr. 22, May 13, 27, June 27-28, 30, July 13, 19, Aug. 1, 16, 18, 23, 25-26, Sep. 4, 10, 13, 16, Oct. 3, 6, 9, 12, 24, Nov. 2, 8, 13-14, 19, Dec. 20

Addiction — Feb. 22, Mar. 15, 30, Apr. 14, June 26, July 1, Sep. 9, Nov. 18, Dec. 6,7

Adrenaline — Sep. 18, Oct. 28

Ambition — Feb. 8, Mar. 19, Apr. 5, Aug. 12, Sep. 14

Anger — Feb. 18, 27, Mar. 2, 7, Apr. 14, June 14-15, 17, 25-26, Aug. 11, Oct. 17

Arrogance — May 5

Awareness — Jan. 12, 16, 20, Feb. 14, 28, Mar. 10, 18, May 1, 11, 26, 28, June 6, 30, July 18, Sep. 24, 30, Oct. 18, 19-20, 25, Nov. 11, 28, Dec. 8, 20

Awe — Feb. 1, Apr. 6, Oct. 27, 30

B

Balance — Mar. 18, 26, May 14, June 12, Aug. 27, Oct. 6

Beauty — Mar. 5, Apr. 1, 6, 10, May 7, June 25, 30, July 2, Sep. 19, Nov. 16

Becoming — Jan. 11, 15, 31, Feb. 17-18, May 3, 20-21, 30, July 2, 12, Aug. 15, Sept. 7, 29

Belief — Jan. 11, 17, 22, Feb. 3, Mar. 5, 14, 30, Apr. 10, 18, May 7, 25, 29, 31, June 4, 10, 17, 22 July 13, 29, Aug. 11, 13, Sep. 10, 20, Oct. 3, 21-22, Nov. 1, 25, Dec. 4, 16, 20, 25, 30

Busyness — Nov. 3

C

F

Failure — Jan. 14, 21, Feb. 8, 17, 23, 27, Mar. 1, 29, May 17, 29, July 6, 20–21, Aug. 21, 26, 30–31, Oct. 10, 13–14, 19, 24, Nov. 4, 8, 24, Dec. 14, 18

Fear — Jan. 5, 14–16, 20, Feb. 1, 5, 8, 12, 16–17, 20, 23, 27–28, Mar. 6, 11, 13, 17, Apr. 6, May 6, 10, 13, 29, June 1, 5, 9, 12, 14, 17, 25, 27, 30, July 14, 28, Aug. 6, 15, Sep. 1, 18, 20, Oct. 7, 23–24

Feelings — Jan. 5, 8, 10, 27, Mar. 14, 23, 30, Apr. 4, 19, May 1, June 1, 6–7, 29, July 3, 10, 14, Sep. 25, Oct. 24, Dec. 22

Forgiveness — Feb. 7, June 25, Dec. 28

Freedom — Jan. 30, Feb. 1–4, 10, 12–13, 26, 28, Mar. 4, 15, Apr. 19, May 19, June 9, 12, 25–26, July 25, Aug. 31, Sept. 7, 11, 29, Oct. 3, 8, 25, Nov. 11, Dec. 14, 18, 24, 26

Friendship — Feb. 28, Apr. 8, June 12, Aug. 18, Oct. 26, Nov. 26

G

Gifts — Apr. 12, May 15, Oct. 24, Dec. 6

Goals — Jan. 11, July 14, 19, Sep. 4, 20, Nov. 14, 22

Gratitude — Jan. 27, Mar. 7, 30, April. 11, May 19, 22, June 4, July 31, Oct. 27

Grief — Mar. 16, 23, 25, Apr. 4, 12, 27, May 13, June 3, 11, 25–26, July 3, Dec. 10, 12

Growth — Jan. 9, 16, 20, 31, Feb. 7, Mar. 1, 8, 22, May 1, 9, 17, 21, 28, July 18, 21, 27, Aug. 9, 23, 25, 29, Sep. 8, 14, Oct. 1, 21, 25, 28–29, Nov. 6, 12, 25, 27, 30, Dec. 5, 7, 19

Guilt — Jan. 15, Feb. 2, 10, 16, Mar. 26, Jun 7, 16, 25, July 10

H

Happiness — Jan. 4, 7, 9, 10, 12, 16, 25, Feb. 25, Mar. 4, 21, 27, June 5, 23, July 16, Aug. 5, 20, Sep. 13, Oct. 3, Nov. 7–8, 10, 17, 23, 28, Dec. 1, 3, 7, 18, 25, 28

L

M

N

O

P

Pain — Feb. 7, 9, 18, 22, Mar. 11, 13, 18, 23-24, 30, Apr. 3, 14, 17, 26, May 9, 13, 19, June 1, 5, 9, 17, July 6, 11, 14, 29-30, Aug. 9, 26-27, Oct. 17-19, Nov. 9, Dec. 2, 12, 23, 26

Panic — Aug. 15, Sep. 18

Parenting — Jan. 14, May 1, July 7, Dec. 19

Passion — Jan. 26, Mar. 12-13, Apr. 1, 11, 17, 19, May 4, 14, July 25, Aug. 4, 11, 17, Sep. 20, 30, Oct. 18, Nov. 19-20, Dec. 22

Patience — Feb. 17, Apr. 1, May 26, July 22, Sep. 14, 17

Perfectionism — Nov. 17, Dec. 19

Power — Jan. 9, 24-25, 27, Feb. 1, 10, 19, 28, Mar. 18, Apr. 15, 28, May 5-7, 9, 12, 20, 28, June 1, July 6, 12, 19, Aug. 11, 18, 20, 26, Sep. 7, Oct. 2, 6, 9, 11-12, 22, Nov. 11, 14, 18, 20, Dec. 9

Prayer — Apr. 22, May 26, June 4, Nov. 3

Present — Jan. 15, 26, Apr. 7, May 22, Aug. 23, Oct. 24, 28, Nov. 11, Dec. 7, 23

Process — Jan. 12, 15-16, 20, Feb. 17, 26, Mar. 5, 21, April. 26, May 3, 11, 16, 20, June 7, July 2, 22, 29, Aug. 5, 19-20, 25, Sep. 8-9, 15, Oct. 6, 12-13, 28, Nov. 6, 10, 27, 30, Dec. 3, 5, 14

Procrastination — Feb. 25

Promises — July 17

R

Reality — Jan. 1, 16, 19, 30, Feb. 9, 19, Mar. 3, 5, Apr. 12, 20, 25, May 18, 26-27, June 10, July 4-6, 27, Aug. 6, 15, 20, Sep. 7, 221, 23, 26, Oct. 5, 10, 18, 22, 25, 30, Nov. 24, Dec. 15-16, 18, 20, 23, 25, 28

Recovery — Mar. 30, June 16, July 3, Sep. 9

Regret — Jan. 14, Feb. 25, June 25, Aug. 27, Nov. 8, 28

V

W

ABOUT THE AUTHOR

Chad Prevost has advanced degrees in creative writing, literature, and theology. A workshop leader and entrepreneur, he has started and participated in writing and literary arts communities in Atlanta, Austin, Chattanooga, and New York. He also has experience writing as a journalist for startups in tech and logistics. He is the author of several books of poetry, as well as interactive-fiction for young adults. He has innovated writing processes to foster reflection and insight, narrative strength, and authentic voice since 2004. Chad supports the Oxford Comma.

THE Big Self SCHOOL

The Big Self School is a personal growth learning community.

We teach classes and offer coaching to help changemakers deepen their self-awareness, emotional literacy, and relationship skills so they can strengthen their impact and improve their lives.

FIND US AT WWW.BIGSELFSCHOOL.COM

who do you think you are?

Who Do You Think You Are? is a short, daily podcast takes you on an adventure in thought leaders from contemporary thinkers to sources from antiquity. We want to learn from, be challenged, or just reminded what others have already spent lifetimes achieving — the least we can do is read and listen to what they have to say to us right now.

Available on:

Printed in the USA
CPSIA information can be obtained
at www.ICGtesting.com
LVHW041537310723
753892LV00026B/148